ARMAGEDDON ROAD

Armageddon Road

A VC's Diary, 1914-16

Billy Congreve

Edited by

TERRY NORMAN

WILLIAM KIMBER · LONDON

First published in 1982 by
WILLIAM KIMBER & CO. LIMITED
Godolphin House, 22a Queen Anne's Gate,
London, SW1H 9AE

© Terry Norman and Major Christopher Congreve, 1982
ISBN 0-7183-0189-7

Typeset by Print Co-ordination, Macclesfield
and printed in Great Britain by
The Garden City Press Limited
Letchworth, Hertfordshire, SG6 1JS

Contents

List of Illustrations

List of Sketch Maps and Diagrams in the Text

All maps and diagrams, except for (3) and (6), are the work of the diarist. Since the diarist was in an excellent position to have the requisite knowledge of each operational area, it may be confidently assumed that his maps and diagrams are quite accurate. His cartographic talents were discovered during his time at Sandhurst where he won a special commendation on the subject. The original sketch maps, drawn in selected colours for instant comprehension, are minor works of art as well as of major historic importance. Reproducing them in more than one colour, however, would have been economically prohibitive. Mechanical tints have, therefore, been substituted wherever it was deemed appropriate.

Acknowledgements

Rarely does the opportunity occur to compile the war diaries of a holder of the VC for publication, especially when the diarist was also the recipient of the DSO, the MC and the Legion of Honour. For this reason, I am indebted to Major Christopher Congreve who kindly gave me permission to edit his eldest brother's diary, as well as allowing me access to his father's diaries and papers for background material. Equally, I should like to thank Billy Congreve's daughter, Mary Gloria Congreve, for her invaluable contribution that included previously unpublished photographs of the Great War.

The generous assistance given to me by the staff of the Imperial War Museum should not go unsung, nor should Tom Fairgrieve's help from Delville Wood on the Somme, Major Tom Craze's support at the Royal Green Jackets' Museum and Joan Neale's research work at the Public Record Office, Kew. It is also my pleasure to thank Sir John Glubb for his approval to quote from a page of his book: *Into Battle*. Finally, I should like to express my gratitude to my literary agent, Charles Messenger of Donald Copeman Ltd, whose help and encouragement knew no bounds.

T.N.

Introduction

Read any autobiographies by Great War front line veterans and wherever staff officers are mentioned, it is usually in the form of ribald comment or downright abuse. Generally applied with a thick brush, such castigation painted all staff officers alike — whether they served at brigade, division, corps or at army level. A distorted and unfair picture perhaps, but front line soldiers daily faced the stark reality of living or dying; and the anonymous men who influenced their fragile existence always seemed so far from the immediate danger. Yet even front line soldiers would admit that there were exceptions amongst staff personnel. Major William La Touche Congreve was one of those exceptions.

Known simply as Billy to his family and friends, six feet four inches tall and only twenty-five years old when he was killed, he carved out an unselfish niche for bravery. He was awarded the Military Cross for gallantry at Hooge in 1915, followed by the Distinguished Service Order for his virtual single-handed capture of over seventy Prussians at St Eloi in April 1916. The French decorated him with the Legion of Honour and finally, but posthumously, for his continuous acts of endurance and gallantry on the Somme, Billy Congreve was awarded the Victoria Cross.

Young men of his calibre and generation constantly placed themselves in harm's way in the line of duty. It was, therefore, inevitable that he would not survive the war unless he was extraordinarily lucky. Providence, however, had already looked kindly on him for nearly two years on the Western Front. In that time he had lost many close friends whom he had known in more peaceful days. His incredible luck vanished on 20th July 1916. On that fateful day, Billy Congreve was cut down by a sniper's bullet.

He was patriotic, God-fearing and much loved by his men. Until that bullet struck him, his military career was very much in the ascendant. Recognised for eventual brigade command and being a professional soldier, he would doubtless have crowned his career as one of Britain's top military leaders in World War II.

The eldest of three brothers, Billy Congreve was born in his grandfather's home at Burton Hall, Cheshire, on 22nd March 1891. Everything pointed to his joining the Army, as he was raised in a family atmosphere that was steeped in military tradition. His father was a dedicated Rifle Brigade officer, and his mother was the daughter of Captain La Touche — an officer who had distinguished himself in the Indian Mutiny. Billy Congreve's father, Walter Congreve, had won the Victoria Cross at Colenso in 1899 and was destined to become one of the most brilliant corps commanders of the Great War. Knighted for his services, he was eventually made a full general and ADC to King George V. Sir Walter Congreve ended his years of devotion to duty as Governor of Malta. He died there in February 1927, much mourned by the island's people.

With few exceptions, each generation of Congreves left its mark on the pages of British history through the centuries; small wonder that Billy Congreve followed in their footsteps. His was a happy childhood that was mostly spent at Burton Hall and, later, at Chartley Castle which his father purchased in Staffordshire. In 1904 Billy Congreve went to Eton where he was an average scholar; after which he attended a crammer in London and won a place at Sandhurst. There, he excelled and nearly won the Sword of Honour — coming second in his entry. He was commissioned in the Rifle Brigade and, afterwards, was posted to the 3rd Battalion of the Rifle Brigade in Tipperary in 1911. In spite of the undertones of Irish politics, he spent three congenial years in Ireland as the threat of war increasingly clouded the politics of Europe.

It was in Ireland where he commenced his diary in the summer of 1914. He a young lieutenant, watching, impatiently waiting and recording. not fully realising that he was about to participate in one of the most destructive wars known to mankind.

His diary, lucidly written with explanatory maps in six leather-bound notebooks, survived his death. Except for a two-month period in 1915, when some entries were destroyed by fire, he kept a complete diary from 28th July 1914 to 17th January 1916. Why he did not continue was perhaps due to pressure of work after his promotion to brigade-major in December of 1915.

As is to be expected from such a resourceful officer, his diary is remarkable for its insight into the fighting that took place in those early months. It is also a mirror of the optimistic endeavours of his generation who went to war willingly before conscription, praying that it would not finish before having the chance to see action. As we know, as the survivors of Billy Congreve's generation know, it continued for over four horrific years. In so doing, it changed the social and political pattern of Europe.

Because of his untimely death, Billy Congreve was not to share our view of the outcome, nor of the consequences that stemmed from it. We, on the other hand, are in a privileged position to share his ideals and enthusiasm when the Great War was curious and new, and soberly observe his reaction when movement gelled into trench warfare. Through his pen we feel his anguish as friends fatten the ghastly casualty lists, and we witness his incredulity at the Christmas Day truce. Above all, he unconsciously shows us what was expected of a junior staff officer — and a gallant one at that.

'I should like to do something that would be really for good; it's fairly easy to acquire merit, there are so many ways open, but to do something big that will do good for the country or the people — that's a wonderful thing.'

Billy Congreve

'I don't think there was ever anyone like him; he was absolutely glorious, and even when he was ADC, all the men knew and loved him — which is unusual. His friendship has done more for me in many ways than I can say; it was the most priceless thing I had. He was the bravest and most gentle fellow in the world, and I can imagine the smile with which he greeted the "sudden turn" when the bullet got him.'

Tribute from a fellow officer

'Billy's was the finest record of the War.'

Field-Marshal Sir Henry Wilson

CHAPTER ONE

Tipperary–A Long Way to Go

Hardly anyone in Ireland could miss the passions roused by the subject of Home Rule, least of all where young Lieutenant Congreve was based in Tipperary. Ever since the House of Commons introduced the third Home Rule Bill in 1912, both Nationalists and Protestant Ulstermen had raised private armies in readiness for a civil war. However, early in 1914 and with Home Rule firmly opposed by the mass of Protestants led by Sir Edward Carson, a compromise had been suggested by the British Government. Ulster would be temporarily excluded from Home Rule proposals for six years. Carson rejected the offer out of hand. Nothing but the permanent partition of Ulster would do.

Prime Minister Asquith and members of his cabinet were in turmoil. Stung by Carson's rebuff and perturbed by reports of gun-running, plans were drawn up to increase the British Army's influence in Ireland. Asquith's intentions upset numerous Army officers, especially those with Irish-Protestant roots. Threats of resignation emanated from many quarters. At the Curragh Camp near Dublin in March 1914, over fifty cavalry officers proffered their resignations *en bloc*. Civilians in various walks of life added their objections and, in April, an illegal large shipment of arms and ammunition was imported quite openly for Protestant use. The British Government back-pedalled on the six years' temporary arrangement; a move that generally appeased the north, but inflamed the more rabid Irish Nationalists.

It was against this sensitive backdrop that Billy Congreve began writing on 28th July. His mind was on Ireland, but wider events were happening. Exactly one month before, a Serbian youth had shot dead a married couple in a Bosnian town called Sarajevo. The dead husband was the Archduke Franz Ferdinand, heir apparent of Austria-Hungary. On 28th July 1914 Austria-Hungary declared war on Serbia and Europe's destiny was on the march. For Billy Congreve, a truly historic day on which to commence his diary

*

28th July 1914, Moore Park Camp

Battalion training all day. Everyone was very full of 'scares', but these are chiefly to do with the Ulster question. It looks as if Civil War is almost a certainty.

After dinner we were all playing bridge when suddenly Meysey[1] was sent for. We all felt something was up and played on rather *distrait*. He came back looking very important and said the orders were that we were to march to Cork at 5 a.m. next morning. Great excitement. I think that we all felt rather hysterical, and such a muddle there was, as this meant the beginning of the 'Precautionary Period', and of course all the papers were in Cork! We all started packing, and Meysey left at 10 p.m. for Cork in a car. Eventually most of us got to bed about twelve. At 3 a.m. we were all up and wondering who had to go where. At 3.45 a.m. Meysey returned somewhat wearied, and the officers and men for duty in the Precautionary Period were warned. I, to my surprise, got a budget of papers which said that I had to go to Gyleen by the 4.30 train (that was in half an hour!).

We got to Cork about 8 p.m. and were informed that we had to go by the 8.45 to Queenstown, so there was no chance of getting anything from barracks. At Queenstown, we got into a launch and this took us to the fort which holds the east entrance to the harbour. By about 3 p.m., I managed to get my equipment — tents, kettles, etc., and, of course, food — and marched off to this place Gyleen which is about four miles by road.

Sergeant Cox, Corporal McDonnell and Corporal White are my NCO's (and a good lot too) and twenty-five men, counting machine-gunners and their one gun. I found that my duties were to guard the tiny landing place, and patrol the coast line — my first independent job!

Gyleen itself is a collection of thatched cottages clustered on the sides of a little valley which ends in the 'harbour'. It is no longer a fishing village, and its population are almost all old men and women. The few active inhabitants are farmers. However, we managed to buy some fish from a boat which came in.

31st July

The villagers are at present very suspicious, as they think we are here to stop gun-running, though I am fairly sure it's Germany and not Ulster. Anyhow, I shall tell them this, or things may be tiresome. I feel I have sufficient of the Irishman in me to overcome their doubts.

Heard a lot of gun firing from [Queenstown] harbour. The picquet and sentries now all know their jobs and things are going very smoothly. The nearest pub (about 100 yards!) is run by a pair of girls whose dirt and language are both prodigious. Their remarks when Sergeant Cox, Corporal McDonnell and White and I went in to dry ourselves by their fire made me quite 'hot'. I guess it will be as well to put it out of bounds to the men!

The guns we heard today were fired by [Fort] Carlisle to bring boats entering the harbour to a standstill. The *Inniscarra*, through ignorance or swelled head, near got herself sunk, for she refused to stop.

2nd August

They brought me news of a probable mobilisation tomorrow; also the following items from the wireless receiving station at Carlisle:

(1) 5 a.m. Message begins, 'Martial Law declared in Germany who is reported to be fighting Russia. Bank rate 8 per cent'. (The latter part of this message leaves me unmoved.)

(2) To a passenger, SS *Olympic*: 'Have darling girl two days old. All think the image of father, thanks ring, love from baby and self'.

(3) 2 a.m.: Marconi reports telephone communication between London and Paris stopped suddenly this afternoon.   French Government has taken over service .

(4) London Associated Press and Reuters Agencies reports that Germany declared war on Russia 7.30 last night (1.8.14). France mobilising .

(5) Private message, signed Brown, begins: '2 a.m. Germany's ultimatum to Russia and France which expired yesterday (1.8.14) has been extended until noon, Monday. Our King in direct communication with Czar and Kaiser hoped will have good results. Reports states German ambassador leaving St Petersburg for Berlin'.

(6) Partial German message reads: '. . . enormous crowds collected about 4.30 this afternoon (1.18.14). The public was informed by adjutants and police officers that mobilization has been ordered — whereupon indescribable enthusiasm broke out in Berlin and all big towns'.

(7) Partial English message reads: 'An ultimatum has been sent to French Government today (Saturday, 2nd), asking what attitude France would adopt if Germany and Russia were at war. Reply considered unfavourable by Germany. German ambassador believed to be leaving Paris tonight'.

All this news looks pretty black. The men much interested. I expect we shall start mobilising tomorrow.

Monday, August 3rd

Germans have apparently invaded France and Luxembourg[2] , so if we don't go in now we are about as chicken-hearted a lot as ever existed. Please goodness we are not going to sit down and watch France 'done in'. Nobody will ever help or trust us again if we stay out now.

A naval reservist here got his orders today midst great excitement and wailing! Yesterday he was breathing fire and murder against Carson; today he said, 'The first — German I meet, I will smash his head in,' so it looks as if this might be a good solution to the Irish question.

Tuesday, August 4th

The papers today are more hopeful as to our position as an ally of France and Russia. I should love dearly to have a go at these bombastic Germans. Tom Grenville came in this afternoon and said that we were expected to mobilise at any moment.

5th August

Got a note from Tom, saying that Germany declared war on us[3] at 9.30 last night and that we were now actually mobilising.

Heard from Dads. He says Geoff [4] sailed on the *Hannibal* some days ago. I wonder if he will see anything? I also heard from Norman Leslie who says Kitchener is to be War Minister which sounds a good egg[5] . Two cruisers came into the harbour tonight. We were all medically examined today and made wills — at least the men did. I didn't, as I have nothing to make one about.

All the village is very perturbed. They follow us about and weep copious tears and utter long-winded blessings. Mr. Hegarthy came up to me with a somewhat alcoholic manner, and mysteriously ushered me into his holy of holies, a stuffy, dirty hole. Here he gave me whiskey of great merit (?) and potent beyond words, and a box of cigars. I had to take all this and many words of affection besides. I hope I played my part well.

6th August

I received my relief orders and am to be relieved here at 4 a.m. There is a big spy scare on all round. I've just had special orders to watch for them here. I wonder if Hegarthy is also a spy as well as a delightful scoundrel?!

Later. Tender farewells from the village. 'Never had they seen so well-behaved a lot of men!' I had my hand kissed by a tearful old lady, and felt a hero at once! It was quite an ovation.

7th August

I was not relieved till nearly 7 a.m., and when the relief did turn up, it did so in driblets and was all stale drunk, as also was the officer in charge. I've never seen such a dismal horrid crew and feel very sorry for my friends the villagers. Eventually we got into Cork about noon.

14th August

This has been a truly painful week, waiting for orders to move, getting reservists tuned up, etc., etc. All very weary work and depressing. Rumour has it we are to be left in England as Home Defence, which will be *too* awful.

All moves of the Expeditionary Force have been kept marvellously silent. Here we are, now ready to move, and believed to be going today — yet it is now 1.30 p.m. and we have had no orders. Even when we do go we are told on no account by letter, etc., to state our port of disembarkation. Till we reach port, it's unlikely we shall know whether it's England or the Continent we have reached!

I should laugh if we did not go after all, though in some ways I should weep with rage. Everybody keeps on saying goodbye and then meeting again the next day. I have given up saying goodbye — it's a rotten thing to have to say at best. WNC[6] is, I believe, at Edinburgh. Poor Cis[7] is very low, but has John[8] and Elsie[9] to comfort her. It must be hard to be a woman now. I am mighty sorry for them all, but should be a deal more sorry if we were not to go, or if we went, to find ourselves too late.

The Navy apparently have the Germans bottled up in the Kiel Canal and in the Baltic, and so far we have sunk one minelayer and one submarine. No news of Geoff for ten days. The *Hannibal* is, I believe, an old ship, so he ought to be unlikely to get hurt. Geoff says, 'She's very old, but has *awful* thick armour.'!

Editor's Note: A 14,900 ton battleship, HMS *Hannibal* was launched at Pembroke Docks on 28th April 1896. Her length was 390 feet with a breadth of 75 feet. She carried four 12-inch guns, twelve 6-inch guns and eighteen 12-pounders.

14th August (continued)

We declared war on Austria yesterday — I think it was. The Germans can't get the Liège forts down[10] and seem to meet with constant checks. Looks as if the mighty war lord wasn't so mighty after all. If *only* we can get out in time to give him a whack, I don't care what happens.

17th August

At last we have our orders to move. We had a real good send-off from the people. Our ship is the *Patriotic*, a good, big and very clean boat. The men have blankets and are lying about all over the decks.

It was rather fine leaving harbour and steaming down the river to Queenstown. We all hung over the side waving to the people on shore, who did heavy shouting work and much flag waving. We have a sweepstake as to where we are bound for. I've got Plymouth, which seems a possibility.

Later — It's Holyhead we are for, and where we go from there nobody knows. Every boat we pass blows its siren and the crew cheers. Several motors followed us all the way down the river.

20th August

We got to Holyhead early Tuesday after a lovely crossing. We only took about an hour to disembark and to entrain, and to start off for Cambridge. I wired to Cis from Chester that we should be going through Stafford at 11.30, which we did — about 70 miles an hour though! It was bad luck. I caught a glimpse of poor Cis on the platform and managed to throw a weighted letter almost at her feet. I heard from her last night that she got it all right and that John saw me, so it was not quite a failure.

We were cheered all the way along. The men never seemed to tire of looking out of the windows and waving handkerchiefs and flags. We arrived at Cambridge about 6 p.m. and marched into camp there. It is on a sort of common in the town and our tents are only fifty yards from the main road, so we have plenty of visitors, chiefly female! Norman [Leslie] performed a fine and typical feat today. I found him sitting on the grass outside his tent, his back to the crowds, stark naked and washing hard. He then stood up and demanded I should pour water over him, which I did. The crowd was immensely interested, but he was quite unabashed and dried himself outside too with a *very small* towel! I don't suppose that the staid aunts and young ladies of Cambridge have ever seen a naked gentleman having a bath on their common before, and within fifty yards of the main road. The local policeman was for once utterly defeated. I could see the struggle going on inside him between his usual duty and the novelty of the situation.

Everyone is exceedingly kind, and really we would be very happy but for the fact that we are so longing to get away to business.

1st September

I dined at Caius and had a great talk with Professor Ridgeway, a wonderful and almost blind gentleman. He is a great Ulsterman in spite of being a South Country Catholic. He fears trouble over there in a few days, if Parliament tries to make Home Rule law before the end of the war.

The 1st Battalion[11] (4th Division) left Harrow on Friday. We *must* go very soon now. The Germans are through Brussels and are very close to Ostend. I wonder what our scheme is . . .?

4th September

Still waiting. A week ago tomorrow we were shifted from Cambridge to here — Newmarket — as being a better camping place and where we eventually entrain if we ever do.

Much has happened on the Continent; the result being that the Germans are within thirty miles of Paris. We heard from the 1st Battalion that they have had a bad time of it. They were hurried up to the front (near Mons), slept the night in a wet cornfield and, at 6 p.m., were engaged. All morning they were marching, counter-marching and fighting and, at 5 p.m., found themselves divided into two halves. One half of the battalion took up a position in a sunken road under heavy shrapnel and machine-gun fire. At 5.30 there was a council of war held by Sam Rickman to all officers and company sergeants. There were three possible things they could do: 1. To surrender; 2. To die where they were; 3. To try and get back.

They naturally decided on the latter course. Leaving everything but rifles and swords, they went across three-quarters of a mile of fire-swept ground, but lost heavily.[12]

Sam is believed to have a mortal stomach wound. Coryton, Lane and de Moleyns were also hit — of course none of them knew where the other half of the battalion had got to. So far we have no other news of them and nothing has come out in the newspapers.

Cis, John and Maggie turned up at Cambridge for the weekend and good it was to see them. Cis is off on Red Cross work to Belgium this week. I have kept John and he is living in my bivouac — as happy as the day is long. He comes out with 'Wumps'[13] on our field days. Godders[14] takes him on the machine-gun limber, and everyone spoils him.

8th September
On Sunday, John and I biked into Cambridge to see Dads, and spent the day with him. We biked back to Newmarket in the evening. About 9 p.m. came a wire to say we were to be ready to move tomorrow (Monday). Yesterday we packed everything up. I sent poor little John off into Cambridge, and at 5 p.m. we entrained. We left about 6.15 and went straight to Southampton and then aboard a 'trooper', an 8,000-ton immigrant ship called the *Lake Michigan* of Liverpool.

This morning we were allowed on shore. Godders and I went to see Dads[15] on the *Georgia*, an even worse ship, I think, than ours. He seemed fit and happy, and had heard from Cis, who is off today from Folkestone. We three went to see some captured Germans, seven cavalrymen. They were caught a few days ago in France, and will go to Dorchester where there are, I believe, already a thousand of them. A captured officer of theirs says that they will be done in a month. If so, we are only just in time. Certainly the papers seem more cheerful today. The Germans have apparently left Paris alone and now we have taken up the offensive.

I believe we go to the mouth of the Loire — St Nazaire? We shall see tomorrow. The weather is glorious and we are at present steaming out past the Isle of Wight.

Editor's Note The 1914 British Expeditionary Force, commanded by Field-Marshal Sir John French, totalled one cavalry division, six infantry divisions (two to a corps), and four squadrons and one aircraft park of the Royal Flying Corps. Both Lieutenant Congreve and his father were members of the 6th Division which left Southampton on 8th September. In common with the other five infantry divisions, its backbone comprised artillery, engineers and three infantry brigades: 16th, 17th and the 18th Brigade. Four battalions with approximately 30 officers and 990 men to a battalion, made up each brigade's infantry complement. The 17th Brigade, under the command of Brigadier-General W.R.B. Doran, CB, DSO, consisted of the 1/Royal Fusiliers, 1/North Staffordshires,

2/Leinsters, also the 3/Rifle Brigade of which Lieutenant Congreve was an officer.

The 6th Division was the last one to leave for France that summer. Due to the initial success of the German advance threatening the Channel ports, it was deemed necessary to delay its departure until the main British base had been shifted from Le Havre to St Nazaire. That the security of the Channel ports should ever be called into question, came as a shock. No country, except for Germany, had seriously considered an invasion route to France via neutral Belgium. Least of all Belgium, since her neutrality had been guaranteed by Germany in the Treaty of 1839. Great Britain had also signed the 'scrap of paper'. Because she did, she was now at war.

France was certainly unprepared for such a violation, having always thought that a German invasion would strike from the direction of Alsace and Lorraine — provinces annexed by Germany as part of the victory spoils of the 1870-71 Franco-Prussian War.

France's mistake was a case of the heart ruling the head, and the two provinces were dear to her heart. Even when the unthinkable happened, France found it hard to believe that it was the enemy's main thrust coming through Belgium. She was still in some doubt when the Hun's massive right wing drove into the advancing left wing of the French forces. The left wing composed of the French Fifth Army and, on its left, was the BEF in the vicinity of Mons. When the Fifth Army reeled away, both British flanks hung in the air.

The leading British brigades, unsure of the Fifth Army's predicament, faced the enemy troops that swarmed towards them. It was then that the numerous pre-war days spent on the rifle ranges came into play. They checked the enemy's progress with such withering rifle fire that many Germans thought that they were facing innumerable machine-guns. When the overall situation asserted itself, there was nothing the BEF could do but to fall back to avoid being trapped. After retreating over one hundred miles, both British and French forces turned and stood their ground just north of Paris. The original German plan — the brainchild of a certain Count von Schlieffen — called for a grand sweep around the north and west of Paris.

It was not to be. Weakened and exhausted from his ordeals, the invader turned in front of Paris. At long last the enemy had shown his flank. On 6th September, General Joffre who was the French Commander-in-Chief, launched his counter-blow on the

River Marne. Fed with troops from Paris, the Allies drove the
Germans back for mile after weary mile under a burning sun
towards the River Aisne. It was at that point in the war that the
ships carrying the soldiers of 6th Division arrived off St Nazaire.

Since a division consisted of just over 18,000 officers and men,
some twenty ships took the division to St Nazaire, but only seven
could dock at any one time. The *Lake Michigan* with the 3/Rifle
Brigade aboard, arrived in the St Nazaire roadstead in the small
hours of Thursday morning, 10th September. There, at anchor,
Lieutenant Congreve and his comrades awaited their turn to
disembark:

13th September
We were kept on board till yesterday morning, when we went in
and disembarked, a longish job, as the quay was a long way below
us. I and others made several journeys into town and laid in vast
stores of eatables. Many times was I asked for my silver cap badge
as a souvenir. There were a lot of our wounded in the town. I saw
Musters of the 60th who was hit in the chest by a shrapnel bullet.
Luckily for him, it hit a bone and glanced off. He was in the
retreat and never saw a German the whole time. The marching, he
said, was awful: twenty-five miles a day and in very hot weather.
About 4.30 we started to entrain in pouring rain.

I managed to sleep all right last night, and about 6 a.m. we
reached Tours where we had breakfast. I ran up and got some
boiling water out of the engine and made some chocolate for
Godders and I — jolly good it was. All day we have been rolling
along. About 5.30 this evening, we passed Paris.

All the way up we have seen French soldiers in their blue coats
and red trousers, and at the halts we had great talks with them.
They seem very intelligent fellows and I take it were all reserves of
some type. It was amusing to see the scramble for the train when
it suddenly started. Luckily it was so cumbersome a show that one
could let it go for a hundred yards and still catch it. Everywhere
we were given apples and cigarettes by the people. The country
was pretty at first and it was hard to believe war even existed,
except that one saw sentries everywhere guarding the line. There
was a constant demand for souvenirs and a lot of men are now
minus their cap badges.

14th September, Coulommiers
We reached here early this morning. It was pitch-dark and raining,

so detraining was a beastly job. After a lot of hanging about we got to some huge sheds — a sugar refinery — where we have had some sort of a meal. The Germans were here some few days ago, and I believe surprised some of our men in these actual sheds.

Our fighting line is about forty miles off. There are small parties of Germans still hanging about between us and them — lost, I suppose. The Leinsters have just found the bodies of four small girls — I suppose killed by the Germans before they left here. I can hardly believe it though.

I took a walk through the town, a small place and little signs of damage. A few shop doors burst in and windows broken. I fancy this was about as far south as they got, and also they were not here long enough to do much harm. WNC turned up before we left Coulommiers and was very fit. He says we are on the extreme left of the army, or will be, but that there is a French army on our left. He is to be in Doue tonight, behind us. The 16th Brigade are somewhere in front of us.

We left about twelve noon; it was then quite fine and marched to this place Busseroles [*sic*], passing through Boissy, St Germain, Doue and St Cyr — about twelve miles and not bad going. I found my impedimenta quite heavy enough[16]. We saw some of the 18th Brigade in billets at Doue.

This is the only place I've seen where the Germans have done serious damage. They set fire to a big farmhouse which is still smoking. All very deserted and quiet, most of the people having fled. The Germans were actually here on the 6th, 7th and 8th, and there was a small fight — the Germans holding the right bank of the River Morin. We drove them out, losses being twenty Germans killed and ten British including *un capitaine*. This is all what the villagers say. The dead are certainly here, buried.

Editor's Note This action occurred about mid-day on 8th September in the small village of Becherelle, situated in a steep valley through which runs the tiny river of the Petit Morin. The 2/Worcesters, in the vanguard of the 5th (Infantry) Brigade, moved down the valley slope to Becherelle and crossed the bridge there to the other side. After a brisk engagement, they killed and captured several Germans at a nearby farmhouse.

It is the same farmhouse to which Lieutenant Congreve refers in his entry of 14th September. With all the frantic marching through various villages, it is quite understandable how he came to misinterpret Becherelle's name. The 2/Worcesters' action allowed

the 2nd Cavalry Brigade to cross the bridge and pursue the enemy
with appreciable results. This local engagement formed part of a
wider action that covered nearly two miles of front, an action that
became known as the forcing of the Petit Morin. As Billy Congreve
and his battalion rested in Becherelle, the Battle of the Aisne had
begun in earnest many marching miles ahead of them:

The whole battalion is bivouacked here in a big mill. Rather
crowded we are, but it is not bad. Norman, Godders and I are
occupying a corner together. I think there are rats too. We are
feeding at a farmhouse on eggs and rabbits. There is also some
excellent cider. A week ago, six German officers billeted
themselves in the same house and seemed to have behaved all right.

I believe we leave at 5 a.m. tomorrow and I guess we shall have
a long march. We have outposts out tonight and, about 6 p.m.,
heard firing, but believe it is only peasants out hunting and killing
stray Germans. They make sort of organised hunts, and goodness
knows what they do to a live German if they catch him. There are a
good many still in the woods around here. Seven came in yesterday
and gave themselves up, half-starved and miserable they were.

15th September
Bézu St Germain — we got here pretty beat at 11 p.m. last night.
Originally we were told that we were to billet in Azy, but we
marched through there and halted east of the town for about three
hours. The last part up to this halt was very trying to the men and
a good many fell out. We were told that we must go on to Bézu, as
Sir John French[17] had wired back that he urgently needed the
division. We must have done twenty-five miles yesterday, but I
haven't had time to measure it yet. A lot of our march was along
the Marne and very pretty it was. We saw many evidences of war,
old bivouacs, trenches and graves, some dead horses too, which
were none too pleasant to halt near. We heard gun firing from
twelve noon onwards, and now hear that we might be fighting
today — possibly!

We bivouacked last night just as we were, and a bad night it was,
for though the day had been fearfully hot and dusty, it changed at
night. It rained all night and is going on still. We were in an
orchard and had plenty of straw. I personally kept dry, as I dug
myself into the stack and put my Burberry over my legs, but most
of the men and other officers have not been so lucky and are
soaked through. I feel rather superior being dry this morning, also

I carried a man's equipment the last eight miles yesterday in addition to my own. Lewis is the man. He has very bad sores, but is a wonderfully plucky little man. My platoon are good fellows and none fell out. It is now 5.30 a.m., and we have had breakfast of sorts. We move again at seven.

Later. A very tiring day. We have marched about another twenty miles and, as none of us slept well last night, we are all very weary. We came up via Breny and are now billeted around Visigneux. The company is in a farm hidden in a little hollow. Some are sleeping in lofts and some outside.

The enemy, or rather his main body, are about eight miles off and, I believe, are retiring. We saw our first guns in action today, also a fine lot of shrapnel bursts at a hostile (?) aeroplane which was apparently untouched. I hear our casualties were 5,000 today, and I daresay we shall have our turn tomorrow. We passed a great number of wounded going back in motor supply lorries, presumably to Breny which seems to be the nearest railhead. I saw a few 1st Battalion wounded at Breny, and hear that George Morris[18] and Sammy Rickman are both dead.

Editor's Note Although Lieutenant Congreve was not aware of it, GHQ had decided that 6th Division should be temporarily disbanded and distributed among formations already engaged in the Aisne fighting. The 17th Brigade, comprising 3/Rifle Brigade, 1/Royal Fusiliers, 1/North Staffordshires and 2/Leinsters, was scheduled to become corps reserve to Haig's I Corps on its march to the forward area.

17th September
Just had time for a wash and bacon and tea when we were hurried off. I had a splendid night on some straw. My platoon also shared the straw and I was much enraged when the dirtiest young scoundrel in my platoon, Bailey, had a nightmare and rolled on to me — his feet hitting me in the face.

There was tremendous rifle fire on the left all night, and today there is a terrific battle going on there. It sounds so close. The gunfire is incessant. We are, I think, in reserve, but it's hard to find out anything. We marched this morning east instead of our usual trek north, and have only come a few miles to this place (Villeblain), where we are in billets.

It has stopped raining now and the guns are still going strong. Apparently we shall move to the firing line now if things go ill, or to make a counter-attack. Tonight the 5th Division sent in an urgent requisition for tools, so things look tough. We breakfast at 7 a.m. tomorrow. I am sleeping in a cement-floored loft by myself — most luxurious! I shan't be bothered by Rifleman Bailey's feet.

18th September
Saw Dads, as usual these days, very fit. He told me privately that we move tonight to take over trenches from the 19th Infantry Brigade somewhere over the Aisne, and that we shall sit there under shell-fire until the French get things going. The French offensive on our left is held up, owing to the fact that the German Army is reported moving down from the north-west and the French have got 'to clear up the situation'.

The prospect of sitting in trenches for some days is none too pleasant. I shall take as much in the way of warm things as I can carry.

20th September
We did not go into the trenches on Friday after all, but Dads was sent off east of our position. On Saturday we marched to Courcelles, arriving long after dark. We had to go a long way round, making it a march of seventeen miles with the last few in pitch-dark over cobblestones. All day while marching we could hear the guns on our left.

About 1 p.m. we marched off to just outside Vieille Arcy. Here we halted about 6 p.m., and it sounded as if we were very close indeed to business. The shells of our guns kept yelling overhead and one could see the enemy's shrapnel bursting, especially after dark. There were also extraordinary heavy bursts of rifle and machine-gun fire — a jolly sort of Sunday evening!

We had been brought up here to relieve the Guards Brigade, who in the last three days have had twenty attacks on them, and have piled up the corpses in front of their trenches till they can hardly see out of them. The smell is, I hear, horrible. However, we were eventually told to bivouac where we were on the edge of the road. I think I shall be fairly comfortable with my thick Burberry and water-proof sheets which we have had issued to us.

I had a good tea with old Godders, and we got well warmed before we were ordered to put out our fires. It is curious lying here and to know of the fighting so very close. The noise is terrific.

CHAPTER TWO

On Divisional Staff

The delay in reaching France, compounded by the inadequate docking facilities at St Nazaire, ensured the late arrival of the 6th Division to the Aisne battleground. It meant also that the division's three infantry brigades were fated to join those BEF divisions already engaged in the fighting. Losses had been heavy since 14th September, but the men of the 16th, 17th and 18th Brigades would help to make up that deficit.

A wide and unfordable river, the Aisne winds a gentle course through a long flat-bottomed valley that is dotted with small towns and villages. The high ground on either side rises to about four hundred feet above the valley base and has numerous spurs and re-entrants. Patches of woodland cover a fair percentage of the slopes and the top of each plateau. On the north side, where concealment proved an easy task, the natural features made an ideal venue for the retreating enemy to stop, regroup and to defend with artillery support. Such support was particularly valuable for the defenders, since all bridges over the Aisne in that disputed area could be brought under direct or high-angled artillery fire. As it was, all bridges had been partially or totally demolished by the Germans prior to their retirement to the plateau on the north side.

Nevertheless, divisions of the BEF had managed to cross the Aisne, and the fighting was especially severe on 14th September when the British tried to storm the heights. For Brigadier-General Hunter-Weston's 11th Brigade, the battle had actually started on 13th September. After a forced march in driving rain, his infantrymen were the first of the BEF to reach the Aisne. They crossed it by way of a broken bridge before dawn on that day. In the vanguard were riflemen all keyed up to attack a contingent of tired Germans, who were seen to be entrenching themselves on the plateau. Hunter-Weston personally stopped the attack from taking place, because the men of his brigade were still the only ones on the hostile side of the river, and Hunter-Weston was reluctant to commit them without back-up. The crossing of the Aisne by the main body of the BEF was postponed until later in the day. It was carried out under an enemy bombardment.

With 13th September almost gone, it was decided to attack the heights the next day. The delay, however, gave the Germans a welcome respite to dig in and to consolidate their positions on the northern plateau or, to give the plateau its correct name, the Chemin des Dames. It meant also that the three corps of the BEF were faced with a fairly rested German First and Second Army, commanded by Generals von Kluck and von Bülow respectively.

Arguably, a golden opportunity to shorten the war had slipped away. Had the Chemin des Dames fallen into British hands on 13th September, a demoralised and diminished enemy would have had little choice but to retreat still further to the River Meuse, close to the Luxembourg border.

Sadly, it was not to be. Moreover, with the enemy entrenched on the heights, it was a grim premonition of things to come.

Meanwhile, as the battle raged on, the three infantry brigades of 6th Division were individually despatched to other divisions. The 16th Brigade was transferred to 1st Division in Haig's I Corps on 18th September and, two days later and still in reserve, the 17th Brigade which included Billy Congreve's battalion, was directed to Courcelles to join 2nd Division. His father's 18th Brigade had crossed the Aisne on 18th September and, by 4 p.m. that day, had relieved two brigades in Major-General Lomax's 1st Division near a village called Troyon.

On Monday, 21st September, the 3/Rifle Brigade had not received additional orders by daybreak – a fact that grieved Billy Congreve. An incident later that morning grieved him even more. He had heard that Major-General Hubert Hamilton who commanded 3rd Division in Smith-Dorrien's II Corps, wanted him as an ADC. His battalion commander, Lieutenant-Colonel R. Alexander, had refused to release him however.

'The one chance I may ever get of really seeing things,' he wrote, dismally, as he sheltered under a corn stack from the pouring rain. Moments later the GOC of 6th Division, Major-General Keir, rode by. He suddenly spied Lieutenant Congreve and reined his horse. Keir informed him that Hamilton had again asked for him. When the 6th Division commander saw that Billy Congreve would like the position, he rode over to Alexander and told him that Lieutenant Congreve was to go to 3rd Division as ADC to Hamilton.

Just as he was in the act of gathering his kit together, he heard that his brigade had been directed to relieve 5th Brigade:

*

It was horrid my leaving them all, just as the battalion was off to the trenches, but the offer was too good to lose. Godders, I shall miss desperately. Harris[1], too, is a sad loss, but I hope to get hold of him again soon.

I left the battalion just going into billets in Dhuizel and we motored to Braisne where I reported myself to HH at his headquarters. He at once gave me an outline of my job and it isn't very complicated. Headquarters consists of about 100 men, servants, grooms, clerks, etc., and eighty horses. These I have to look after, also the messing arrangements. We are a total of about twenty-five officers, and live in two messes. I look after one mess and Thorpe (A and S Highlanders) the other. He is the other ADC, and seems a very good fellow. I can't say how I miss little Harris. HH is very good to me, and seems glad to have me with him.

23rd September

The war goes well, or rather the battle all along our lines. We hold the Germans in spite of desperate attacks on their part. Generally these take place in the evening, and their shell fire is more or less continuous and is marvellously accurate and deadly. Each evening brings its attack on a different part of the line. These attacks are always beaten off with huge losses and are never made in great force. Perhaps their scheme of things is to keep us busy here while their main army withdraws or concentrates elsewhere. Whatever it is, we are besieging them. On each flank the French press on, very slowly, but forward.

At a big army conference in Braisne today, Sir Archibald Murray[2] told HH that it was difficult fighting with allies and a most heart-breaking job. They come to him and say, 'At 5 a.m. tomorrow, we will fight. Will you fight too?' Later the time is changed to 7 a.m. At 7 a.m., there is no sign of French movement. Eventually a message comes: 'We are sorry, but won't be able to fight today after all.' He gave an instance; that the French told him that at 7 a.m. today, an army corps would be passing through Soissons. When 7 a.m. came, the head of the corps was still twenty miles south of Soissons.

Sir Archibald looked tired and ill, but said that he was very fit. I also talked to General 'Putty'[3], who was still smiling as ever.

General Keir said that Dads was having plenty of fighting and that he was doing very well. The first night his brigade was in the trenches, however, there was nearly a disaster. The Germans made a strong attack. Eventually things were righted again, but the 18th Brigade had 600 casualties that night — a pretty hot start off[4]. Since 13th September, 4,500 wounded men have passed through here alone, of whom about 1,600 are of the 3rd Division. All but the life and death cases are sent straight by train to base — changed again now from St Nazaire to Le Havre.

Editor's Note If a benchmark is required for the evolution of trench warfare in the Great War, look no further than the Aisne. The ingredients present at the Aisne predetermined the demise of mobile warfare until late 1918, because no previous war had introduced so many destructive weapons with the men to use them. Aircraft, initially employed as 'eyes' for the artillery, also gave a new dimension to warfare.

Mix these new ingredients with the old tactics that pivoted on the traditional attacking spirit of the infantrymen, and everything became a recipe for attrition. With attrition came heavy casualties that were unheard of before. Heavy casualties meant temporary respites for the licking of wounds under artillery fire, frequently brought on target by the eyes in the sky or from observation posts on the heights overlooking the battlefield. For evenly matched armies where lofty decisions demanded no retreat, there was but one answer — to dig in, and dig in deeply until ordered to prosecute the next infantry attack. And that is precisely what occurred on the Aisne. Furthermore, it was a bloody taste of what lay in store, although very few realised it at that moment in time.

On the question of German artillery fire, which had a disconcerting habit of achieving a high degree of accuracy than thought possible from just aircraft or balloon observation, brought forth suspicions of spies at work. Many civilians were rounded up and found guilty of spying, some of them on very flimsy evidence. Others were caught red-handed, as Billy Congreve describes:

*

We are much bothered by spy scares. The Germans seem to have an uncanny knowledge of what goes on this side of the river, and it certainly must be largely due to spies, and not only to aeroplanes. In Chassemy village, it was noticed that one man had horses and cattle left him. This looking suspicious, he was arrested and searched. On him they found a large sum of money — much larger than he could have come by honestly; they then searched his house and found in the cellar a German working a telephone, the line of which went over the river. Both were given short shrift. Altogether in the last ten days we have caught and shot sixty spies, most of them bribed peasants. They are usually handed over to the French authorities for justice, which is less merciful than ours, as a matter of fact. It is extraordinary that Frenchmen, who one would think had a good reason to loathe Germany, should help them — yet many do.

We keep on taking prisoners and they seem to be glad to be caught. Nearly all state that the German 'morale' is very bad. We also obtain a lot of information from their letters and diaries which are found on prisoners or on their dead. The following are some extracts:

Letter of lieutenant, dated from Rheims, 14th September:

As you see, I have been away from my regiment for several weeks, engaged in a very bloody battle which has lasted since Sunday. I have been wounded. My regiment which started with sixty officers has now only five. More than 2,000 men are *hors de combat*, with the result that my gallant regiment is only a fragment. It is the same with the Saxons fighting at our side. To speak candidly, the army to which I belong has passed through terrible experiences during the last four weeks. Let us hope it will soon be over.

Letter from lieutenant of the 26th Regiment FA:

For the last five weeks we have undergone colossal fatigue. The X Corps has been constantly on the move since the first day of the campaign. My battery, especially, is always with the advanced guard. Our horses are for the most part worn out, we are now using Belgian and French horses. There are moments when they simply cannot go on — they just lie down. Add to that the numerous wounds which they receive. From five in the morning until eight at night, we are under the enemy's fire without being able to eat or drink. Even in bivouac at night the troops are not safe.

Another letter from the same officer:

In the X Corps, some infantry companies that started with 250 men are reduced to seventy. Some officers of the Guard who have fought by the side of our corps told me yesterday that some infantry companies of the Guard 'Augusta' Regiment are commanded by 'one year volunteers', because there are no officers left. We occupy a new strategic position. Let us hope that the French will not push forward, for if they do they will occupy Rheims.

From a letter found on a prisoner of the 74th Infantry Regiment, X Corps:

I have just been living through days that defy imagination. It was horrible, it was ghastly. On 5th September, the enemy were reported to be taking up a position near St Prix (NE of Paris). The X Corps, which had made an astonishing rapid advance, of course attacked — on Sunday. Steep slopes led up to heights held in considerable force. We reached the crest and came under a terrible artillery fire that mowed us down. However, we entered St Prix. Hardly had we done so, we were met with more shell fire and a violent fusillade from the enemy's infantry. Our Colonel was badly wounded — he is the third we have had . . . fourteen men were killed around me . . . we got away in a lull without being hit.

The 7th, 8th and 9th September, we were constantly under shell and shrapnel fire and suffered terrible losses. Our heavy artillery was being used for the siege of Maubeuge[5]. We wanted it badly, as the enemy had theirs in force and kept up a furious bombardment. On the night of the 9th the order was given to retreat, as it would have been madness to attempt to hold our position with our few men. In spite of unheard of sacrifices we had achieved nothing. Our 1st Battalion, which has fought with unparalleled bravery, is reduced from 1,200 to 194 men. The numbers speak for themselves.

This fellow doesn't seem very optimistic! I am awfully glad they don't like it — it will teach them a lesson they will never forget, and it's of their own doing this war — every bit of it.

Sunday, September 27th
A scare last night. About 3 a.m., an officer of the 5th Division (on our left) reported that 'the enemy were crossing Condé bridge in great numbers'. We were all hunted out of bed, and very misty and cold it was. I rode to Chassemy with HH, and after waiting there till about 7.30 a.m., we rode home via the Brenelle plateau. The scare was only a scare. However it was, as HH said, 'excellent practice'. I expect someone will get his tail twisted for starting the story.

I had breakfast all right, and then took a map and message up in one of the cars to General Wing (the CRA), who is up in Brenelle. He is a delightful gentleman and always in the thick of everything. He had a shell splinter in his leg a few days ago, but is still doing his job all right.

Nearly all the guns of the division are concealed on the plateau, and very well too. Whenever the Germans 'find' them they shift to another place. At present, this battle has developed into an artillery dual; nothing very fierce, but a constant interchange of shots. Of course the infantry are constantly sniping each other, but that is all that happens here for the moment.

Two days ago, the 3rd Battalion was in action rather heavily with the 2nd Division. As far as I can find out, the battalion was holding trenches with two companies — the other two companies in reserve. The Germans gradually dug themselves in to within 400 yards of our line, so the two reserve companies were ordered to turn them out. The attack failed. A good many men killed and wounded, a bad job.

Editor's Note It was a dawn attack on a German advanced trench that, in the candid words of one battalion officer, 'was not the surprise it was intended to be.' The reserve companies were 'C' and 'D', and they sustained heavy casualties which included the death of 'D' Company commander, Major Anthony Boden, whose body was never found.

On Friday in the afternoon I rode over to see Francis[6], and after some trouble found him and his battery (4 guns) comfortably dug in at Ciry — very far forward! He was very well and cheerful, and has been recommended for a French decoration which, from all accounts, he most thoroughly deserves.

This afternoon who should turn up at HQ but Winston Churchill. He wanted 'to see things', so HH handed him over to my tender care with orders to take him up to the observation station above Chassemy. He was dressed as a Trinity Brother — blue coat, brass buttons, etc. We went up in his car to just short of Chassemy. Captain Guest was driving. The car was a beauty, a 60-hp Rolls-Royce. Half-way there WC asked me, 'Are you quite sure there are no parties of Germans inside our lines?' — (there *had* been a few half-starved wretches found in the big woods). I said I was sure there were none. However, this did not satisfy him and I had to get his revolver out from his coat pocket, a very fierce-looking weapon which he held ready for action on his knee. I was a bit scared of that revolver, as it was one of those patent beasts that you 'pull the trigger and the gun does the rest' sort of thing. However, it didn't get going.

When I got the car behind the Brenelle ridge, I told them to

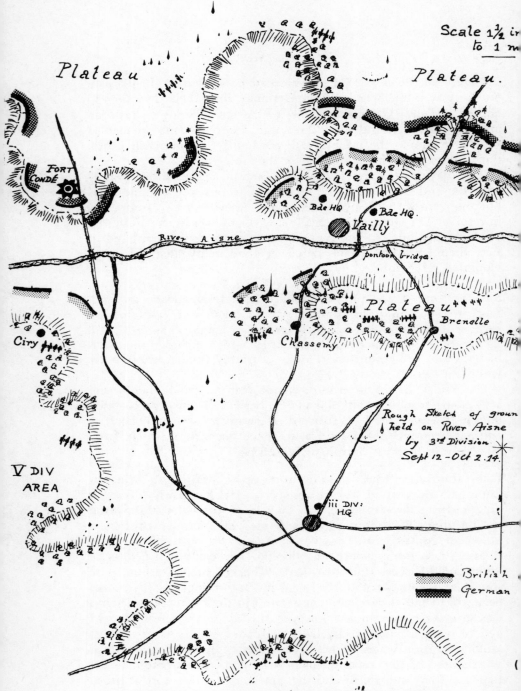

Lieutenant Congreve's diary sketch of area held by Third Division
on Aisne Battlefield 12th September — 2nd October 1914

wait while I went up to see if things were fairly quiet. Only a few shells were coming over, so I took him up to the observation station from where one gets an excellent view over the river. There wasn't much to see, but a few of their shells came gurgling over, and I was glad when they were safely over and bursting well behind us, for I am by no means used to them yet myself. One sees a column of mud and smoke and then the crash of the explosion. We got away without any excitement, after he had grandiloquently exclaimed: 'Now I have been under fire in five continents.'

I must say that he was very nice to me. He hadn't much information to give, except that, 'I am sending out some 9.2 guns.' I got out of the car at Braisne, and he went on to see the Scots Greys at Courcelles[7].

Thursday, October 1st

What might have been a rather serious accident took place yesterday afternoon. The Norwegian minister in Paris[8] got leave from GHQ to come over here and to be shown round. Instead of coming to us to ask his way, he must needs go off on his own, apparently thinking that he could drive his car right up to the trenches. He went up through Brenelle to carry out this plan and set off across the plateau towards the river. He was half-way over when the Germans spotted the car and opened on it with 'crumps'[9].

The first shell made the chauffeur pull up! They began to try to turn the car, and that was as far as they got, for 'crumps' began to arrive in quantities and they fled to the shelter of some neighbouring haystacks, leaving the car to its fate. They saw the chauffeur get hit as he was getting out of the car; whether he was killed or not they did not know. Eventually and with great good fortune they got back to General Wing's HQ unhurt, but covered with mud and dust and bits of haystack. The Royal Artillery sent them on down here and the Duke of Marlborough (who is doing King's Messenger) happening to be with us, took them back in his car.

The minister, a fat middle-aged gentleman, was awfully pleased with himself, but was scared lest it should get into the papers, in which case the Germans would say that Norway had broken her r.eutrality! We calmed his fears, picked straw and mud out of his hair, and sent him off to GHQ with his two ADC's and the Duke, after we had given them tea.

I then took a car and two chauffeurs up to see what I could do to their car, expecting to find it smashed to pieces. We waited till dusk and then walked out to it. The car was intact, but the chauffeur dead, and every piece of glass in the car was smashed to atoms — big, strong plate glass. It was a lovely brand-new Panhard limousine, and beyond the glass, a few bits off the paint and a small hole in the petrol tank, there was no great damage which, considering the number of 'crump' holes around it, was a marvel. Inside the car was a good mixture of glass and mud which we cleared out and, while the hole in the tank was being mended, I finished off the old boy's luncheon basket — chicken there was, and great fat pears, also a huge supply of cigarettes and tobacco for the men in the trenches! There were also heaps of matches. Before he left, the 'minister' said that I might keep all this *'pour les braves soldats'*, so I did so, and sent the car on to GHQ under the second chauffeur, who shed tears.

Saturday, October 3rd
It's been made clear that the Germans have comparatively little opposite to us here, as large bodies of troops have been moving to the north-west where the French are really beginning to go ahead — so it has been decided to hold our present line across the river weakly and concentrate a reserve behind. Last night the division moved from Braisne to where we are now — a place called Arcy-St-Restitue — after a march of ten miles. There was first a big conference of Generals at our house in Braisne, and we moved after dark and got here by 10 p.m. Now we sit still by day and move off again tonight.

Editor's Note Here we have the physical beginnings of the British move northwards that would eventually take the BEF to Flanders. The move had already been discussed between Winston Churchill and Sir John French at Fère-en-Tardenois with regard to concentrating the BEF in the northern region. Such a move would shorten the supply lines of the BEF, offer it a coastal flank and, simultaneously, have the Royal Navy at its left elbow. General Joffre supported the proposed move, provided that it was done quickly. The 7th and 8th Divisions were due soon from England. Once they were re-kitted, they could land in the Dunkirk area for immediate operations towards Lille. There was also the deployment of the Indian Corps who would begin to disembark at Marseilles on 30th September. In their case, they would travel by rail all the way to the north.

Churchill had already sent a detachment, including a brigade of Royal Marine Infantry, direct to Dunkirk on 20th September. Shortly afterwards, the Royal Marines with two Naval Brigades entered Antwerp to help the Belgian Army defend the fortressed city. Rather belatedly, German forces proceeded to shell the outer defences on 28th September with such accuracy and with such an impressive array of heavy artillery that there could only be one outcome. On 29th September the Belgian Army arranged for the evacuation of the city. The civilian population left in droves over the next few days, followed by an orderly withdrawal to Ostend of non-combatants with prisoners and Allied wounded as the actual city came under bombardment. Among them in British Red Cross uniform was Billy Congreve's mother, Celia[10]. On 9th October, it was decided to withdraw the garrison as there was no hope of stopping the German war machine. The following day, Antwerp surrendered.

The so-called 'Race to the Sea' had commenced about ten days before, when the French and Germans tried without success to envelop each other from north of the BEF and the Aisne battleground where the war had turned to stalemate. The French and German determination for each to gain the upper hand gave rise to a rapid northerly movement not unlike the action of an erratic zip fastener. The more the zip travelled upwards, the more the front line locked into place behind.

The 3rd Division, as one of the two infantry divisions in Smith-Dorrien's II Corps, marched towards Pont Ste Maxence where it arrived on 5th October. The town's huge bridge had been blown up during the Allied retreat, so the division's troops crossed over a pontoon bridge to the town's railway station on the other side. There, they were slowly transported by trains to Abbeville on route to Flanders. It was at Abbeville that Lieutenant Congreve learnt that they would stay near the town until the whole division had fully concentrated there for the next stage of the journey.

Sunday, October 11th

I have hardly had a moment to myself for the last five days. We spent all Wednesday in Abbeville. On Thursday I was kept busy at odd jobs and, at 1 p.m., went on with Duval[11] to billet at Le Boisel. We found fairly good places, though it is only a village, and returned to Abbeville about 5 p.m. It was amusing at Le Boisel: I was the first *soldat Anglais* they had seen. One house we went to, the good lady nearly threw a fit when she saw me. She explained on recovering that she thought that I was *un Allemand* and, on realising her mistake, nearly threw another fit — of joy!

We passed an aviation ground on the way back, the 3rd and 4th Squadrons, consisting of about thirty 'planes of all sorts and descriptions. A very workmanlike party they were, with a huge convoy of lorries and a wireless installation. I met Barton (Scots Fusiliers) who is a pilot on a big biplane which is mounted with a machine-gun. He chases any German plane on sight and says it is splendid fun. He thinks that he has bagged one. I rather envied him. A fight in the air must be as good a thrill as one can get on this earth (this sounds Irish!).

We moved from Abbeville at 1 a.m. Friday (the 9th) and marched along in the most lovely moonlight. The aeroplanes which we again passed looked most weird in the moonlight. We got into Le Boisel about 7 a.m. As soon as we were settled in and had breakfast, I was sent off to billet again, this time in a bigger town called Hesdin. I went with Duval and got everything fixed up. We were surrounded with kind people offering us billets, which was most helpful. I picked out two quite pretty girls who were evidently friends, and arranged for Colonel Wilson[12] and his adjutant to go to the home of the less pretty, while I arranged to go to the other's house. The family consisted of Madame and Mademoiselle and *une domestique.*

The girl is called Marie-Louise, so I called her Mary. Both she and Madame were wondrous kind, partly I think as the master of the house was a colonel of a Zouave battalion and was away fighting somewhere. I was frightfully tired and went to bed at once after dinner, though first of all I had to be shown some of the family treasures. We had to move at 4 a.m., so at three I was up and heard a knock on the door. Outside I found the three ladies of the house, ready to conduct me to a bath! We formed a triumphal procession and I had a glorious tub in front of the kitchen fire. My first real tub since St Nazaire! It was good, and then feeling simply grand I found tea and bread-and-butter waiting me, also a postcard with their names on it and a photo of Marie-Louise. I was sorry to go off into the cold dark morning.

We had a tough long march to Pernes. Pernes was an awful sight, streams of refugees from Lille — mostly men — crowds of our men and French soldiers. In addition, cattle was being slaughtered all over the place. We moved from Pernes about 8 p.m. and marched to Gonnehem where we halted for some time, and eventually pushed on to Hinges.

Everywhere are these crowds of refugees. Apparently the Germans make prisoners of all and sundry between the ages of eighteen and fifty, making them work either on defensive lines or in the fields. Now the French are turning all men of these ages out of the towns which may be occupied by the Germans. It was pitiable to see all these poor people with nowhere to go and very weary and footsore. We are very close to the Germans now. I think we have been brought up to help the forward movement on Lille, taking over the line from the French.

Editor's Note Lieutenant Billy Congreve was right. Sir John French and General Foch had agreed a plan at Foch's headquarters at Doullens on 10th October, whereby the BEF would assist the French to outflank and envelope the German right wing. The British Army — still arriving in Flanders — would pivot forward on the French left flank at Vermelles, south-east of Béthune. On 11th October, as Foch became Commandant le Groupe des Armées du Nord (GAN), Smith-Dorrien's II Corps began its advance on Lille. The Germans, having occupied Lille and then lost it in their retreat, re-occupied the city during the night of 11th/12th October. The centre of the French coal, iron and engineering industries, as well as the point where five main railway lines met, the recapture of Lille was a bitter blow to the Allies. Lille was to stay in German hands until mid-October 1918.

12th October

We moved about 8 a.m. this morning, leaving behind all the transport etc., but ready to come up when necessary. Headquarters at first was at Le Cornet Malo. HH had gone off to ride around the line when I got there, so I went to look for him. I rode as far as the Marmuse cross-roads when I heard rifle shots just in front of me and, as some bullets started coming down the road, I dismounted and waited a bit. General Wing then came up and we rode on together to Zelobes and Vieille Chapelle where the Germans were last night. There was a good deal of firing going on down by the canal where the 8th Brigade were entrenching themselves.

There were, as usual, a lot of dead horses — and the church was in flames with the spire knocked about; probably intentional, as churches make good positions for artillery observers. This country here is deadly flat and uninteresting. Few hedges, numerous roads and many dykes and ditches — nothing could be more unlike the

Aisne, and not unlike our country around Peterborough, fewer hedges though.

I saw signs of German brutality today for the first time. We found a poor old man hiding in a hay stack. He must have been a good eighty years old and was half mad with terror. No wonder, for his face was a mass of blood. Some brute had evidently hit him, probably with a rifle butt. He was too terrified to talk and had apparently been hiding for some time. We handed him over to two French soldiers, who led him away to get him bound up. It's almost incredible that soldiers should so treat an unarmed *ancient* like that, yet I fear there was but little doubt.

There was heavy fighting for us today. The Germans held the village of Fosse most obstinately. Although we eventually drove them out (chiefly by gunfire), we lost a good many men doing it. We have held La Vieille Chapelle all day against various attacks, and our line is over the canal tonight. We also hold Lacouture and Richebourg L'Avoue, and the 5th Division[13] are on our right. The 6th Division are somewhere on our left near Hazebrouck, covered by the 2nd Cavalry Division. The 1st Cavalry Division links our left and 2nd Cavalry Division's right. We also have on our left some French cavalry under General Conneau. Firing has died down now and I am just off to Corps HQ (now at Hinges) with General HH.

Editor's Note The two British cavalry divisions had instructions initially to cover the concentration of II Corps. On 9th October, both divisions were formed into a cavalry corps under General Allenby. On the same day they were first ordered to make good the line Merville–Hazebrouck, next the high ground about Mont Noir and the Mont des Cats, after which the canal line Comines–Ypres. By the 11th, with little resistance, Allenby's newly-formed cavalry corps reached its first objective. Meantime III Corps was arriving from the Aisne and detraining at St Omer, on the left of II Corps. Only the 6th Division had arrived by the evening of 11th October with part of the 4th Division. To cover the detrainment of the remainder of the troops, III Corps was ordered to advance to Hazebrouck which was thirteen miles east of St Omer.[14]

13th October

I had a good though short night on a mattress outside HH's room and we rode out together at 5.30 and went to Vieille Chapelle. He was very cheery and I think he likes getting to business again. The

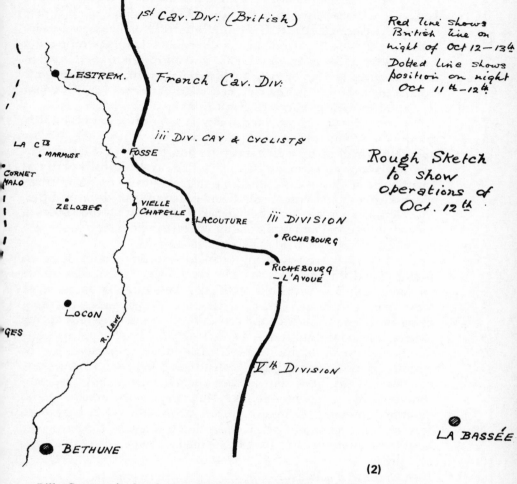

1st Cav. Div: (British)

LESTREM.

French Cav. Div.

iii Div. Cav. & Cyclists

LA Cⁱˢ
• MARMUSE
• FOSSE

CORNET
NALO

ZELOBES

VIELLE
CHAPELLE
• LACOUTURE

iii DIVISION

• RICHEBOURG

• RICHEBOURG
— L'AVOUÉ

LOCON

R. LAWE

GES

Vᵗʰ DIVISION

BETHUNE

LA BASSÉE

Red line shows
British line on
night of Oct 12 – 13ᵗʰ
Dotted line shows
position on night
Oct 11ᵗʰ – 12ᵗʰ

Rough Sketch
to show
operations of
Oct. 12ᵗʰ

(2)

Billy Congreve's sketch that shows II Corps' advance in his sector from
night of 11th/12th Oct.(dotted line) to night of 12th/13th Oct.(solid line).

7th Brigade HQ was still at Vieille Chapelle. The church spire fell in
last night and it is now only a pile of smoking ruins. Then we went
on to the 8th Brigade[15] in Lacouture. Both had had some sharp
fighting — the Worcesters got one company badly cut up. They
lost five officers (two killed) and a lot of men. There were several
of our own and German dead about.

We are to push on hard today and are already at it hammer and tongs — we are advancing due east. The Gordons are in Fosse which the Germans cleared out pretty quickly on being shelled by our howitzers (4.5") from here. A German aeroplane dropped a bomb close to Corps HQ last night. Also a lot of notices printed in French advising the French to surrender at once, as they were bound to be beaten in the end, also stating how well the Germans looked after their prisoners! I don't think!

We moved our HQ up here today (Lacouture) and have fairly good billets. Our progress is rather held up on the left; we are apparently held up by German cavalry and Jägers — the latter fight like tigers and shoot mighty straight. The cavalry consist partly of Death's Head Hussars. We caught a few of them; very smart their fuzzy busbies look with the skull and crossbones in silver on front. The Germans are good at this fighting — they put all the houses in a state of defence, and it takes a lot to shift them out.

Editor's Note When advancing eastwards on the north side of La Bassée Canal the previous day, the three infantry brigades of 3rd Division with 5th Division's 14th and 15th Infantry Brigades on their right (the other 5th Division's infantry brigade — 13th — being on the south side of the canal) were opposed by four enemy cavalry divisions, supported by more battalions than the total number of men comprising two British infantry brigades. By the evening of 12th October, the 15th Brigade had entered Givenchy, but lost it the next day after a terrific enemy bombardment followed by a counter-attack. Due to enemy resistance, as described by Billy Congreve, the 3rd Division could only push forward one mile on 13th October. Casualties in II Corps over both days amounted to about 1,200 men.

14th October, Lacouture
As bad a thing happened this morning as ever could happen. Hammy is dead, and we lose a splendid soldier and I a very good friend. He and Thorpe were out to the north of Vieille Chapelle; he had gone to see personally why our left wing was hung up. They were dismounted and standing on the road when a salvo of shrapnel burst right over them. One bullet hit him in the forehead, and he died almost immediately. He never spoke or opened his eyes. There were several other officers there besides Thorpe, yet nobody else was hit.

We brought his body back here tonight in a motor ambulance.

We had to wait till night, as the road was still being shelled. During the day I had a rough coffin made and a grave dug under the walls of the old church here. At 7.15 p.m., when the ambulance arrived, we put him into it just as he was, wrapped in a blanket. I had to take the spurs off his poor feet though, as they would not fit, and then we nailed on the lid. I then put a guard around him with fixed bayonets and left him.

At 8.30 we all assembled. There was a representative from each unit and Sir Horace Smith-Dorrien turned up also. Poor Lindsay, Hammy's servant, kept breaking down. It was a pitch-dark night and had been raining hard all day, so there was mud everywhere and a cold wet 'feel' in the air. The rifle and machine-gun fire was very heavy, and it sounded but a few yards away, so loud was it and so still the night. Stray bullets now and then knocked up against the church and gravestones, but somehow nobody bothered about them.

Just before the chaplain arrived the firing almost ceased, but while the short service was being read it commenced again, louder and nearer than ever, so loud indeed that the chaplain's voice could hardly be heard.

The scene was the strangest and most beautiful I have ever seen. The poor church battered by shells, the rough wooden coffin with a pewter plate nailed on the lid on which we had stamped his name, a rough cross of flowers made by the men, the small guard with fixed bayonets and the group of twenty or thirty bareheaded officers and men. Above all, the incessant noise, so close, sometimes dying down only to seem to redouble itself a few minutes later. A ghastly sort of light was given by a couple of acetylene lamps from a car. It was soon over, and then each officer and man stood for a moment by the grave, saluted, and went back to his work.

Sir Horace, in that rather wonderful voice of his, said: 'Indeed, a true soldier's grave. God rest his soul.' Nobody else spoke. I wanted to cry. I stayed and saw the filling in of the grave, and now I must see to putting up a cross.

CHAPTER THREE

The Crunch at Neuve Chapelle

Major-General Hamilton's death came on the fourth day of what is termed as the Battle of La Bassée. This particular battle was one of four principal bloody struggles, all fated to take place within days of each other with a good deal of overlap as November approached. They happened when the Allies attempted to swing forward to outflank and envelope the German right wing. The swing forward, however, clashed simultaneously with a huge German movement when the enemy also shifted forces north. These forces included troops released by the fall of Antwerp and four newly organised corps, all of which were hurried forward to turn the Allied flank and to reach the Channel ports.

The names and dates of these battles (and the dates are simply reasonable guides, because there were no clean beginnings or cut-off points) in which the BEF strongly participated were: La Bassée (10th October—2nd November), Armentières (13th October—2nd November), Messines (12th October—2nd November) and First Battle of Ypres (19th October—22nd November). About the bloodiest of them all, the First Battle of Ypres virtually finished Britain's Regular Army and encompassed Langemarck (21st—24th October), Gheluvelt (29th—31st October) and Nonne Bosschen (11th November).

Just before 10th October, Sir Henry Rawlinson's independent force (under Kitchener's control) of 3rd Cavalry Division and 7th (Infantry) Division[1] landed at Ostend and Zeebrugge, and had arrived at Ghent via Bruges on 9th October. On the same day, Rawlinson's force was constituted as IV Corps and placed under Sir John French's command. Meanwhile a German cavalry corps had entered Ypres on 7th October, but quickly retired south on encountering a strong British presence in the area. By 15th October, the Belgian Army had withdrawn to the banks of the Yser as Rawlinson's force covered its flank by occupying the country between Bruges and Ypres. The Germans moved into the vacuum, occupying Bruges, Ghent, Ostend and Zeebrugge as well as less important places in their path. Retiring on Ypres, the 3rd

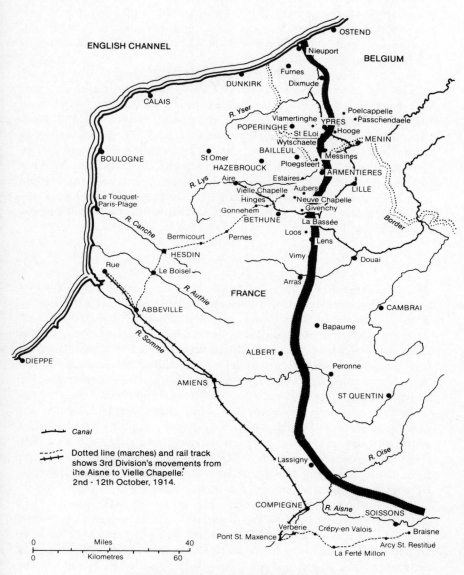

THE FRONT LINE ON 15TH OCTOBER, 1914

(3) The Aisne to the English Channel

Dotted line and italicised place-names shows 3rd Division's movements
from the Aisne to Vieille Chapelle: 2nd–12th October 1914

Cavalry Division of IV Corps entered the city on 13th October. The 7th Division arrived the following day and positioned itself just outside the city across the Ypres–Menin road. South of Ypres, Pulteney's III Corps entered Bailleul on the morning of 14th October.

The brigades of Smith-Dorrien's II Corps fought continuously all day on both sides of La Bassée Canal, but only limited progress was made in conjunction with the French 7th Cavalry Division on the left of 3rd Division. Much of the enemy resistance came from Jägers and dismounted cavalry who had established themselves in farms and in village houses. On 15th October, brigades of 3rd Division, with field guns situated amongst the infantry, began a determined advance to drive the Germans from their entrenched positions and fortified villages in an effort to reach the La Bassée– Estaires road. In his inimitable style, Billy Congreve describes the situation:

*

Thursday, October 15th
Since I last entered up our movements, we have not managed to push forward much. It's very difficult country to advance over, the deep broad dykes and ditches make it very bad. Add to this these hard fighting Jägers, and the difficulties are many. We have lost heavily, especially in officers[2], so much so that the Royal Scots[3] this morning were commanded by a second-lieutenant, so Thorpe has gone out to take over command of them.

French cavalry have pushed into Riez Bailleul, with the divisional cavalry squadron further north. Coming up into line with us fast are more French cavalry and the 4th and 6th Divisions[4]. General French's HQ is now in St Omer. Today, we have been attacking the La Bassée–Estaires road hard, and hope by tonight to have driven the Germans over it.

The French cavalry on our left are very little good. They naturally hate fighting on foot, and it is a pitiful sight to see these huge cuirassiers in their 'tin tummies' going to attack or to hold trenches. Imagine the gentlemen outside Whitehall going to attack on foot in full dress uniform. This is 1914, not 1814, and yet the French are dressed more or less the same as they were then!

I've been up in the church spire here a good deal of the day, and though one could see a long way — long past the German line of defence — it was awfully hard to spot any movement. We could

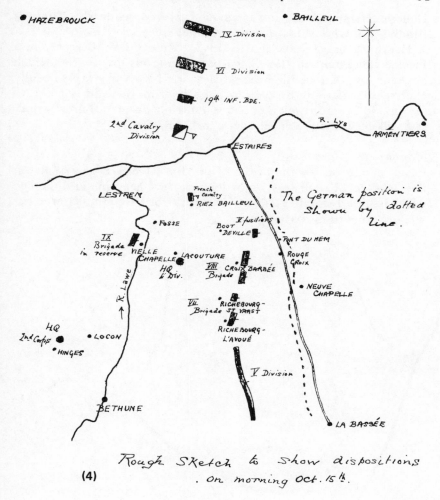

HAZEBROUCK

BAILLEUL

IV Division

VI Division

19ᵗʰ INF. BDE.

2ⁿᵈ Cavalry Division

R. Lys

ARMENTIERS

ESTAIRES

LESTREM

French cavalry
RIEZ BAILLEUL

The German position is shown by dotted line.

FOSSE

V fusiliers

BOUT DEVILLE

PONT DU HEM

IX Brigade in reserve

VIELLE CHAPELLE

LACOUTURE

ROUGE CROIX

HQ 6ᵗʰ DIV.

VIII CROIX BARBÉE Brigade

NEUVE CHAPELLE

R. Lawe

VII Brigade

RICHEBOURG-ST VAAST

HQ 2ⁿᵈ Corps

LOCON

RICHEBOURG-L'AVOUÉ

HINGES

V Division

BETHUNE

LA BASSÉE

(4)

Rough Sketch to show dispositions on morning Oct. 15ᵗʰ.

now and then see our men moving forward in extended formation, and the shrapnel was bursting over the German and our lines almost continuously.

General MacKenzie[5] turned up today to take over command and brings two ADCs with him. I fear I must therefore retire to the battalion again. I think I shall try to get to the 1st Battalion, as I believe they are shortest of officers. It's tiresome, just as I have settled down here, and I don't know what to do with Viscount,

General Hammy's old horse which he loved so dearly. There is Lindsay too who wants to stay with me.

Hammy's grave looks quite tidy[6]. While I was there today a French inhabitant of the village offered me his 'own' cross which he kept by him in his house ready for his own grave (a really cheery sort of thing to keep in one's bedroom). I did not like to say no, so it's been put up, and is a terrible ornate affair of wood, but will do well enough till I get another ready.

Monday, October 19th

I am to stay on for the present, but don't feel very overjoyed at the prospect. I shall stay on as long as they need me and then go back. I think I should go now if it wasn't for Viscount. Thorpe has already gone to his battalion.

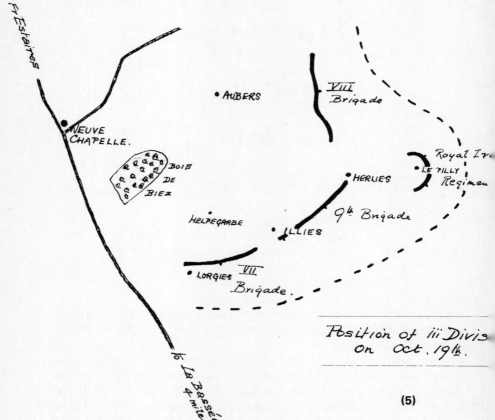

(5)

On Friday we moved from Lacouture to this place — Neuve Chapelle. The villages on the way here are fearfully knocked about, especially Croix Barbée. There seems little chance of pushing on today. The division as far as I can make out is now on a line something like this [see map on previous page—*Ed.*]

We can apparently get no further for the Germans have brought up strong reinforcements, and also have a strongly prepared position which we are now up against. So it looks like another siege unless we are strongly reinforced here.

The fighting was hard all the way. Aubers, Helpgarbe, Herlies, Le Pilly and Illies were all taken with difficulty at some considerable loss to us, but we hope more to them. They never waited for our men to get at 'em with the bayonet, though the 9th Brigade got a few 'stuck' in Herlies I believe. A beastly habit the brutes have is to go on shooting until our men get within a few yards and they then throw up their hands. I am glad to say that the British soldier, soft-hearted as he undoubtedly is, gets tired of this sort of thing and will, I think, deal harshly with this type.

25th October
The last few days have been very busy. After a good deal of consideration it was agreed that our former and forward line was too extended to hold — we were and are too weak to shove ahead — so now we are back on a strong position which we dug before withdrawing. The turn of the tide of our advance was clearly shown by the almost complete loss of the Royal Irish in Le Pilly. Apparently they pushed on too far (as can be seen in preceding sketch) and were heavily attacked and surrounded. There are about seventy survivors all told — a bad business.

The Germans have been following up their attack on Le Pilly and are evidently strongly reinforced, but so far they have done no good to themselves and we have killed a lot of them. The arrival of some of their beastly heavy artillery has begun to make things nasty for us though, and we have by no means got off scot-free. Of course our headquarters has had to shift back again to Lacouture, a place I hoped to have seen the last of, and not one of very happy memories.

Editor's Note Here we have trench warfare slowly superseding that of war of movement as two vast battlegrounds developed: one on the north of the River Lys (Ypres salient, where Haig's I Corps came into line from the Aisne on 21st October); and La Bassée/

Armentières on its south, where II and III Corps with Conneau's cavalry and the recently-arrived Indian Corps unknowingly faced a numerically and materially superior enemy. Unknowingly, because both Foch and French had seriously underestimated the German strength above and below the Lys. As French issued an operational order on 16th October for a general advancement, so (below the Lys) the German Sixth Army under Crown Prince Rupprecht simultaneously advanced in conjunction with the German Fourth Army which was above the Lys.

The inevitable happened. Outmanned and outgunned, the Allies fell back on the south of the Lys, although III Corps had captured and managed to hold on to Armentières and some area around it. As for the tragedy of the 2/Royal Irish Regiment at Le Pilly, which the battalion had taken on the 19th, their fate was sealed when it was believed that Conneau's cavalry had occupied Fournes, roughly a mile north-east of their position and thereby covering their left flank. In fact, Conneau had failed to take Fournes. When Smith-Dorrien started to retreat his left for fear of being enveloped on 20th October, the 2/Royal Irish stayed in Le

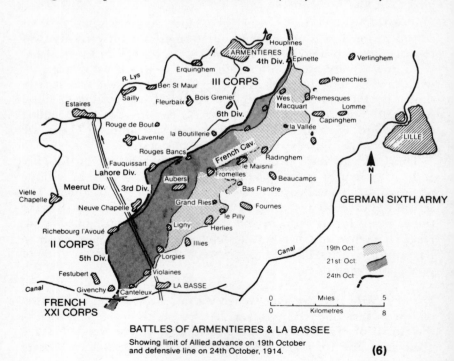

BATTLES OF ARMENTIERES & LA BASSEE

Showing limit of Allied advance on 19th October
and defensive line on 24th October, 1914.　　　　**(6)**

Pilly, not realising that they were in an isolated position. After a crippling bombardment in the morning of 20th October, they were attacked by three battalions of the German 14th Division. It was a one-sided contest, and the fighting to take and to hold the village cost the battalion 17 officers and 561 men.

During the night of 22nd/23rd October, Smith-Dorrien's II Corps retired to a newly prepared line that went from east of Givenchy (now in Allied hands) up to a little west of Rouges Bancs. The line ran just east of Neuve Chapelle which came within 3rd Division's right flank that connected with 5th Division's 14th Brigade. Little realising – in common with the rest of 3rd Division – that the Germans were preparing a major assault on Neuve Chapelle, Billy Congreve continued his entry for 25th October:

Cornwall and I are now great allies. He is in the Royal Field Artillery and is here as Intelligence Officer. He speaks goodness knows how many languages and is as brave a fellow as ever I have met. He is keen too, and that's always good. On Thursday (22nd) he and I went out to try and get some information about the situation on our extreme left at Fauquissart. The night before, Wednesday the 21st, there were rumours of Germans massing there. At 5.30 a.m. we motored out and, leaving the car some way back, walked up to the trenches. It was a misty but fine morning. The position there was:

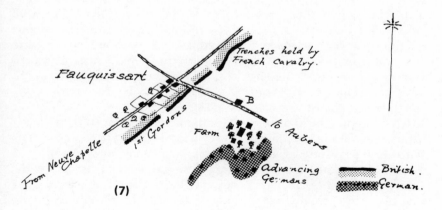

(7)

The left trenches were held by French Chasseurs who were firing into the mist, apparently at nothing in particular. The 1/Gordons held the other trenches and, not only were they without sentries, but nearly all officers and men were coiled up asleep at the bottom of the trenches. They had made no attempt at any form of head cover, no patrols out or a picquet in the farm in front. I found an officer called Thomas whom I knew at Sandhurst. He wasn't able to give us much information, so Cornwall and I decided to go forward to the house marked 'B' to see what we could see. It was about a hundred yards in front of our trenches.

We got up there all right and it seemed deserted enough. I was just going upstairs to make certain, when out of the mist (which was now clearing off) we heard a loud and clear *auf, auf*. Cornwall said that this was German for 'up', 'up' and, sure enough, a few hundred yards off were some advancing figures unmistakably German, doubling forward in no particular formation, and keeping as much under cover as possible. Cornwall and I cleared back to the trenches rather hurriedly. By dint of some kicking and shaking, we got them on their feet and shooting, even though there was no attempt to give proper fire orders and not much interest shown by the men.

The Germans at once stopped and took cover when we opened fire, and then continued to advance again one by one with 'short rushes'. Eventually they began to build up a firing line about 300 to 400 yards away. They were extraordinary hard to see against the mist, for the grey-green uniforms they wear are an excellent colour. I got out my telescope and marked down one bold fellow with great care. He was hiding behind a turnip which had a very leafy top to it. I then pointed this out very carefully to Cornwall who had a shot at the place. I saw the shot strike short, so we put up the sight fifty yards and he fired again. I, with my eye glued to the telescope, saw a violent movement behind the turnip. I sincerely hope that the shot was as good as it looked. We might have had some pretty shooting, and I was longing for my shooting specs, but we had to get back to make our report.

That night (the 22nd) the Germans made one of their heavy attacks all along our front. Everywhere we repulsed the attack with heavy losses to the Germans, except just south of the Fauquissart crossroads where the Germans walked right into the Gordons' trenches. As usual they must have been all asleep. Only one place in their line was broken through. The Middlesex[7] who were in reserve, came up under Colonel Hull and drove back the intruders, making everything secure again.

At dawn next morning, Cornwall and I went up and there was no difficulty in seeing the place where the Germans had broken through, for the place was marked clear enough with dead bodies of our men and Germans — mostly Germans, I am glad to say. Apparently only one company had broken through and we found twenty-three of their dead and one young officer.

The first body we found was that of a poor young subaltern of the Gunners who was in the trenches observing. He had been bayoneted and then apparently rushed over by a good many feet. He was a sad sight — Nixon was his name.

After finding out what had happened, Cornwall and I examined all the dead Germans, taking all their papers to examine later. We collect a lot of useful information in this way as to the movements of the various regiments and corps etc; also a good idea of the personal feelings of the Germans. Nearly every German keeps some form of diary — which I think goes to show the higher education of the Germans. A good many of them had been bayoneted. Horrid wounds our bayonets make, and these Germans must have put up a good fight. It is all rot the stuff one reads in our papers about the inferiority of the German soldiers to ours. If anything, the German is the better, for though we undoubtedly are the more dogged and *impossible* to beat, they are the more highly disciplined. Of course, here we are up against some of their best regiments.

Most of the dead Germans had got stiff during the night, and it was difficult to get papers and things off them. I had no idea a man was so unwieldy when dead. I don't think I have ever handled a dead man before; somehow one doesn't mind out here, for death loses its terrors and awesomeness. Their equipment was very good and the amount of ammunition these fellows were carrying is extraordinary. Even some of their pockets were filled with it, and also their packs, which are made of untanned cowhide.

The officer was interesting. His name was Lieutenant Meyer Zu Wambergen and he was Adjutant of the 57th Regiment. I noticed that he had on the ribbon of the Iron Cross which he wore between two buttons, so I searched him carefully and found the Cross in his purse. Unfortunately, he had no diary. He died an Iron Cross death all right, leading his men inside the enemy's line. He had a Frenchman's sword and field-glasses. I wonder if I shall ever have the chance of finding out more about him?

This morning (the 25th), Cornwall and I were sent off to try and find out exactly how things were going in Neuve Chapelle, which had been constantly under attack from the Bois de Biez, and where the Germans had apparently got a hold on parts of our

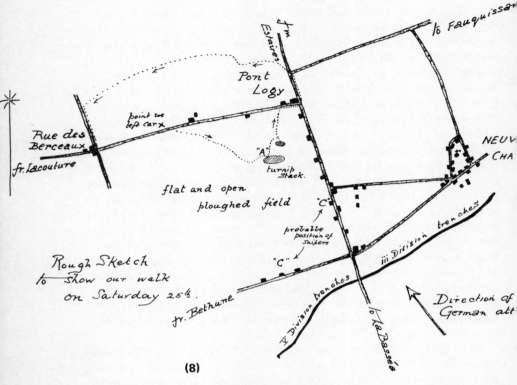

to Fauquissart

Estaires

Pont Logy

point we left car X

Rue des Berceaux

fr. Lacouture

"A"

turnip Stack.

NEUV
CHA

flat and open ploughed field

"C"

probable position of snipers

iii Division trenches

"C"

Rough Sketch
to show our walk
on Saturday 25th.

V Division trenches

fr. Bethune

V Division trenches

to La Bassée

Direction of
German att

(8)

trenches. We went by car to where I have marked 'X' on the sketch, and where we had to leave the car owing to the fact that a German 11-inch shell had pitched right on to the road. It knocked a hole about ten feet deep and, to get along the road, one had to walk in the ditch.

On leaving the car, we turned into a ploughed field to walk across the corner straight to the village. After going not very many yards bullets began to zip over, but we did not bother, as we thought they must only be stray ones. A few yards further on, we came to the conclusion that whether stray or not, they were beginning to come unpleasantly close. In addition, there were big bits of 11-inch shell singing by us. The actual bursts were a good six hundred yards off (on the line of our trenches), so they had some way to come.

Eventually we decided that things were rather unhealthy, and we came to the conclusion that all the bullets were not stray ones. Just as we both thought this, we also realised that we were near the middle of the very flat ploughed field. By good fortune, however, there was a turnip stack not many yards away ('A'), so we ran to it quick and under it and felt happier. There was then no doubt that we were being fired at, and not from a great distance either, for whenever we tried to look over the top or round the edge, zip came another bullet. Evidently some snipers or sniper had, during one of their night attacks, found their or his way through our lines by accident or intent, and now lay up in one of the houses marked 'C'.

We tried to spot them through our glasses, but found it unwholesome, so we were rather hard up to know what to do. Tummy crawling seemed the only solution. There was another pile about fifty yards off. Cornwall set off for this and I followed. We arrived there without being seen. We then decided to run for it to the road where we knew there was a ditch. I went first this time and got there without being fired at. Cornwall followed and had two shots after him, while I sat laughing at him from the depths of my ditch. Shots followed us along the road, so we decided for home, the whole place being too 'busy'.

We returned by making a detour behind. Even there we were unlucky, for a stray crump came yelling along and burst about twenty yards off, covering us in mud. Somehow we found ourselves lying in a very shallow ditch. We got back to the car, having done nothing of any value, but it adds zest to life, this new work. We must get those snipers cleared out somehow or other.

Editor's Note On 25th October, detachments of the Lahore Division moved into the trenches at Neuve Chapelle, their presence bolstering the declining manpower of the defenders. The Indian infantry arrived in the nick of time, because enemy action at Neuve Chapelle would shortly rise to a crescendo. The very next day — a Sunday — the Germans launched a major assault on the village. It took the form of a massive bombardment in support of an attacking force of six infantry regiments and two Jäger battalions. Why so much effort for one small village is puzzling, unless the Germans believed that its capture would place them astride the main communications line between II and III Corps. Whatever the reason, the brunt of the assault fell on the 3rd Division battalions and their recently arrived Indian comrades.

27th October

The Germans seem quite determined to break through us at Neuve

Chapelle, and their efforts get more and more vicious. The battalions of the 7th Brigade, who are holding these trenches, are nearly done for, for this incessant shelling with these big shells is very terrible. They have hardly any officers left and the men are few and rather nerve-broken. It is getting on for three weeks' hard and continuous fighting now — always under fire by day and driving off desperately hard pushed attacks by night. Our men are really wonders, but things begin to go ill now. Trenches are lost and then retaken a few hours later, each time fewer men. The Wilts, West Kents and Royal Irish Rifles are the chief sufferers, and the devil is we have no fresh troops to shove in to help. However, I suppose all comes right in the end.

On the 25th the Germans bombarded our trenches especially heavily (while Cornwall and I were up there being played with by that sniper), and I have never seen a better display of explosive destruction. There were shells bursting in the village and around it twenty and thirty a minute, each shell sending up columns of black and pink smoke some fifty feet into the air and making the whole place shake and jump. The whistle and crash of 'em seemed incessant. Each hole they made was big enough to put the Ford car into and lose it! The actual trenches being outside the village escaped a good deal, but in several places all semblance to a trench was gone, and the inmates buried; yet the others stuck it out and were ready to shoot more Germans when the shelling finished and the attack began.

28th October

A very anxious night. A heavier attack than ever developed against the poor old 7th Brigade — the Germans having massed as usual in the Bois de Biez[8]. The RIR, Wilts and Royal Scots were driven out, leaving the West Kents and 5th Fusiliers to be enfiladed by the Germans who occupied their trenches[9]. It was really a case of physical exhaustion as much as anything else that told in the long run. The men just went to sleep.

A strong counter-attack is to commence this morning, so we hope to regain our line and turn out the Germans who are now in between the 5th Fusiliers and West Kents. This gap includes the village of Neuve Chapelle, so I expect we shall have some house fighting — always dirty work. Cornwall and I have been ordered to go out and see how things go, and to keep on sending in reports to Headquarters. We ought to have an interesting morning. I wonder how the natives[10] will like modern weapons as used by the

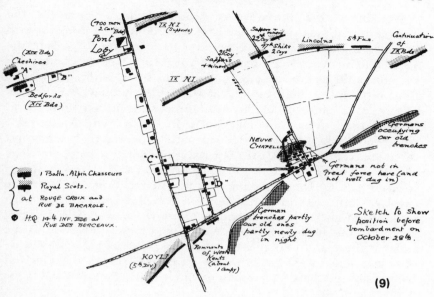

(9)

Germans? They are mad keen and look all right, but I wonder what they will think of shrapnel?

29th October

My word, we did have an interesting day yesterday. Nearly too interesting. The [above and following two] sketches will show how things were at dawn yesterday, at mid-day and at 9 p.m.

At about nine, Cornwall and I reached the house marked 'A' on first sketch and left our horses and grooms there, taking two orderlies on with us to carry back messages. We went straight to the little house marked 'B' and spent some time there, as we were anxious to try and find out where the Germans had been lying up who tried to snipe us that day. Although we were again sniped at close range, not a sign of a German could be seen. We knocked a hole in the roof for the telescope, but in spite of the fact that a bullet smashed the tiles close to this hole — not far from my head — we could see nothing. It was most uncanny. We had to give it up at length, the only German we could see being a dead one in the middle of the field. We went up the ditch to Pont Logy and, here, could see native infantry sitting, ready to advance, and also found 400 men of the 2nd Cavalry Brigade in reserve.

We knew that the advance would begin as soon as the bombardment was over — the attack to be pushed home by 9th Brigade, native infantry[11], the sappers and miners[12] and the Sikhs[13]. The West Kent remnants were to attack when the 9th Brigade and native infantry came up level with them. The Lincolns[14] would help the attack with rifle and machine-gun fire. The reserves consisted of the Alpin Chasseurs and Royal Scots at Rouge Croix (over a mile away). The Bedfords[15] and Cheshires[16], who were only to be used if absolutely necessary, were about three-quarters of a mile off. The only immediate reserve were the cavalry at Pont Logy.

After talking for a few minutes to 'Chaser' Forsyth[17] and the cavalry, Cornwall and I went down a very deep and muddy ditch to 'C' to await the bombardment. There was a little rifle shooting going on, but nothing serious. At 'C' we found a few men in the *auberge* there and two gunner subalterns, who said that they were observers. They were in a hopeless place for observing, nothing but houses and gardens all around them. In fact, they seemed to be doing 'damn all'.

We had only been there a moment when the bombardment started. For half an hour Neuve Chapelle was a beastly unhealthy place. Every gun we had was turned on to it, and also a brigade of French 75's under that great little man, Commandant Creuse. We were so close up that we could hardly hear ourselves speak; it was one incessant crashing. A fine sight, the white of the shrapnel and the yellow of the lyddite, also a good deal of black smoke from the Germans, who also chimed in. So we sat, waiting for it to stop and wondering when a shell would come our way. None did, however, and then our guns lengthened their range 500 yards everywhere and the Indians advanced.

At first, Cornwall and I could not find a good place to watch from. We tried several houses. I got a fright at one place. I jumped through a hole in a wall into a little garden and came very near on top of a live German. He was badly wounded and making no end of a fuss, grunting and groaning. He had been out there all last night, and when his friends retired they had taken his rifle and had not attempted even to make him comfortable, far less carry him away. His leg was badly shattered, probably by shrapnel. I made him comfortable, and gave him his pack and opened it, but had to leave him where he was, as we were in a hurry.

All the houses were so broken about and there were so many trees, hedges and orchards that finding a place was difficult. We did at length though, and got forward to 'D'. All seemed to be going well. The house we went into was more or less undamaged and was occupied by two of our wounded men, hiding in the cellar. It struck me at once that the native infantry had very few supports and that they had very little touch, if any, with the sappers and miners on their left, who we heard at this moment already entering the first houses of Neuve Chapelle at the northern end with great and weird yelling.

To the south we had a good view of the West Kent trenches. They were well held and we could see the men putting on their equipment; I thought probably preparing to co-operate with the right of the native infantry when the latter moved up level with them. The German shrapnel was bursting over these trenches very accurately, but apparently not doing much damage.

The native infantry suddenly seemed to lose direction. They had been advancing at right-angles to the 'C'-Neuve Chapelle road, but then came under fire from the German trenches south of 'D' and wheeled to the right. This seemed to take the dash out of the attack. Up till then they had had few casualties, but now began to suffer heavily and the stretcher bearers were very busy. Of the sappers and miners we could now see nothing, as they were into the village. There also seemed some movement in the German trenches, probably reserves and supports moving in. We had an excellent view of these trenches, and we could see them firing away at the native infantry. Many of their bullets came high and hence in at our windows, which made observation no easier or pleasant. I felt much more inclined to lie down on the floor.

By this time the native infantry were lying down in a sort of shallow trench about fifty yards from our house, facing the German trenches. How we longed for them to get up and advance in short rushes as white troops would have done. If only they had, I believe they would have got into the Germans. As it was, they started crawling like great khaki slugs and about the same pace. Fancy starting to crawl 300 or 400 yards from the enemy's trenches! It was an extraordinary sight, looking at it as we were from so close.

One man I watched — he sort of fascinated me — was a great bearded turbaned fellow. He shoved his rifle along in front of him and crawled just as I have many a time after rabbits. He advanced perhaps a yard a minute. I remember reckoning that he would at that pace reach the German trenches in about six hours!

He was going along like this and had just pulled up his right leg

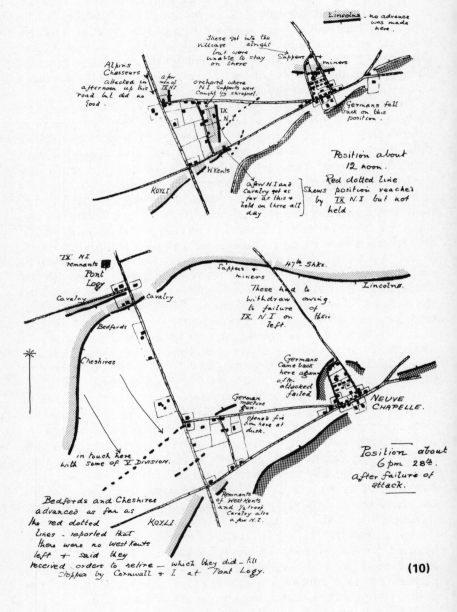

Major William La T. Congreve, VC, DSO, MC.

Billy Congreve at the age of seven.

to get a shove forward, and his arms were stretched out in front of him, when suddenly he seemed to relax and collapse, though the position of his body and limbs did not change. I could hardly believe that he was dead, he looked so natural, but dead he was. I suppose shot through the head, for he never moved again.

After a bit the crawlers began to give up. One after another they were being picked off by the Germans, for the ground was flat and there was no cover at all, so they began to crawl back to the shallow trench. One big man, I suppose, considered it beneath his dignity to crawl backwards, so he coolly rose to his feet, picked up his rifle, and walked slowly and steadily back to the trench. I found myself counting the paces he took. I had counted eleven, and twelve would have taken his to safety. He was walking as steadily as he would have on parade, and then suddenly up went his arms and he fell forward flat on his face.

There were many lying there by now and, worst of all, there were white officers down. In fact, nearly all the white officers. Things were beginning to look bad. Every minute's delay was a minute gained to the Germans who had undoubtedly been shaken by the attack, but were now shooting mighty straight and coolly. So Cornwall very gallantly said that he would go and try to get the native infantry to advance, and off he went. I hardly expected to see him again.

I dodged back through the houses to send a message to the effect that the attack was hung up, and supports were needed at once if we were ever going to get the natives on. I got the message off from 'C' and then returned to the house again. The firing was much heavier on my way back. There were bullets everywhere, or so it seemed. Just as I got to the house a bullet cut the strapping on the inside of my knee and cut the skin — it made me hop about proper for a moment. I couldn't see Cornwall anywhere. The natives were still in the trench and all the crawlers who were not dead were also back again, leaving an unpleasant line of motionless figures to show how far the advance had been.

I acquired a rifle and two bandoliers of ammunition from one of the wounded men and, going up to the top window, I started trying to pick off some Germans — range about 450 yards. I longed for my spectacles. What I did in the way of damage I could not see. There was one German who looked as if he was leaning up against the back of the trench. I could see down to his waist. About five rounds I let off at him, but he did not seem to care. Eventually I came to the conclusion that he was dead, so I kept on

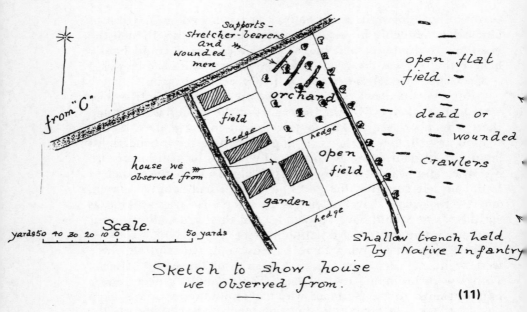

Sketch to show house
we observed from.

(11)

sniping at the helmets I could see.

What I knew would happen did happen. The German shrapnel started to arrive. My word, it scared me. It burst beautifully just on a level with the tops of the apple trees in the orchard — where all the stray natives had collected and where the stretcher bearers were at work. In a few seconds that orchard was a proper little inferno, branches and cut-in-half trees flew about and the men there were almost wiped out. One poor fellow just below my windows had most of his face torn away. I thought that my house might get its turn, so I went down and, as the man was able to walk but could not see, I led him back to 'C'. It seemed an awful long way and the poor fellow's wound was terrible. I do not know why he was not dead.

We arrived all right, but I found that all the telephone wires had been cut, so I could send no further messages through. However, I set my orderly off down the ditch to Pont Logy with a message, saying how things were going. There were no signs of any supports coming up. It was then about 11.30 p.m. I did not quite know what to do when suddenly Cornwall appeared, unhurt. At the same moment a troop of cavalry came up the ditch from Pont

Logy. We arranged that the troops should go up to support the natives with Cornwall to show them the way. We also arranged that I should go back along the ditch to find supports of some sort, so off I went.

German shrapnel was bursting all over the place now, and the ditch was full of wounded and unwounded natives. The wounded were all making for home and nothing I could do would stop them. I even tried to persuade them with my revolver — that did send a few back — but I was much hampered by my lack of their language and they were terrified by the shrapnel.

At Pont Logy I found the cavalry and a lot of officers who said they had strict orders to stay where they were, so as to occupy a second line of defence. So they were no good, and I went off up the road to Rue des Berceaux. It was comparatively quiet after where I had been. There were a few stray bullets coming over, but they no longer even bothered me.

I found the Bedfords (where I have shown them on the first sketch), but they said that they could not help me. I went on to Rue des Berceaux where I found General Maude (GOC 14th Infantry Brigade)[18] . I told him all I knew and all I had seen. He at once said that I might have the Cheshires, but seemed very dubious as to their exact whereabouts. He also knew very little about the situation, which did not surprise me.

He gave me a note for the OC Cheshires and off I went to look for him, taking the opportunity to send another message to Headquarters to say what I was going to do. I wasted a precious half-hour before I found the Cheshires, for the guide I had was a fool. However, at last I did find them, sitting in a ditch about 12.20 p.m. All that the Cheshires consisted of was a most hopeless CO and an equally poor adjutant, and only half a battalion, the rest being 'lost'. Goodness know how — the CO didn't. It was not a cheery start off.

I got them moving and led them up to 'B' where I met Cornwall again. He had been hit by a shrapnel bullet on the chin and three bullets through his Burberry; he was only 'bluggy' though and quite cheerful. He had got hold of the Bedfords, so we put both battalions along the road and started them off in extended order to advance across the field towards 'C' and to support the West Kents, who were now being counter-attacked. We saw them start all right, and it made me laugh to think of Cornwall and I, whose united service cannot be eight years, playing about with battalions.

Cornwall then went back to see General Maude while I returned to Pont Logy and sent a message back to say what was happening. I found some French Chasseurs who had come up, so I put them in to advance up the main road on the Bedfords' left. It was about 4 p.m. now, and I was mighty weary. However, I thought I had best go up to see if any of the West Kents were left, so got into that awful ditch again. There were dead and wounded men all along the ditch, so it was worse than ever to move along. Some of the dead were quite trodden into the mud.

I went up past 'C' and found the left of the Bedfords on the road as I have shown in the third sketch. They had not suffered many casualties and reported that the West Kents were still holding on. I told them to push on at once and occupy the West Kents' trenches, also to get in touch on the left with what was left of the native infantry and the troops of cavalry. I then came back.

While I was sitting at the bottom of the ditch for a moment's rest, some form of beastly shell landed in the ditch with me and covered me with lumps and stones. I thought I was dead, but was all right. One man close by said, 'Oh, Gawd, that's a near thing.' I agreed, but it was quite an unnecessary remark. Halfway down the ditch I came across a half dead native. He was in great pain, shot through the stomach. I was carrying a long knife. I have not the vaguest idea of when and where I picked it up and, as I stepped over him, he caught hold of my arm and tried to get hold of the knife. When I refused to let him have it, he made signs that I should cut his throat for him, which cheerful job I was not for at all. I managed at length to get some French Chasseurs to carry him back to Pont Logy.

It was getting dark now, and when I got to Pont Logy I found to my horror that the Bedfords and Cheshires were retiring, goodness only knows why. I felt inclined to sit down and cry, but hadn't time. The men said that they had had orders to retire. There were very few officers about and what there were seemed useless. The officer commanding − a captain − saluted me and called me 'Sir', which showed he was pretty far gone. Eventually Cornwall and I, after great efforts, got them together and started them digging on a line shown in the 6 p.m. sketch. As we stood on the road (it was almost dark), a German machine-gun opened fire down the road from the direction of 'C' that cleared us off in no time.

We saw the digging well started, arranged with the cavalry to dig themselves in behind, and then felt we had done about all there was to be done. Returning to our horses — it seemed a year since we left them — we cantered off down the road. Immediately a machine-gun started on us from somewhere over by the KOYLI. We fairly flew then, and were soon out of range of the brutes for the first time since 9 a.m. We went back to the 7th Brigade HQ in Richebourg-St-Vaast where we found Colonel Maurice[19] and told him everything. He said we had done jolly well, which was good hearing. Oh, but it was a badly run show. If only that attack had been supported we should have got all those trenches back again. As it was, there was a great loss of life and no good done at all.

CHAPTER FOUR

Ypres Salient

In the afternoon of 29th October, a British patrol edged cautiously into Neuve Chapelle and found it empty of enemy troops. The Germans had indeed withdrawn from the ruined village — a village that had cost them in excess of 5,000 casualties. Other battles had commenced further north, however, and more German divisions were needed; so was the heavy artillery that had mercilessly pounded the fronts of II and III Corps. That too went north beyond the River Lys.

On the Allied side, most of 3rd Division were in the process of being relieved with the rest of II Corps. Taking their place to face an entrenched enemy outside the village was the Lahore Division, whilst the Meerut Division took over the remainder of II Corps line. Everything now pointed to the north where Haig's I Corps, Allenby's Cavalry Corps, Rawlinson's IV Corps with French Army divisions, plus a few units of Belgian troops, were gripped in conflict with the enemy along a sixteen mile front that formed a salient on the eastern side of Ypres. That salient was already germinating into the most sanguineous battleground of British military history.

Meanwhile and still in the vicinity of Neuve Chapelle, and blissful of what lay ahead, Billy Congreve decided to have a final look at the village defences:

*

31st October
The trenches there are now in the hands of the Gurkhas, Jats and Seaforths. Cornwall and I went up to see them this evening. The line is not a good one and I thought the Seaforths not a very good show. They are holding the ditch made famous in my memory and it is not a good place. They are also not holding the houses where Cornwall and I observed the fight and which, as far as I can see, the Germans can walk into at any moment.

We went all the way up to 'C' and found two wounded natives

in the cellar of the house — we made arrangements to have them removed. The CO we found in a house close by with nothing at all between him and the German trenches. He seemed surprised when we pointed this out! There was actually an old woman in the house he was in. It is dreadful she should be there. Of course she can get no food, but what is given to her by the men. She is bound to be killed sooner or later if she stays there, but it is terribly hard to make these poor people leave. As usual, Cornwall and I were given a dose of shrapnel on the way home.

General Mackenzie went home this morning; I presume owing to the mess made of the attack. Anyhow he's gone and General Wing, who was made major-general a few days ago, now commands. I only hope that it is permanent. Mackenzie was, I thought, not of great merit, though very nice to me. He was not physically fit.

I have just heard that Norman has been killed — some days ago.[1]

1st November

Left Lacouture at 7 a.m. About 6 a.m. last night, I was up in the church tower when the Germans suddenly started shelling Richebourg St Vaast. I thought it might be serious, as the nerve-worn remnants of 7th Brigade were in there. Sure enough, while I was watching, crowds of men and waggons began to stream along the road and over the fields in no sort of order. One can hardly blame them. I rushed off and went in a car to try to collect them. Just as I was off, three crumps came into Lacouture. Sergeant Brear, my transport sergeant, was seriously wounded. No other damage was done, but I felt glad that we were leaving next day.

We made arrangements for housing the 7th Brigade and I went up to Richebourg. On the way I met what I took at first to be a drunken man, but found him to be Major Ashworth who was commanding the South Lancs. He was covered with bits of plaster and dust. It turned out that he had been asleep on a bed when a crump landed and burst in his room! How he was not killed I cannot think. The first thing he knew was that he was lying in the street under several feet of ceiling etc. He took me to see the place in which he had been asleep. It was a fearsome sight, everything smashed to blazes. As I've said, the shock had made him drunk, as it were, and he had to go to hospital. Bursting shells do seem to have a curious effect on people. Some are sort of mentally paralysed, and some even physically so. I have seen a man alive and unhurt, but absolutely incapable of lifting a hand or of

speaking. It's curious.[2] A few men and horses were killed in the
streets, but nothing very serious, and we collected everybody by
dark and got them into fresh billets.

We are now in Meteren and have moved northwards. All the
division is broken up. Some still with the Lahore Division (8th
Brigade), some under III Corps. As much of it as possible is resting
— a thing it sadly needs. Part of the 9th Brigade has been taken off
in buses (the good old London motor omnibus!) to help the
cavalry somewhere near a place called Messines. The Divisional
Artillery is still with the Lahore Division.

Editor's Note Billy Congreve's passing reference to Messines is of
significance, because it was in the Zandvoorde—Messines sector that
the Germans launched a surprise assault at dawn on 30th October.
Their objective was the capture of the Messines ridge. If successful,
they could then break through to Ypres between Zandvoorde and
Hollebeke astride the Ypres—Comines canal. Ypres was the key to
the route to the Channel ports, as far as the Germans were
concerned — and the Allies held it. On the Allied side, especially
for the BEF, Ypres had to be held in order to feed men and
material into the salient.

The German assault commenced with five new divisions, backed
by a fearsome array of heavy artillery, commanded by General
Max von Fabeck. Opposing Fabeck's Army Group were Haig's
depleted I Corps and, at Messines, Allenby's dismounted and
depleted Cavalry Corps with one Indian brigade. Fabeck's
ambitious plan also included a simultaneous break-through to
Ypres from along the Menin road via the tiny village of Gheluvelt.
All told, Fabeck meant to destroy the BEF along a seven mile
front and then grab Ypres. Although he drove Allenby's men off
the Messines ridge to a new line about a mile around it, forcing the
British to give up a depth of two miles in the lower half of the
salient, he failed in his overall task. The new line held — thanks to
the bruised, battered and often bewildered British Tommy. Yet
the fight for Ypres was far from over. More men from both sides
would be sucked into its maelstrom, including Billy Congreve.
Meanwhile, since 3rd Division was so fragmented, he had very
little to do. He therefore decided to visit his father who still
commanded 18th Brigade in Keir's 6th Division:

2nd November
I found his headquarters south of Armentières, not far from Croix

de Bacs. He was very fit and had Alan with him as brigade-major, Wallace having been badly wounded a few days ago while doing some foolishness with Charlie.[3] They were out to look at dead Germans and promptly were fired on by live ones — Wallace having his leg smashed. Charlie helped to carry him in without getting hurt himself.

Dads and I rode round some of his second line trenches and then had lunch. Afterwards, I set off to find the 3rd Battalion who were in the trenches on his right. The first person I saw was old Meysey sitting in a dug-out with 'Snipe' — the latter being in command during the absence of 'Jellunda'[4]. Meysey looked lovely in a red beard and woollen cap. Snipe was not, I thought, very cheerful.

I next found Charlie[5], also with a goodish beard and looking very fit; also old Martin[6] with a bullet hole in his cap and fatter than ever, apparently quite pleased with life. At last I found Godders who had a bad eye, but otherwise all right. It was grand to see him and the others, and to know them to be all right, but it was sad how many good fellows were gone. Poor old Norman Boy and Cherub.

I had one bad blow. I had gone up quite confident of bringing Harris back with me. When I got there I heard that he was dead, killed ten days ago in an attack[7]. He was shot through the head, I think the same day as Norman. I had a long talk to Godders and Charlie, and would have loved to have stayed with them, but it was not to be.

6th November

At about noon, orders came that we were to move headquarters to Dickebusch and to take over from the 7th Division who are apparently in sore need of a rest[8]. I went on to billet with Duval in his car. It was a most hopeless job, for every house and cottage was full either of Frenchmen or our own fellows. I gave it up at last, but not till it was dark. A fearsome evening, very thick and wet mist, and cold. The road was crowded with transport, all of which was getting tied up and bogged down in the mud. Eventually it turned out that the part of the line we were taking over was just east of Ypres, so there was no need for billets in Dickebusch.

Monday, November 9th

Things are a bit straighter now. I keep all the transport back at La

Clytte and HQ is in a house on the Ypres—Menin road, about a mile from Ypres.

Cornwall and I rode in on Saturday morning to HQ via Ypres. It is a jolly old town with a big moat and wall all round. The town has been little shelled by the Germans. All the squares have a few 'crump' holes and a good many of the houses are knocked about, but the Cathedral and town hall are only touched by a few splinters. A civilian stopped us and told us that in the hospital were a lot of wounded Germans, and there was great difficulty in looking after them. We found the hospital and went in.

There were fifty-three Germans, all pretty badly wounded, and twenty-five civilians, two or three doctors and a few fat-faced old Belgian nun-nurses. They were in a bad way and full of woe. No water and no bread, as a shell had cut off their water supply, and one had actually burst in in their laundry, hoisting the old lady in charge of the washing about a hundred yards into the square. We promised to get the authorities to evacuate them — which we did do, but I don't think that they have been yet removed.

The division now consists of the 7th, 9th and 15th Brigades — the 8th Brigade still being away down south. We have Zouaves on our left and the 2nd Division on our right. It's the same old trench game, but I have not yet seen them. From what I can hear, the trenches run largely through woods[9]. Cornwall and I hope to go there soon. Alas, we are not going to keep General Wing as our divisional commander. General Haldane[10] (lately promoted) has been appointed and, I believe, brings two ADCs with him. So I simply must go now, though Dads has made me promise to stay if I can.

5 p.m. Cornwall and I are just back from a visit to Ypres. As usual we drew fire. He and I, when we go anywhere together, always seem to irritate the Germans! No sooner had we gone into the Cathedral — we were really standing inside the huge doors — when we heard the whistle of a shell coming; then there was a crash that in the Cathedral sounded tremendous. A huge hole appeared in the roof and the centre of the building was full of brick and dust and smoke. Another shell followed the first. Neither burst, and the reason for this we discovered later, but they did plenty of damage.

The Cathedral is a lot more restored than I thought. The restoration must have been in progress when the war started, as there is a lot of scaffolding still up. We decided to postpone our examination of the inside and left hurriedly. The old verger was dancing about with rage and misery, for these were the first shells to actually hit the building. He wanted to go in to see the damage, but we stopped him. Poor old man, it is dreadful for him to see his treasure being slowly knocked to bits, for now they have started I expect they will go on till it is only a ruin.

On leaving the Cathedral, we went to the Hotel de Ville or Halle[11] which is really a lovely old place. The walls are all painted with frescoes, and the old woodwork and stonework would please Edward[12] . No sooner were we inside than 'crash', and into the very part of the building we were in came another big brute; again not exploding, but going through two three-feet walls and making a beastly mess. The third wall stopped its career and it finished up in a pile of straw (for soldiers had been billeted on the floor). This at once set fire, so we rushed out to get some water and met the 'fire brigade' arriving — consisting of three men, the verger and a boy.

I did not at all like the look of the shell, as it was lying there red-hot. If only I had thought a moment I might have realised that a red-hot shell would not explode, but one doesn't always remember little things like that! We put out the burning straw and came away before worse should happen, as they now really seem to be going to shell in earnest and we were only there for 'fun'. Those Belgian town guards and firemen are gallant fellows. There are only a few who have not left the town now, and their water supply is mostly cut off and broken; yet whenever a shell arrives, they rush off to try to minimise the damage — forgetting or heedless of the fact that one shell usually means another in the same place. I much admire them and their devotion to their old buildings.

10th November
This morning I stopped at the Halle and found the shell is an 'incendiary'. This, of course, is the reason that there was no explosion. The fuse in the base of the shell starts off some combustion, which fuses a hole in the wall of the shell and also makes the whole of the shell red-hot. Out of this hole some form of molten liquid comes out — it's a cunning contrivance.

For some days past they have been shelling all along the main road with a very big howitzer shell. Today, about 5 p.m., there was a fearful crash and the whole house seemed to jump about a yard to one side, then sort of stagger back again. There was not much left in the way of glass to smash, but what was left came crashing down. Colonel Maurice, who had been leaning over a table by the window, looking at a map, was covered with glass. I really thought that they had managed to hit the house at last. Going to investigate, however, I found that one of these big 'super-crumps' had landed about sixty yards beyond the house. It made a grand hole 13 feet deep and 35 feet across. Horses were tied up all round, but beyond being covered in mud were unhurt.

I was lucky enough to find the base fuse of the brute, which shows us what the gun is. It is the Austrian Skoda gun which fires a shell of 850 lbs — diameter 12.4" or 31 cms. We call them 'Weary Willies', as one seems to hear them coming for so long. This poor château is in a bad way now. Once a nice château villa outside the town, with grounds of its own and a good garden, now everything spoilt everywhere. There is a good deal of shelling going on.

Editor's Note On 10th November, Major-General Wing's 3rd Division line was extended north of the Menin road to Veldhoek Château, then along the front of Nonne Bosschen Wood to the south-west corner of Polygon Wood. The 2/Duke of Wellington's (West Riding) held Veldhoek and, from there to Polygon Wood, some 812 officers and men of what remained of the 1st (Guards) Brigade looked to their front. In the whole of 3rd Division's sector, including every officer and man that could be drummed up in the way of reserves, some 7,850 battle-worn British soldiers were about to face the enemy's best, namely the Prussian Guards of General Winckler's Composite Guard Division (1st and 4th Guard Brigades) together with General Pletenburg's 4th Division. All at full strength — some 17,500 strong — supported by 228 guns.

The force facing Major-General Wing was part of Germany's biggest offensive yet to take Ypres. Bad weather had already led to a twenty-four hour postponement, but word of the postponement did not reach the Duke of Würtemberg's Fourth Army which launched its attack between Langemarck and Dixmude as previously planned. The Allies were warned. On 11th November in the fog of a damp dawn, the enemy opened up with the most vicious bombardment yet known on the British line at Ypres. The Germans badly wanted Ypres and, on 11th November, they were even more determined to take it and crash their way to the Channel ports. The Allies had different ideas and, in General Wing's section of the line which would take the heaviest enemy onslaught, Billy Congreve was there to record his impressions of that day of crisis:

11th November

A proper day this has been, beastly wet and cold, and the fiercest fighting we have yet had. The Guards Corps (Bill's Own) arrived to turn us out and get through to Calais. They haven't yet though. We have traced twelve battalions of it so far. They were told that the infantry of the line could get no farther ahead, so they were being brought up 'to finish us off'. The result has been desperate fighting and the complete failure of the Germans, up to date.

Before they attacked they gave our trenches and supports and guns the most terrific bombardment. I have never seen the like before. It was one incessant crashing like at Neuve Chapelle but more so — much. The shrapnel played up and down our lines exactly as one waters a line of flowers, backwards and forwards. Also there were heaps and heaps of crumpets, crumps and super-crumps — all over the place they were. This went on till 10 a.m., when a silence fell except for our guns, and the Germans came on. They told us (a prisoner officer did) that they expected to see what was left of our men after the bombardment run, but they were badly shocked, for they were met with bayonets and such musketry 'as they never dreamt could be possible'.

The attack went on all morning and well into the afternoon, when finally it began to slacken. The wood fighting bewildered the Germans. They lost touch with each other and then lost courage and, finally, it grew dark and we still held on all right. Just a few places had been pierced and they still hold one or two small parts of our trenches — nothing to what it might have been. Their losses must have been enormous.

We took some prisoners. I counted fifty men and four officers myself and at least half this number were wounded. An officer told me that they had often given the French a similar bombardment, lasting an hour or two, and had then attacked and that they were never waited for — and this was the first time they had failed to get the front line trenches. These guards had been marched up from Arras where they had been fighting French troops, and their attack (a carefully arranged affair) was meant to finally crush 'this rabble of English'. Oh, my poor dear old Kaiser Bill, what a mess you have made of things.

Our line is now, of course, a bit different, but not very much so. In all, we lost about 300 yards of trenches which are still held by the Germans.

Our casualties were heavy though, amongst them being General Shaw[13] , his staff captain Harter, and his signal officer Deakin, all

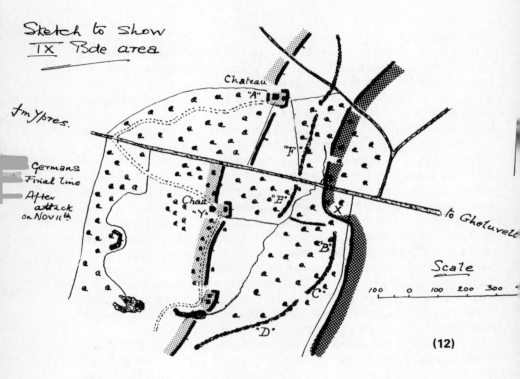

Sketch to show IX Bde area

fm Ypres.

Germans
Final line
After
attack
on Nov 11th

Chateau
"A"

"F"

Chau
"Y"

"E"

X

"B"

"C"

"D"

to Gheluvelt

Scale

100   0   100   200   300

(12)

hit as the result of the same shell which burst just outside the door of the little estaminet they were using as HQ. I was up there a few minutes afterwards, none of them bad except Deakin who had several holes in him. However, they all have to go sick and Colonel Douglas Smith of the Royal Scots is commanding, with Forsyth as signal officer and Crichton as staff captain. It has been an anxious day.

Editor's Note It certainly had been an anxious day. The 1st (Guards) Brigade and the 2/Duke of Wellington's had their line broken, but restored with the help of the Royal Scots Fusiliers, whilst 9th Brigade lost 40% of its fighting strength. Worse still, 9th Brigade had not commenced the day's fighting at full strength. Indeed, that day, brigades had been reduced to battalion size, and some battalions fell in numbers below that of normal peacetime companies. Yet they had contained the best troops that Germany could throw at them and, again, Germany was denied entry to Ypres.

12th November

All fairly quiet in the night, but for frequent arrivals of 'Weary Willies', 'Black Marias'[14] and others of the hateful brew. Cornwall and I about 10 a.m. went up to find out how the left of our line (the 9th Brigade) was, as this is where all the heaviest of yesterday's fighting took place.

We went up to the château marked 'A' [Veldhoek Château] where we found Courage[15] and his hussars in the support trench. In the wood, just before we reach the château, we found some cheerful-looking Zouaves in their wonderful trousers and short coats. Some were in dug-outs and some, I believe, up in the front trenches sandwiched in amongst our own men. One had just been badly wounded in the knee and was being helped back.

Cornwall and I got up without being shelled, but we found Courage and his men sitting 'mighty small' at the bottom of his trench. I stood outside talking to him until he said, 'For goodness sake, come in' (he always is a little fussy) 'as that's just where they are shelling.' So in I squeezed and, no sooner was I down, than whizz-bang — came shrapnel just where I had been, so I felt glad for his fussiness.

Courage said that they kept up this game for hours, so it looked as if Cornwall and I were fixtures, for I find that once one gets into a trench one is never very keen to leave it again if things are happening outside. However, I timed these shells and they came in bursts of two and three every three minutes, so after we had all Courage's news we waited till one salvo was over and ignominiously bolted back through the woods.

Nothing much doing the rest of the day. No further attacks, but a lot of shelling as usual. Our men are splendid, but they get dreadfully weary and 'broken'. It is a wonder to me how they do stick this shelling. Oh, if only we had not lost so many officers.

13th November

I came in about 9.30 a.m. from Poperinghe and found that nothing had happened during the night. Colonel Maurice has sent me up here[16] to do temporary staff-captain vice Harter. So here I am, in a most uncomfortable windowless house and it's raining and blowing a gale outside. I am quite happy though, and have plenty of work to do.

Colonel Douglas Smith is still commanding the 9th Brigade. He is an unmoved and very pleasant Scotsman, and sits smoking his pipe quite at peace with the world.

15th November
A busy night on the 13th[17], the whole of our line had to be slightly drawn back owing to the taking and holding of those few trenches by the Germans. Units had to be sorted out, for everyone was hopelessly mixed up. I was out until 2.30 a.m., and Costeker[18] was out all night.

As I have said, this new line was the result of the Germans holding one of our trenches as shown[19] and which I have marked with an 'X'. 'B' was held by the 5th Fusiliers[20] with the 1st Lincolns on their right at 'C', and the 1st Bedfords (15th Brigade on their right at 'D'). 'E' was a new and hastily-made trench (now held by the 1st Royal Scots Fusiliers), occupied when the 4th Royal Fusiliers were driven back from 'X'. The 2nd Sussex were shoved in to join up the line from the right of the Royal Scots Fusiliers to the 5th Fusiliers. North of the road there was a mixture of various regiments (the trenches marked 'F'); north again of 'F', taken by the 1st Division.

This situation was an unpleasant one, especially for the 5th Fusiliers who, through all the heavy fighting and when the Royal Fusiliers retired, had stuck to their trenches in a most gallant way. The situation there was most extraordinary — the Germans and our men being within talking distance of each other and in the same line. Snipers were naturally busy. CQMS Gillborn[21] bagged eight Germans himself in twenty-four hours, sometimes at under fifty yards range.

Whether they would have been able to stick out another strong attack in such an awkward position was doubtful. It was impossible to retake the lost trenches as we had no men to do it with, so it was agreed to draw back the line to freshly-dug trenches. All went well in spite of the Germans being so close to us.

We found some of the trenches in the new line to be not deep enough, some were even full of water. So we had to get up tools and collect as many men together as possible to finish the digging by daylight.

Early on the 14th, we received news that the few skirmishers left in the old trenches had been driven in and the Germans had occupied our old line, and were coming forward to find out the position of our new line. About 10 a.m., a wire came in to say that a trench known as the 'stable trench' had been captured by the Germans, who were now entrenched between the stables and the château.[22] The Royal Scots Fusiliers had been holding this stable trench and, once taken by the Germans, our line was easily

His mother, Celia Congreve. As a nurse in the Great War, she was awarded three medals for bravery. One of the awards was the French *Croix de Guerre* (an honour seldom conferred upon women) in recognition of her courage and coolness when the hospital area where she was nursing came under shell-fire and aeroplane attacks.

General Sir Walter Congreve, VC, KCB, MVO.

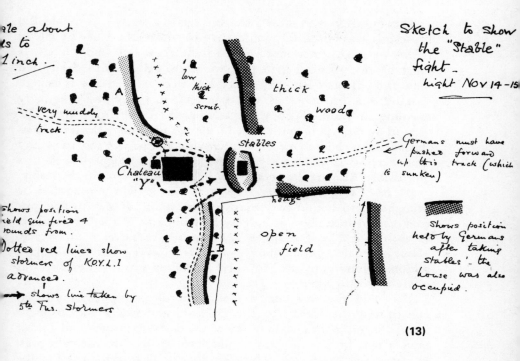

(13)

enfiladed from it. This is exactly what had happened and things looked dirty.

All day our men in 'A' and 'B' suffered considerable loss and, at 7 a.m., a counter-attack was arranged to retake both stable and trench. The KOYLI[23] were given the job, and the scheme was for them to put sixty picked men behind the château who, at a given moment, were to rush round both sides of it and storm the stable and trench. The trenches on the right ('B') were to open a heavy rifle fire at the same time in order to make the Germans think that the attack was coming from there.

At 7 p.m. it started. The sixty men rushed into the darkness (they had only fifty yards to go) and never returned. The Germans opened a heavy fire; and I think that our opening fire was a mistake, for it put every German in the vicinity on the look-out. What actually happened nobody yet knows — probably most of the storming party were killed or wounded and the rest captured. Anyhow, none came back and it was horrid sitting still waiting to get news. Eventually a patrol sent from 'B' about midnight reported that the stable and trench were still in German hands.

The question was now how on earth were we to tackle the
brutes? It was absolutely imperative to retake the place by dawn;
if not we might once more have to withdraw our whole front. It
must be remembered here that we were dealing with dead-tired
men and officers. For days they had been shelled and attacked,
soaking wet for most of the time and, in many cases, actually
standing in water. Also there were very few officers left. The
ground was deep in mud and, in the wood, going was terrible as
the shell-fire had made an abatis with all the broken trees and
branches, so anything big in the way of a night attack was
impossible. Also artillery could not bring indirect fire on the stable.

At last, at 3 a.m., it was decided that a field gun should be
brought up to within fifty yards of the stable. It was to fire four
rounds into it, and an assault by a small party of the 5th Fusiliers
to go in and take it 'at all costs'. Poor 5th, so battered and weary.
Major Yatman, commanding them, was a tower of strength. I have
seldom admired anyone more. He never got downhearted and was
ready to go anywhere.

The field gun was manhandled up through the deep mud that
constituted the 'drive' to the château, and was finally brought
into position just as dawn began to break. It was touch and go, for
once dawn broke, the gun would have to be left where it was.
However, all went well. The four rounds were duly fired at the
dimly outlined stables and the gunner subaltern swore that each
round hit the mark.

No sooner was the first round off than a terrific fire was opened
by the Germans from all directions, but *not* from the stables!
None hit the gunners and the gun was safely brought back. The
firing of the fourth round was the signal for the 5th 'stormers', led
by CQMS Gillborn. It was completely successful, both stable and
trench being retaken. A good show and, my word, what a relief it
was to us. Gillborn died of wounds during the day, and too late
for him to know of his award of the DCM.

In the fighting for those infernal stables we must have lost 150
men and officers. The place itself was found to be a shambles. It
was a bad night. I was tramping round in the mud and water trying
to find people most of the night. The Germans guessed we were
going to attack and kept on firing up lights, which make things as
bright as day for a few moments. It was a weird scene, the mud,
the woods all smashed about, the lights.

Editor's Note The defenders were men of the Prussian 2nd Guard

Grenadier Regiment. The field gun, an 18-pounder, was under the command of Lieutenant A.F.B. Cottrell. As for CQMS Gillborn, DCM, like so many other dead soldiers, his grave lay in disputed territory which was fought over for years. Little wonder that his last resting place disappeared without trace. His name, however, is commemorated on the Ypres (Menin Gate) Memorial with the names of the other 55,000 British soldiers who fell in the salient and who also have no known grave.

For the remainder of 15th November, Billy Congreve — still at 9th Brigade headquarters and holding the rank of captain — noted that the shelling was worse than ever in his sector:

Today (15th)
Our house was simply rained on by shrapnel, the shells bursting just outside and the smoke from them drifting in through the broken windows. We sat there, and every moment I expected one to come through the roof. Goodness knows how it escaped. Wonderful to relate that nobody was even hit, except two pigs who were killed two yards outside the back doors. It was an ill wind, for we have had splendid pork chops ever since — shrapnel-killed pork! Quite a new diet!

18th November
On Monday most of the brigade were relieved by cavalry and we withdrew our HQ to Hooge, a few hundred yards down the road. I wasn't sorry to leave our little home, for I bet it will be hit full pitch before long.

The night before, while Costeker and I were up in the woods arranging reliefs, he was hit. The Germans were very jumpy and kept on opening rapid fire. By great ill luck, one bullet had hit Costeker in the arm. I bound him up with my first-aid dressing and, as we had finished our job, we came home and I sent him off to hospital first thing this morning.

A new brigade-major, Wavell[24], came out in the course of the day; also Buchanan to take over from me, so I am back here as ADC again. It has been a strenuous few days and I have seldom been so cold and miserable as I was at times. If it hadn't been for pork chops, I should have been very unhappy!

20th November
A good deal of shelling and alarms, but no attacks. The 'stable'[25] is still a source of great trouble, as also is a gun the Germans have

called a *Minenwerfer*. It is some sort of mortar that they have in their trenches and which throws a 200 lb bomb of high explosive. It goes off with a most awful row and sends out clouds of filthy black oily smoke. Its effects are also very unpleasing – filling trenches, killing and burying men. As usual, we have nothing capable of dealing with it and there seems to be no way of getting at the brute. The Ordnance will probably send us something of the same sort in a month or two, which will be typical of the way we go to war.

Last night the General, Colonel Maurice and I rode off in the snow and dark to see the brigades. The Germans usually shell the road we have to go by (the main Ypres–Menin road) after dusk, and we had the bad luck to just hit off one of the moments. We had just got down to the level-crossing – a particularly unhealthy spot – when I heard the well-known bang of that infernal field gun that shoots down the road. It always sounds as if it was only a few yards off, firing straight down between the trees. We heard the bang, pause, then the whistling scream, then crash, and a blaze of white light just over our heads. Nobody was hit, but we decided to wait behind the level-crossing till they gave over, which they did in a few minutes. It is a perfectly beastly sensation being shrapnelled in the dark on a horse.

This morning we were up and riding out into the dark (about 6 a.m.) and it was already snowing. These last few days it has steadily been getting colder and colder – now there is an inch of snow and a hard frost as well. My word, it *is* cold and for the poor devils in the trenches, it must be terrible. When we went to see them this morning they were all terribly stiff. Some were so numbed and rheumaticky that they could only just hobble, and some actually had to be lifted out of the trenches and carried back. What a deal of misery this Kaiser has caused.

At last we are being relieved – by the French – and go off to rest and get up strength again. I believe we go to Westoutre, half-way to Bailleul.

Editor's Note When the latest German offensive had spluttered to a halt on the bullets and bayonets of the desperately thin khaki line, being the proud remnants of Britain's Regular Army[26], so Foch assumed responsibility for the salient. The change-over began on 15th November and was completed by the 22nd – the official date given for the conclusion of 'First Ypres'. On that date and having been promoted to full general, Haig departed for England on five days leave whilst his weary I Corps rested. As Billy Congreve had calculated, the battered but unbowed 3rd Division left the salient for Westoutre on 21st November. Before leaving himself, Billy Congreve helped the French troops to settle in along 3rd Division's old line:

21st November
We managed to get the reliefs finished last night. I had been out all day taking French officers around to arrange the taking over. They struck me as being wonderfully quick and sure of themselves. I had lunch at a regiment's headquarters near Poperinghe — a very good lunch it was too. The little colonel was most charming. He said he thought I was very young to be doing the work I was, which rather offended me. All the taking over went off without a hitch; and we were mighty glad to turn our backs on the Ypres salient, never, I hope, to see it again.

CHAPTER FIVE

Entrenchment of Trench Warfare

Midnight of 22nd November found the BEF seven miles south of Ypres, positioned on a twenty-one mile front from just north of Kemmel down to Givenchy. Although local actions flared, died, only to flare again, there were no immediate signs of great assaults in the making. The reason was painfully obvious; all armies were busily licking their wounds and being reinforced. By the end of 1914, for instance, twenty-three Territorial battalions would have joined the BEF.

Such reinforcements were sorely needed, as the old Regular Army was but a mere skeleton of its former self. To take one example, who on 4th August could have possibly believed that, within a hundred days, more British officers would die than had been killed in the previous one hundred years? Yet it happened.

The 3rd Division had particularly been hurt and went to rest at Westoutre on 22nd November for four days, after which it would take over roughly two miles of front that faced the enemy-held village of Wytschaete. The new headquarters for 3rd Division was Mont Noir Château, situated on top of a ridge of hills that ran from Cassel to Kemmel. It was there that Billy Congreve awaited his new divisional commander:

*

22nd November
General Haldane and his ADC Fraser have arrived. He wants me to stay on as his other ADC. Both seem quite nice. General Wing is off on ten days' leave home and is pleased as Punch over it. Lots of people are now going on leave which seems rather wrong in a way, though of course those who are out resting have nothing to do. I shall not go unless I am told to, though I have been told that I may. Fraser has gone off with General Wing.

23rd November
Very quiet days these. We ride or motor off in the morning to see

our war-worn warriors, presenting various medals to those who are left to get them. Various generals turn up and tell them how splendid they are, including Sir John French, who came out today and waded round in the mud. The men look better already. Shaving and washing and plenty of sleep work wonders. Heaps of 'comforts' are now arriving from home and cigarettes galore. In fact, I think they only lack beer! We are now getting in drafts fast, so by the 27th we should be quite a useful unit again.

25th November

We are going to keep the château as our night headquarters and use the Scherpenberg Hill as a day headquarters. This latter is a high conical hill with a windmill and farm on top of it, and one gets an excellent view of Wytschaete, Messines and Ypres. On a real clear day, one can even see as far as the sea somewhere near Ostend.

28th November

We took over a part of the line last night. We now have one brigade in the front line with the other two in reserve, so each man has only three days in the trenches and six in billets, just as the Germans and French do. Always so far we have had to have the whole division in the front line, with the result that the men never get any rest at all. This new departure is a great improvement.

Our line, a baddish one in many ways, was taken up after our cavalry and the French had been driven off the Wytschaete—Messines ridge and where they dug themselves in under fire. A very different thing from a carefully chosen defensive position. The great difficulty (a universal one at the present time) is the mud and water. Some of the trenches are always flooded and the ground is so spongy that drainage is nearly impossible. We are trying all sorts of dodges to get rid of the wet — brushwood, planks, sacks filled with straw, pumps and, lastly, barrels. The latter are really the best: beer barrels sawn in half with seats nailed across the top. Each man has one to stand on or to sit in! It's a miserable type of existence though, bad for morale and bad for health. However, it must be as bad for the Germans — please goodness it *is*.

Our left is marked by Vandenberg Farm, and our right is just south of Point 76[1]. The French join up to us on our left, and the 5th Division on our right.

My word, but the Scherpenberg is an awful cold place. Every bit of wind hits it and all the winds in the world seem to live and have their being in this corner of Belgium.

29th November
Feeling rotten today, an awful sore throat. Fraser comes back tonight. Nothing doing on our front, except sniping and shelling. I am going to take to bed.

3rd December
The King is going up the Scherpenberg today[2]. I wish I could go and cheer too.

4th December
I have been in bed these last few days, but have only missed King George and no operations. I believe it must be this filthy water. The General wants me to go away to get right again. I do not like this idea of going home. It is unsatisfactory somehow, but . . .

5th December
Left Mont Noir in René's car at 7 a.m. and reach Boulogne at 10.30. The boat left at 11 and, at 3.50, I walked into Queen Anne's Gate where Brown showed absolutely no surprise[3]. He at once offered to get the bath ready! It is rather gloriously wonderful to be home again.

14th December
Left London at 1 p.m. and got here at 9.15 p.m. Again René Duval's car was at my service. It's rather awful being back again in a way.

15th December
Yesterday we made an attack and, as we only put two battalions[4] into it, the attack naturally failed. We had about 400 casualties. It is very depressing. I should have thought that we had learnt our lesson at Neuve Chapelle about unsupported attacks, but it seems not.

The truth of the matter is this I believe: Sir John French wanted to see the Army on the offensive, so an attack on the Petit Bois was arranged. Then later, for some reason or other, it was decided to also attack Maedelstede Farm. Sir John, Sir H. Smith-

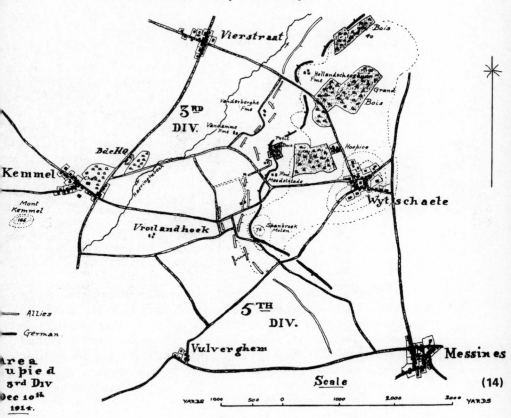

Dorrien, HRH The Prince of Wales and many other lights of the Gilded Staff sat about on the Scherpenberg, and watched the preliminary bombardment by ours and the 5th Division's artillery — and then saw these two unfortunate battalions go to more or less certain failure. The reason why? Because it was considered time to be able to report some form of victory. It failed and the reason is obvious.

'A', 'B', 'C', 'D' and 'E' are the German trenches — 'B' in Petit Bois and 'D' round the Maedelstede Farm. RS are the Royal Scots and GH the Gordons. These two battalions were ordered respectively to take the wood and the farm. What happened was that for half an hour or more our guns gave the German trenches a very heavy and accurate fire with shrapnel and a smaller amount of HE. The results of which made the Germans laugh at us.

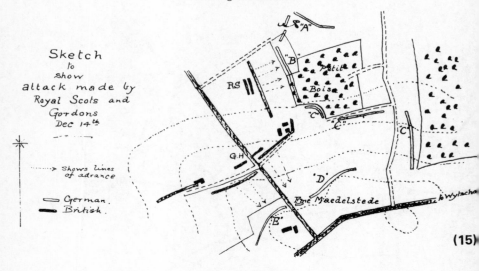

Sketch
to
show
attack made by
Royal Scots and
Gordons
Dec 14ᵗʰ

------> Shows lines
of advance

▭ German.
▬ British.

(15)

The effect of field gun shrapnel on trenches is almost nil when the trenches are well and carefully made, and there was too little high explosive to do any good. The Germans so little minded this type of bombardment, which to us on the Scherpenberg looked like an inferno, that they kept up a heavy rifle fire the whole time from the bombarded trenches. The two battalions then attacked. The Royal Scots actually got into 'B', taking two machine-guns and thirty-five German prisoners, but they were then so heavily enfiladed from 'A' — and fired on from the back of the Petit Bois — that further advance into the wood was impossible. Eventually they had to be content with holding on to part of the captured German trench.

This enfilade fire that came from 'A' held up the attack. This could have been found out by a proper reconnaissance *before* the attack. It was not done and, as 'A' was neither being attacked or shelled, the Germans holding it were able to shoot our fellows down one after another.

The Gordons left their trenches to attack 'D' and 'E' and fared even worse. The mud on the ploughed field which they had to attack over was *so bad* that they could only just move out of a walk. On leaving their trenches they at once came under a terrible rifle and machine-gun fire from 'C', 'D' and 'E'.

Imagine sending a battalion alone to attack a strongly wired position up a hill and over mud a foot deep, under frontal and enfilade fire. It was a regular Valley of Death. The losses were, of course, very heavy. They were very, very gallant. Some almost reached the German trenches, where they were killed. One or two even got into the trenches where they were killed or captured. A few lay in little depressions in the mud till darkness and then crawled back. Those who got there could send no communication to the supports etc in the rear. Several men tried to get back, but were all shot. They lost seven out of nine officers and 250 men.

Such was the attack ordered by Sir John French. Next day, I read in the paper: *British troops hurl back Germans at Wytschaete.* A beautiful epitaph for those poor Gordons who were little better than murdered.

I had a long talk with Hume Gore about it. He led his company over the plough, losing a good many men. Luckily the fact of the field being a plough, gave cover in the sort of waves of the ground. They eventually managed to get within forty yards of 'D' (in other places, some of the Gordons actually reached the trenches). Here, he lay down with about forty men in a little hollow. They could move neither backwards or forwards. The right-hand men of this little party were all killed as they lay there by some 'dead-shot' of the Germans who picked off eighteen — one after another. When darkness came, they retired one by one, leaving their dead and wounded (who could not walk) behind. He eventually returned with about twenty men out of his company. He said, 'If only we had been only a little supported, I could have taken that trench — but what good could I do with twenty men?'

However, it is done now and Sir John French will be able to tell the English papers how he won a victory and captured sixty prisoners (this is the actual number that GHQ put in their report — real figures were thirty-five). One more thing, I am sure that if the division had been allowed or ordered to go in as a division, we should have captured the whole line.

Editor's Note As well as hoping that it would make good propaganda for home consumption at upper echelon level, this ill-conceived attack — and others like it — was, incredibly, a recent policy by GHQ to maintain the morale of the British Army by making small and sporadic attacks on the German trench system. Billy Congreve was not the only individual to be appalled by the unnecessary waste of human lives. His father, still GOC of 18th Brigade in 6th Division, also commented in his diary on 20th December when hearing of a similar disastrous attack on

Ploegsteert Wood: '. . . these small isolated attacks seem to me deadly. There was the same experience in the north on the 14th. Horrid losses and nothing done with them . . .' Returning to the attack that Billy Congreve witnessed, it is sufficient to add that having been brought up to strength before the attack, both battalions were again mangled and in a thoroughly needless way. Losses came to 17 officers and 407 other ranks. The 2/Royal Scots and 1/Gordons were later relieved by the 2/Suffolks and 4/Middlesex.

16th December

Now we are all just going to sit tight and bother the Germans as much as we can, and wait till the fine weather comes.

They are shelling Mont Kemmel very heavily today. This hill has even a more commanding view than our Scherpenberg and one can see even more of the German and our lines. We have artillery observers up there, so naturally the Germans shell it. There is a sort of watch tower on the highest part — this the Germans make a dead set on and shell it unmercifully. They have so far put only one shell through the tower, but the ground all round it is a most extraordinary sight; just as if hundreds of earthquakes and cyclones had visited it, so smashed up is it.

18th December

Went over to see Dads. He said he would be at Ploegsteert. I rode and when I got there an orderly told me that he was back again at the old HQ in Pont de Nieppe, on the Bailleul—Armentières road. I found him at last and it was good to see him again. There was yet another of these useless and rotten local attacks last night up in 'Plugstreet' Wood. Again, a costly failure. I should think that even our Great General Staff will learn soon. Yet there may be some deep meaning which justified it and that we don't know.

The 1st Battalion were in the attack and did very well, but lost 'Tip' Prittie[5] and the 'Master'[6]. Several others were wounded. It appears to have been a repetition of our failure — bad artillery preparation and mud up to the men's knees.

I had lunch with Dads and Alan[7]. Later on we three walked up to 4th Division's HQ where General 'Fatty' Wilson[8] reigns supreme. He was very upset about this unfortunate attack, but otherwise all right. I then rode home in the dark along that brutal *pavé* road.

Editor's Note The attack referred to by Brigadier-General Congreve in his diary entry of 20th December, had its origin in Sir John French ordering a vigorous attack along the British line in conjunction with a French attack at Arras. The French, however, decided not to attack. Nevertheless the British divisions involved were ordered to prosecute the attack as planned.

The 4th Division's attacking front was between Le Gherr and St Ypres with 1/Rifle Brigade, 1/Hampshire Regiment and the 1/Somerset Light Infantry of 11th Brigade participating. The Germans were prepared, probably due to the 11th Brigade using the telephone for the synchronization of watches. There was also the problem of a severe shell shortage, a problem so acute that a 6-inch howitzer battery which 4th Division had loaned to II Corps was returned to them with the following message: 'Please inform General du Cane[9] that II Corps place 10 rounds of 6-inch howitzer of 4th D.A. at disposal of III Corps'. To underline the problem, offers of additional guns for the bombardment were turned down because of the ammunition shortage for what were already available. The attack in 4th Division's sector resulted in a total of 226 casualties of which 1/Rifle Brigade's share was 27 killed, 52 wounded and 30 missing.

19th December

The German gunners seem to be a good deal more active. Cornwall and I went up to the top of Mont Kemmel where one really gets a grand view. The tower is now only 'standing on one leg'. Very little more and down it will come.

Rain and wind still are the order of the day and though the trenches are desperately bad, we are doing our best to cope with it, but it is uphill work and a horrible existence for the men. One of the great difficulties is to keep the parapets bullet-proof. There has been very little revetting done so far, with the result as shown [see sketch on page 94].

Owing to the country being so flat, the drainage question is very difficult. Open drains, having little or no 'fall', get waterlogged at once. Communication trenches become as bad. In some cases these get so bad that men have been drowned in them. I was told the following by an officer a few days ago:

The company was going up to do a relief at night and, on completing the relief, the company commander found a man missing. A short search was made without results and it was concluded he had stopped one of the stray bullets going about, as

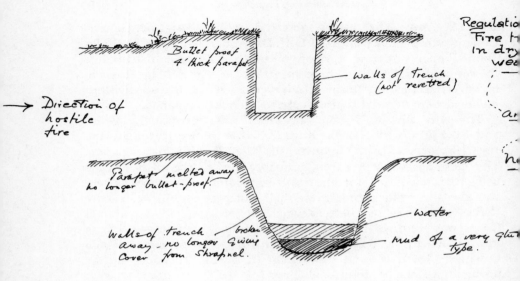

they always are. Two days later this same company was relieved. While moving back again in the dark, groans were heard and eventually traced to a disused water-logged communication trench where the missing man was found, up to his shoulders in mud and quite incapable of movement. He had got into the trench in the dark by mistake, went in up to his knees, floundered along a few yards when he went to his waist, and there he stuck and gradually sank. It took them four and a half hours to get him out, then he died about ten hours later from 'exhaustion and exposure'. It is quite likely that many a 'missing' man has met a similar fate, which is a horrid thought.

As I have said, we have tried most ways of overcoming the difficulties. In order to form a firm 'bottom' to the trench, we have put in brushwood, sacks of straw, timber, ammunition boxes etc, but all are gradually swallowed up under the men's feet. In many cases, dead French and German soldiers are found buried in the parapets and walls and bottoms of trenches. In one particular place in our line there is a trench called 'dead boot ditch', and one is shown by the inmates with some pride a protruding Boche's foot where it sticks out from the side of the trench. Everyone is quite friendly with the gruesome boot. Even if they wished to, they are unable to extricate it and re-bury its owner!

It is interesting to think what a section of one of these trenches will look like when dug up in years to come by some research party — dead British, German and French soldiers, rifles, equipment, bully beef, biscuits, spades, ammunition, 'Tickler's' jam, all mixed up with wood, straw and mud and forming various strata.

The best things to keep the men dry are sawn-in-half beer barrels. The men float about in these. An excellent picture of this is in this week's *Country Life* — on my suggestion![10]

20th December

They are shelling the top of Kemmel heavily today, and are evidently determined to finish off the poor tower. I suppose they feel sure we use it as an observation station, just as we credit them with using Wytschaete tower and which we also try to knock down.

21st December

Sir Horace came up this morning and there was much 'palaver talk'. The whole cry at present is for heavy howitzers and plenty of them, but I doubt us seeing them for months yet.

Yesterday a man of the 5th Bavarian Regiment (Reserve) was brought in badly wounded and exhausted. He had been wounded on the 14th, and had been lying out in the Petit Bois since then. On being wounded he managed to crawl into a dug-out a yard or two in front of our trenches and, there, he lay groaning most horrid. Our fellows at night tried to bring him in, but the fool made such a squealing when they tried to move him that he had to be left where he was, for each squeal brought a heavy fire from the Germans who were only a few yards off. Our men threw him food, and they say he liked bull's-eyes best. On the 20th, a doctor managed to give him morphia. They finally got him in by crawling out and tying a rope around him and then hauling him into our own trench, whence he was taken to the hospital where Cornwall saw him and reported him cheerful in spite of five bad wounds. I hope all Germans don't die so hard.

24th December

Cornwall brought back a gloomy account of the trenches he was in yesterday (F1 and F2). We number all our trenches now, which is a good plan. The front is divided into sectors, and the trenches in the sectors are numbered. Cornwall says that not only are the trenches bad, but the men do not work enough at them and the officers are content to sleep in their dug-outs all day, which is very bad. This sort of life does tend to make everyone fatalistic and slack.

He says that there are a lot of French soldiers of the 153rd Regiment lying about there still. They are terribly mangled — feets, hands and other bits all over the place. Apparently they were caught in a very heavy crumping there.

Xmas Day, December 25th
The War Diary sums up the day pretty well. It says 'Foggy and quiet'. The fog is bad and it is cold too, with the roads hard frozen. At breakfast we each received a card from the King and Queen, a very nice one too. The men are especially pleased. They had heard about the 'Princess Mary's' gift, but this Christmas card was kept very secret.

We have issued strict orders to the men not to on any account allow a 'truce', as we have heard rumours that they will probably try to. The Germans did try. They came over towards us singing, so we opened rapid fire on to them, which is the only sort of truce they deserve.

Editor's Note The famous 'Christmas Day Truce' occurred in many parts of the front line, even Billy Congreve's old battalion participated. The 3rd Battalion's war diary states: 'Christmas in the trenches will always be remembered by the battalion as a day of perfect peace during which, by mutual consent, both sides declared a truce. There were many interesting features on this Xmas Day, not the least of which was a German juggler who drew a large crowd of Riflemen and Germans in the middle of No Man's Land.' A sergeant in 3rd Battalion's 'A' Company wrote home: 'Today I stood shoulder to shoulder with a German and dug a grave for his late comrade.'

Fraternisation also took place on Billy Congreve's father's front, which led Brigadier-General Congreve to write in his diary: 'After lunch went to Rue du Bois to take some presents mother had sent for the men, and found a very extraordinary state of affairs. The men had arranged a truce between themselves in a.m., and all day they have been walking about together singing and smoking. The officers also walked and smoked together even to a colonel. At 4 p.m. it was arranged that all were to be back in their trenches and, at midnight, firing would commence. My friend said he had a cigar with the best shot in the German Army, who others said had

A pre-war photograph of Billy Congreve in full dress uniform with the rank of lieutenant.

A relaxing dip for the men of 'D' Company, 3/Rifle Brigade, during their stay at Cambridge in August 1914. Photograph taken by Billy Congreve when a lieutenant with 'D' Company. Most of the men seen here never survived the war.

killed more of us than any dozen others, "but I know where his loop-hole is now and we mean to down him tomorrow." '

Christmas lunch at 3rd Division's headquarters was quite splendid, as Billy Congreve describes:

*

We have had a great Xmas dinner — oxtail soup (from a tin), fillet of beef with macaroni, *oie rôti*, plum pudding (on fire), caviare, champagne and port to drink. The chef quite rose to the occasion. It's not a bad Xmas day, but I hope the next I shall spend at home.

New Year's Day, 1915

Again some of the enemy tried to be friendly and came out opposite the Lincolns'[11] trenches. They must have been drunk. The Lincolns opened rapid fire with great success! There is a good deal more shelling by the enemy than usual, but nothing else of interest doing.

Editor's Note The dying days of 1914 had confirmed that mobile warfare had long since gone and, more to the point, no one knew when it would recommence. With both sides at a loss on how to penetrate the defences of the other, it was inevitable that war on the Western Front would stagnate even further whilst military leaders sought ways of breaking the deadlock. Meanwhile, barbed wire increasingly made its appearance and fortifications strengthened with defences in depth in order to dilute the effects of artillery fire and sudden infantry attacks. Reinforcements also flowed to the front. As well as Territorial and Yeomanry battalions, the BEF was also reinforced from 18th December with the Indian Cavalry Corps, quickly followed by V Corps that was composed of foreign service Regular battalions in the newly constituted 27th and 28th Divisions. Sir John French then divided his command into two armies: First Army under Haig and the Second Army under Smith-Dorrien. It would not be long before a third army would be added, after which a fourth by the end of 1915. In his entry of 3rd January, Billy Congreve makes reference to some of the reinforcements:

3rd January

The weather is horribly cold and foggy. The mud really seems to get worse and worse, which one deemed impossible some weeks ago. A party of officers of the 80th Brigade, 27th Division, have come out to see how we run things. One brigade — the 81st I think it is — has in it the 4th Rifle Brigade and two 60th Battalions[12]. A real rifleman's brigade and is commanded by Charlie Fortescue[13].

11th January
On the 5th, the 8th Brigade took over some more front from the French 32nd Division. Our line now runs from Spanbroek Molen to the Vierstraat—Wytschaete road. Eventually I expect we shall take over still further to the north, also the 27th Division will come in and relieve more Frenchmen. I suppose the plan is for us to eventually take over the front up to the sea.

The weather is truly awful and, on the night of the 8th, trench E2 down by Spanbroek Molen was completely flooded out — water pouring in at the loop-holes and the men having to vacate it and dig themselves in as as well as they could.

Today we gave Holland's Farm an awful doing with the 6-inch howitzers. Our men reported that Germans were hurled all over the place, many in pieces. These old 6-inch guns which have now been in the Army for twenty years are splendid. If only we had more like them.

15th January
The General, Colonel Maurice and I went up early to Kemmel and into the gunner observation stations to watch a bombardment of Spanbroek Molen. General Wing was also up there. It was not easy to see at first, but it got light very quickly and it was a good sight to see our shells bursting all over the German trenches. It was just 'frightfulness' on our part; the infantry were to pretend to be getting ready to assault etc, etc. A really quite useless show, but I suppose it was annoying to the Boche.

Here is another of Cornwall's efforts[14]:

Missing
I'm lying wounded where I fell,
Alive amongst the slain.
But all that's left of life is Hell,
I cannot move for pain.
Nor even invoke that wizard spell:
One swift shot through the brain.

I'm in the ditch beyond the wood,
And all my men beside.
We'd broken through the wire, but could
Not cross the bare hillside.
Their Maxim raked us where we stood,
And slashed us till we died.

Till all the others died and I've
A bullet through the chest.
I bleed so fast I can't survive,
I'll soon be like the rest.
They'll never find me here alive:
(I know they'll do their best).

'Missing' — it seems the worst of ends
To moulder like a leaf.
While there at home for months my friends
Will cherish the belief
That I'm still living; doubt but lends
A keener pang to grief.

I'll no more see the pearly dawn,
Or crimson sunset skies.
The colours fade as if were drawn
A veil before my eyes.
They'll seem as fair when I am gone,
The same old sun will rise.

Though the same old world will drift,
Its old apparent ways,
Things will alter, scenes will shift,
And Victory's torch will blaze.
Tyranny vanquished, Right will lift
Its head in happier days.

J.H.M.C.   18 January 1915

22nd January
Today a 6-inch German shell pitched into a house just outside
Kemmel. It killed a woman and child and badly injured a little girl
— again the fault of these infernal Belgian civil authorities. They
go on letting these people live quite close up to the front line and
so they get killed, besides being badly in the way. One actually

sees them working in the fields less than one thousand yards from our trenches.

7th February

Today we are moving yet a little further northwards. We take over 'M' sector from the 27th Division and hand over 'E' sector to the 5th Division. This move takes us up to opposite Bois 40. The 27th Division are but a poor show. When they first came into the line about fifty per cent of them went sick straight off. Though now they have got going a bit better, I do not think much of them and wish they were anywhere but on our left.

I have seen old Kinkie[15] who is much the same as ever; and Reggie Hargreaves[16], who is very happy and, I hear, a splendid fellow in every way. I hope he is all right, but I hear is disgustingly brave, so I suppose is certain to get hit sooner or later, as it's always the best who seem to be hit.

9th February

We had a royal visit yesterday — King Albert turned up. He looks quite a king and seemed a very nice one too. He was very interested in all we pointed out to him from the top of the hill. He had never seen this corner of his kingdom before, and it must have been a very sad thing for him. It was a most lovely day, the best we have had since King George was up here, and the view was wonderfully clear.

To celebrate the occasion we started a visitors' book — and caught the King, Prince of Wales and Alexander of Teck. Sir John French also came up, so we had a great collection of leading lights. I like the Prince of Wales; he is very quiet and small and slight looking, but has a sense of humour. Sir Horace had just got a very smart new limousine car, and he told me he had told Sir Horace that it was certainly *un automobile de cocotte* and that Sir Horace hadn't quite seen the joke! It certainly was very luxurious: satin and all sorts of *luxeries*.

10th February

Out at the hill all day. Sir Bruce Hamilton came up to see us; he is absurdly like General 'Hammy' in voice and manner. He was very nice and says that I may keep Viscount, though in General H's will he was left to someone else.

Our sick returns of the division show that our convalescent homes do much good, as it is much the lowest in the whole army

— the sick return I mean. The men go to these homes and get a complete change of *everything*; their rifles and all equipment are taken to a store to be cleaned and put away, the men go straight into a bath and then are given hospital clothing. They stay in the home a week or ten days and are provided with games, books, sweets, tobacco and, in fact, are made as happy as can be. If they need medical treatment they get it, as the home is in charge of a medical officer; and when ready to go back to the battalion, they get a new outfit to go back clean and rested to the trenches. Our 'home' holds about 150 men and six officers. The General himself supplies a lot of the 'comforts'.

Later — have just got a wire from Dads: 'Maurice very seriously wounded, doctor says no hope.' 10 p.m.

12th February

I went over as soon as I could — about 8.30 a.m. — yesterday to Armentières and went straight to the hospital I knew Godders to be in. I found Wyatt (his servant) looking after him. Godders looked awful bad, paralysed all down his right side and quite unconscious, but his left arm and leg were moving up and down continuously. I stayed nearly an hour and felt hopelessly useless.

Wyatt told me that when hit, he was helping to build up the parapet at a place that he had just been warned of as being watched by a certain sniper. The bullet went in at the top of the head and, besides breaking a bit of his skull away, seriously injured his brain. I spoke to the doctor who said that there was really no chance, and that he thought he would only live twenty-four hours.

I spent the rest of the morning with Dads who still has a touch of asthma. He was, of course, very cut up about Godders, and so was and is Tom Grenville[17]. In fact, we are all miserable. I again went to see him in the afternoon, but he was just the same. Neville Talbot[18] was there too. When he spoke to Godders loud, he opened his eyes, but they looked quite vacant. Tom motored back with me, and a wire has just come to say that they are moving Godders into Bailleul.

13th February

Went down to No 2 Clearing Hospital at 6 a.m. He was being much better looked after by very nice nurses, and his bed was more comfortable. He seemed better himself too. Everyone still seems to think there is no hope, but somehow I believe there is. Sir Anthony Bowlby, the big specialist, saw him today and thought there was no hope, and at any rate there was no chance of his ever getting back the use of his right side.

19th February
Each morning and evening I've been down to the hospital. He seems gradually to be regaining consciousness, but it is dreadfully slow and he hasn't spoken yet. He eats a good deal though, and is very strong. I sit with him, for I feel he may know that I am there.

Saturday, February 20th
Went to see Maurice early. I really believe that he knew me, but still won't speak. The nice sister is leaving today, which I am very sorry for, as she has been so good to Maurice and is interested in him. It has been a vile day — the first thunderstorm that I have seen in this country. A real good one which made the rival artillery quite a secondary show.

Old Kincaid-Smith brought up the honours list today. They have made Dads a major-general which is grand, but he ought to have been one ages ago[19]. Cornwall has a Military Cross and George Cory a brevet. We presented old Courage this evening with a beautiful 'Iron Cross', mounted on some of the ribbons off Madeleine's bed![20] He is also being given the Military Cross.

Sunday, February 21st
Saw Godders as usual — much the same. The new nurse could not give much account of him. I do wish he would speak — sometimes I feel he tries to and, today, when I said, 'Give me your hand' he did so, but that's all.

I hear rumours that the 28th Division lost a trench last night. The 28th Division has come in on the left of the 27th Division and is of about the same type — hurriedly put together Regular battalions, collected from all over the world, given staffs made up in the same way and thrown out here. A most rotten arrangement. General Snow commands the 27th and is about as much good as an old hen, and General Bulfin the 28th.

22nd February
Went to see Godders and took the padre[21] with me. I am afraid he was not so well. He certainly looked worse and the doctors say that he is decidedly so. They fear that the wound is turning septic. Went on to Armentières. Found Dads very well, also Charlie Swan, Tom Grenville and Alan, but Alan very depressed at not being

mentioned in despatches. I found that I was mentioned and, of course, Dads was too. Our names came together, the list being alphabetical.

I had a lot of news of the 3rd Battalion. They are terribly changed since I left them. In November it was bad enough — now there are only a few I know. Charlie is really the only one I care for enough to want to be with them. He, poor fellow, hates the life. The monotony of it gets so bad, especially now that he has lost Godders.

Editor's Note Enemy sniping, shelling and local actions were steadily draining the front of valuable and experienced men left after 'First Ypres'. December's casualties in 3rd Division alone were 33 officers and 717 other ranks. In 3/Rifle Brigade, casualties included the commander, Lieutenant-Colonel Alexander, killed in action on 30th December, having previously recovered from a shrapnel wound. Two days before Billy Congreve penned his impressions of his old battalion, the British Army lost one of its ablest officers in the form of 43-year-old Brigadier-General 'Johnnie' Gough, VC, CMG, Chief of Staff to Sir Douglas Haig. He was shot and mortally wounded when carrying out a reconnaissance of the Aubers Ridge.

25th February
Yesterday, Gillingham and I walked in the rain to Reninghelst, about four and half miles, to have tea with Reggie Hargreaves. Herbert Buller also turned up; he is adjutant of 'Princess Pat's Pets'[22] . Reggie walked back to Mont Noir with us and stayed to dinner. It was good to see him again. He is so exactly the same as when we were at Eton together.

This morning we woke up to find the snow thick on the ground. Maurice a good deal worse. I went down at 6 a.m. and have asked Gillingham to go. Even my optimism is at an end. It seems so cruelly hard that he should die.

We were just sitting down to lunch today when suddenly Hamilton turned up with a lovely lady — the first woman other than 'natives' I have seen out here. A simultaneous exclamation of 'Good Lord' broke from us! She turned out to be Mary Roberts Reinhart, an American who had come out to look round in her capacity as journalist. She was very amusing and we gave her lunch. I don't think she much appreciated our sour red wine of the country. 'Reminds me of eating a persimmon,' she said (whatever that might be).

We told her all we could and she told us how America regarded
the war. She had just seen King Albert. She was granted a private
interview; the people there told her 'to take great care how I
should behave myself, how I was to bob my head and not go
nearer than six feet and all that, and I went into the room where
he was standing by the fire and we shook hands in silence. He said
nothing and I said nothing, for I had been told on no account to
speak first. At last I had to say something, so I said, "Well, you
know, it's you who have to speak first." ' This made the King laugh
and the rest of the interview was most successful. Her description
of it was most amusing. She talked about twice as fast as most
people and with a strong 'twang'. She leaves for America
tomorrow, 'if these submarines will let me.'

Later — I have just got back. The padre tells me that Maurice
died quite peacefully at 12.30. I knew this before I saw him. I feel
I don't much care what happens now.

27th February
I went down to Bailleul this morning and met Dads and Tom
Grenville at the hospital. We buried Maurice in the cemetery. P.T.
and Maurice Wingfield came too[23] . The coffin was carried in a
motor ambulance and we walked behind. The funeral made little
or no impression on me, which is either because I have lately
learned to understand or else forgotten how to.

Editor's Note It is interesting to compare his father's (now a
major-general) diary entry of that day with regard to Captain
Osborne's burial: 'Neville Talbot took the service — a simple one.
We laid him to rest in the French cemetery beside many other
soldiers, French and English. Billy was splendid and quite
collected. I felt like a baby.'

28th February
Motored round as usual with the General. He is not very fit at
present. Everything is very quiet, but yesterday afternoon one of
our own HE shells fell in E2 [trench] and seriously injured five
men of the Wilts. I saw two of them in hospital this morning —
one with his legs fearfully shattered, and the other with one leg
actually blown off. The latter was only a boy. Accidents from our
own shells used to be a common occurrence, but lately when every
gun knows its job so perfectly, these accidents have been very rare.

Our Staff has changed a lot since I joined it. General Wing[24] has gone to command a new division at home, Cornwall has gone to II Corps, Dundas home, Tandy to GHQ, and Colonel Maurice to GHQ. I shall soon be the oldest inhabitant.

The 15-inch howitzer arrives today, or rather parts of it do. It is a huge affair. The breech-block alone weighs one and half tons. It fires a 1,400 lb shell and has a maximum range of 10,000 yards — and *they say* (?!) that the maximum error at this range is only forty feet, but I take this *cum grano salis*. Anyhow it ought to astonish the Boche, but we only have about one round of ammunition *per diem* and two on Sunday!!

Have just heard a rumour that the whole division is to move up to Ypres again. It's damnable in a way — a move is always bad and the Ypres salient is such hell too. However, I suppose we must not grouse. The next few days may mean a bit of work, which is a blessed prospect for I am sick to death of this life.

2nd March

The move scare has not developed any further at present. Yesterday we had the most weird storm. It got dark about 2 p.m. and then blew a gale with snow. Sir Horace was trying to inspect the South Lancs which was tiresome for all concerned. The Germans shelled Kemmel again yesterday and broke all the château windows. This is about the fifth time they have all been broken. Two horses had been buried (not before they needed it) in a field just behind the château. A crump landed right on top of the grave. The result was decidedly depressive, especially for the re-burial party!

5th March

Roger Owen and I motored over today to Armentières. Dads was out when we got there — up at his trenches — so Roger and I walked round to Chapelle d'Armentières where we found the 17th Brigade HQ and saw 'Sparrow' Scott[25]. Roger then went on to 3rd Battalion HQ and I returned to find Dads. He was very fit and cheerful.

General Henry Wilson[26] turned up for tea and was like a sort of delightful whirlwind. I do admire him, more than anyone I know, I think. After tea, eight war correspondents turned up — much to everyone's horror! Ashmead-Bartlett was one of them[27]. Dads is taking them round his trenches this evening. It's about an even money chance on one of them getting hit or lost in a water-logged trench!

General Henry Wilson was very angry about the shortage of ammunition. He said it was an awful disgrace that the French should be able to provide ninety divisions of their own, the Portuguese (whose guns are up with the Belgians)[28], the Servians and the Russians with ammunition — and that we should be unable to provide our measly force of twelve divisions![29] The shortage is so serious that our 4.5-inch howitzers along our whole front are not allowed to shoot *at all*, unless we are actually attacked. It certainly does seem an awful disgrace.

The 15-inch howitzer —'Grandmother' as she is called — was to have fired today. Now it's put off till tomorrow. That is if it is a good enough day for Sir John French and the Prince of Wales to see well, for apparently GHQ are in charge of the gun.

Editor's Note Artillery ammunition, especially high-explosive shells, had always been at a critical level since the day Great Britain entered the war. It was the same sad tale concerning the supply of heavy artillery. The plain fact was that Great Britain was not prepared for a war on such a grand scale, unlike Germany. The gradual reduction of Army Estimates in the years preceding the war by politicians, coupled with the enormous difficulties in putting the country on a war footing, were felt in no small measure by the highest ranking officer to the humblest of soldiers at the front. Moreover, the situation would not greatly improve until 1916.

Billy Congreve's reference to the scarcity of 4.5-inch howitzer ammunition was, doubtless, exacerbated by the hoarding of artillery shells for the forthcoming British offensive that was already in preparation. The offensive was planned for Wednesday, 10th March.

Monday, March 8th
The 15-inch fired four rounds yesterday; the first two at Wytschaete tower which they were just short of. A great column of smoke and flame went up and, I think, gave the Germans something to think about. The next two rounds were at Pt 76 (Spanbroek Molen) and fell within fifteen yards of each other. So the gun is fairly accurate and this is what we wanted to find out.

I saw Sir Horace on Saturday. He said to Crichton[30] and me that he was sorry to see that we had received no decoration in the last *Gazette*. I expressed my conviction that I should have been a good deal more surprised if I had.

It's fearfully cold again today, but not wet[31] . The country is still very water-logged, but the trenches are now kept in a fairly livable condition. Chiefly, I think, because the men work harder and the officers know better how to set about it.

The 15-inch fired at 3 p.m. on Messines tower. The first shot was 300 yards short and to the right, no doubt partly owing to a strong east wind. The second shot hit the tower full pitch. It made a most enormous cloud of pink and yellow smoke which hung about for two or three minutes. When it cleared, we saw that the tower had all the right side blown away. The range was about 8,000 yards, so it was a fine shot. I hope to goodness that there were some Germans close to it! Of course we had up the usual crowd of sightseers — it's really rather absurd.

CHAPTER SIX

Spring Offensive and St Eloi

Although the Western Front had somewhat stabilised as 1915 dawned, with trenches threading an uneven line from the English Channel to Switzerland, events on the Eastern Front told a different story. There, Russia's military position was precarious to say the least. Rumours of ammunition shortages, plus substantiated reports of German divisions leaving the Western Front for the East gave rise to anxiety. The anxiety deepened when Russia appealed to Great Britain on 2nd January for the Allies to ease the Turkish pressure in the Caucasus by a demonstration against that country, Turkey having sided with Germany in late October.

The British Government had already debated various alternatives to the Western Front, since the prospect of a break-through there in the foreseeable future looked very doubtful. It was finally agreed to send a naval expedition with military support to the Turkish-dominated Dardanelles. If successful, it would ease Russia's problems in the Caucasus, turn the screw on Constantinople and give Russia access through the Black Sea again. It would also help to create a favourable impression on the fidgety Balkan States.

From the outset, Sir John French objected to any plan that would dilute his command of men and material. With Germany monopolising a good chunk of his beloved France, it was not surprising that Joffre held the same opinion. Both felt that the Allies should take advantage of the reduction in enemy forces. Sir John French had personally aired his views at a War Council meeting in London on 13th January. At the meeting, he had emphasised the importance of striking at the enemy in the West at the earliest possible moment with all available strength, adding that it was chiefly a question of having enough artillery ammunition, especially high explosives, in order to destroy the enemy defences. Above all he made the point that, until the impossibility of breaking through on the Western Front was proved, there could be no question of making an attempt elsewhere.

The British Commander-in-Chief was determined to launch an offensive at the earliest opportunity, appreciating the politics of the situation as he did. Because of his antipathy towards Sir Horace Smith-Dorrien, he asked Haig to draft a plan in the full knowledge that the First Army commander was in sympathy for an offensive. For a time, it had been the intention to have a joint effort with the French Tenth Army. Sir John's inability, however, to relieve two French corps north of Ypres (a principal condition of Joffre's for a combined operation and, in all probability, the basis of the rumour that Billy Congreve had heard about the 3rd Division moving to Ypres) stopped the Tenth Army involvement at the eleventh hour. It was then that Sir John French decided to go it alone. In so doing, he would inadvertently give greater attraction to the Dardanelles operation that was fated to crumble on the Gallipoli peninsula.

Haig's scheme was for a limited objective offensive, launched along a narrow frontage of his First Army line. Formulated with the blessing of GHQ, Haig intended to break through the enemy lines at Neuve Chapelle and, if successful, to establish the First Army across the Aubers Ridge, after which to funnel cavalry into open country and, hopefully, to threaten the enemy-held city of Lille. There would be subsidiary attacks along the BEF front to keep the enemy busily employed whilst the main operation took place.

On the surface, Haig's plan looked remarkably sound. Enemy strength in the Neuve Chapelle sector was accurately judged at three battalions. Haig had forty-eight infantry battalions and two cavalry corps. He had also collected together more artillery pieces in one place than had ever before been seen on the Western Front. Included in the artillery support were forty 4.5-inch howitzers and, for the first time, a battery of (three) 9.2-inch howitzers would be employed in this British operation. With a numerical superiority of thirty-five to one, and with two artillery pieces to the enemy's one, everything seemed optimistic for 10th March when battle would commence.

Haig knew that his men must capture Neuve Chapelle and move on quickly before enemy reinforcements arrived. He also knew that his stocks of artillery ammunition were only adequate for a four day battle. What he did not know was that although the Germans had half his number of guns in that sector, they had double the amount of artillery ammunition. They also had at least twelve well-sited machine-guns. Another telling point was the late

arrival of two 6-inch howitzer batteries from England. Because of
the time factor, they could not be in a state of readiness for the
7.30 a.m. opening bombardment on 10th March. The result would
be a vital 400 yard stretch of enemy front line escaping demolition.

As for Billy Congreve, his division being part of Smith-Dorrien's
Second Army, he would find himself as an eye-witness to one of
the 'side-shows':

*

10th March

We motored to Kemmel at 7 a.m. this morning. Our guns were
shelling Spanbroek Molen very heavily. An awful row they made,
all going off at once. Even old 'Granny' chimed in, and we heard
her going over our heads just like an express train. I worked out
that the shell travels about 400 miles per hour, slow for a shell,
but imagine half a ton of steel and high explosive coming along
at 400 miles an hour, and landing near you from five miles away.
Gee — some gun![1]

12th March

We are full of preparations for an attack on Spanbroek Molen,
which we have been ordered to make so as to take off pressure
from down south. The 6th Division took a farm called L'Eppinette
last night, but there are no details and, as yet, very little definite
news about Neuve Chapelle[2]. I believe to date that we have taken
close on a thousand prisoners. Our attack on the Molen was to
have come off this morning. The 7th Brigade are to do the work
and there is to be a one and half hour preliminary artillery
bombardment. Now it's nearly mid-day and the fog is so dense
that we can do nothing at present.

Later: About 2 p.m. we received orders to commence the
bombardment and attack at once, whether the mist was lifting or
not. So it took place. The shelling went on for about forty
minutes, and then the attack went in and failed. Apparently our
shelling did too little damage, and the Wilts[3] never got home at
all, being held up by machine-guns and rifle fire. The Worcesters[4]
got into one bit of German trench, but found it unoccupied. They
stayed there for several hours and were told then to withdraw;
bringing nothing with them to show as a result of the attack but a
meerschaum pipe. We lost about 400 men and 20 officers, and *did
no good at all*. Even as a feint to prevent reserves moving south, I

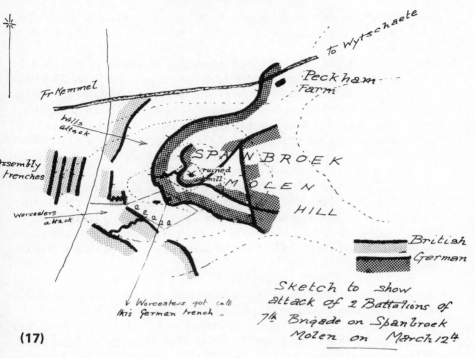

Sketch to show
attack of 2 Battalions of
7th Brigade on Spanbroek
Molen on March 12th

(17)

doubt if it was effective, and the Germans must have seen the
weakness of it. However, it was ordered to be done and there is no
more to be said about it. We are all rather depressed though,
especially Haldane who feels this as being his second failure, for he
is intensely ambitious.

The reasons for the failure are, I think: (1) No small attack on a
strongly fortified position will be successful, unless the preliminary
bombardment is so intense in power and duration as to completely
wipe out the hostile wire and trenches; (2) Any bombardment
against modern earthwork defences is useless unless made with
very many heavy guns on a small front. Wire cutting by shrapnel is
very slow, though effective if the guns are at close enough range —
about 1,200 yards; (3) Weather conditions must be good; (4) The
alteration of time at the last moment is bad; (5) All brigade and
battalion commanders concerned should be *close* up — this was
not the case today; (6) Too much importance cannot be attached
to preliminary arrangements. At least two weeks' hard Staff work

is necessary for any divisional scheme.

14th March

We arrived back from the Scherpenberg about 5 p.m. when a terrific bombardment started somewhere up in the 27th Division area (our immediate left). It was the heaviest I have heard since Ypres days. Until about 5.30 we had no news, and then heard that the 27th Division 'were being very heavily shelled at St Eloi'. Apparently some of our trenches were blown up and, under cover of the bombardment, the German infantry rushed in. Now it is 10 p.m. and we have heard that we have lost about seven lengths of trench and the village. This is rather serious. All the moves are cancelled (we were to have extended southwards tonight) and General Snow has ordered a counter-attack. The 4th Rifle Brigade and Princess Pat's CLI are to do it. I expect this German attack is really only to draw off our attention and forces from Neuve Chapelle.

Editor's Note Positioned at the junction of the Ypres—Messines and Voormezeele—Warneton roads, St Eloi village is less than four miles from Kemmel in a north-easterly direction. Loosely defended by the 82nd Brigade of the 27th Division, it is situated halfway up the side of a gentle hill (with the enemy holding the ridge) and, just inside the British defences, was a large artificial knoll called the Mound. With 27th Divisional headquarters having dithered on the practicability of mining in the local soil, after a young subaltern had reported suspicious mining sounds in February, the Germans exploded a mine under the Mound at 5 p.m. on 14th March. After a violent artillery bombardment, they drove the defenders from their trenches and managed to penetrate the village as well as capturing the Mound. The 80th Brigade, which included the 4/Rifle Brigade and PPCLI, moved up in support as the 82nd Brigade hurriedly organised a counter-attack. At 3 a.m. on 15th March, news came that the counter-attack had failed. It was then that the 4/Rifle Brigade received orders to make the main attack in an attempt to retrieve the situation. Among the officers in that battalion were Billy Congreve's uncle, Major Arthur King, and many friends, including Lieutenant Reginald Hargreaves who was the battalion's bombing and sniping officer. If the battalion was successful in retaking the village, now bristling with enemy machine-guns, the next objective was the recapture of the Mound. The officers and men of the

1/Royal Scots Fusiliers in trenches running through some houses in St Eloi village, April-May 1915. 9th Brigade, 3rd Division.

(*Left*) German prisoners being escorted through the battered streets of Ypres. Photographed by Billy Congreve in June 191 (*Below*) Faces of victor and vanquished: Germans captured in 3rd Division's assault at Hoog on 16th June 1915. Photographed by Billy Congreve inside the ramparts at Ypres.

4/Rifle Brigade went in under cover of darkness, without a preliminary artillery bombardment and with little idea of the exact situation.

15th March

As far as we can make out from the scanty news that has come in, the counter-attack has not been successful. We only got back one of our original trenches. The Germans still hold all the rest and have also established themselves on the Mound. There are, however, no Germans in the village, which is in our hands. The situation is now something like this, but the 27th Division [Staff] are hopeless people to have any dealings with [see map below].

I fancy that our original line will not now be retaken, and that

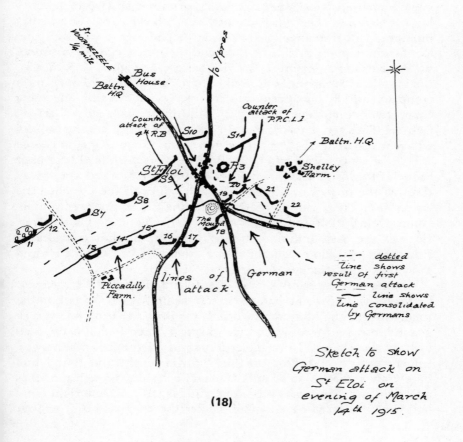

(18)

Sketch to show German attack on St Eloi on evening of March 14th 1915.

the 27th Division will consolidate themselves – or try to – on the line they now hold.

I have just heard that poor Kinkie was killed in St Eloi this morning. He must have been leading the counter-attack, so what better fate could one ask. Many other good riflemen were also killed – and Reggie and Moses both hit[5].

We were firstly told that all the trenches had been retaken, but this is not so. I believe Stopford-Sackville (Tiger)[6] actually got on to the Mound and killed a German machine-gunner there, which was a very fine performance. I am always hearing tales of his gallantry.

Editor's Note With only the elements of surprise and discipline on their side, companies of 4/Rifle Brigade went to their assigned tasks in the darkness. They had retaken one trench before the enemy realised what was happening, after which two companies began clearing the village houses and barricades. From that moment, with the enemy alert, it developed into a grim struggle. Confusion reigned outside St Eloi, and there seemed little prospect of the battalion's supports arriving before daylight. At 5.15 a.m. the battalion commander, Colonel Thesiger, called up Major King's company which had been held in reserve. At roughly the same time, two companies of the 2/Shropshires managed to arrive. Colonel Thesiger then organised a general advance on the Mound which was defended by machine-gun teams. Major King, in charge of the advance, was immediately killed. Meanwhile, Lieutenant Lionel Stopford-Sackville and one rifleman worked their way through the houses on the left of the road until they reached the last house. There, in the dawn light, they shot at the machine-gunners on the Mound with Stopford-Sackville using his revolver. He had the satisfaction of noting that one machine-gun ceased firing. But battalion casualties were mounting and, having cleared the village, the attack was called off.

Among the casualties was Lieutenant Reginald Hargreaves. Critically wounded, he had to be left behind where he fell on the road towards the Mound. An order was issued that no one was to go out looking for wounded, as too many men had already been lost in the attack. Nevertheless, four of Lieutenant Hargreaves' snipers went to St Eloi on the following night and found him barely alive in No Man's Land. He had been shot through the lungs and right leg. His arm was broken, and his left foot and right hand had been shattered by shrapnel. Under the enemy's nose, his four snipers brought him back to the British lines where they carried him on a stretcher to Dickebusch.

16th March

All is now quiet at Spanbroek. In the afternoon I motored with George Cory[7] to Sailly, not far from Armentières. We went to see his younger brother who is in some Canadian regiment. When we got to the Canadian HQ, we found that Bob Cory was in the trenches, so we went up there. The trenches consist of very good breastworks with the Germans 200 to 400 yards off. We hold our line very weakly there. The colonel of the battalion told me that he was holding 5,000 yards of front, but this of course was an exaggeration. They were a very cheery, fine-looking lot, and as keen as anything. Their trenches were quite amusing. All the dug-outs and little forts and bridges had boards up with their names on them, such as 'Grand Hotel Ottawa' and 'Niagara Bridge'! There was but little shooting going on, though as we came away in the dusk the Germans turned on a machine-gun down the road, which wasn't pleasant.

The country there is so flat that it is easy to get about in daylight. We walked up to within 150 yards of the fire trenches along the road, then through a ruined house and down a well-made communication trench — a very different matter to our almost unapproachable line.

17th March

St Patrick's Day: Kennedy sent me some shamrock, also Joe, so I had plenty and sent some out to all the Irishmen I could find on the Staff, much to their joy. I also planted a bit in a pot. I wonder, will it grow? Cameron[8] is very dubious, saying that he knows it will never grow out of Irish soil, but as he is a bigoted Scotsman I think he is probably wrong. In the morning, I went over to Armentières and found that Dads was up in the trenches. Such a lovely day it was, quite a hot sun, so Tom and I set off to find him.

It is a funny business going up to the front trenches there. You walk out of Armentières, which is a big place with slums, into a flat arable country with hardly any hedges. As one passes the last building — in which there sat a fat old lady comfortably knitting — one could see the trenches 800 yards off, and one solemnly walks down the high-road towards them. It is most uncanny why nobody snipes, but the fact remains that they don't. We walked right up and into the breastwork trenches, which are a maze of

parapets, parados and communications. They were fairly dry and
well boarded and, I think, the average distance from the Germans
was about 200 yards. The wire on both sides was extremely thick
— the accumulation of months.

Tom and I, after much wandering, which is exactly like being in
a maze, for one can see out neither to right nor left, found Dads
and Alan. After a little more inspection we walked back along
another road to the town, apparently in full view of Mr German. It
wasn't till we were nearly back at the town that some more
enterprising Boche woke up and sent a few poor shots our way.
The trenches there are a revelation to me, and beats ours into a
cocked hat.

Reggie is worse than I at first thought. They all say in the 27th
Division how wonderfully well he did, and was as brave as a man
can be. General Snow says he hopes to get him the DSO, for if he
lives his soldiering days are done, I fear. They told me in the
hospital today that there was but little chance for him. He is
terribly wounded. He is, the doctors say, most marvellously
plucky, but this damnable gangrene has, I fear, got at him.
Apparently they have not yet brought Kinkie's body in.

18th March
Yesterday there was a tremendous inquisition over the Molen
affair; the C-in-C holding court and Haldane, Ballard[9] & Co being
arraigned. Ballard is apparently the chosen scapegoat, and he
certainly seems to have put up a poorish show. I think General H.
himself thought that he might be 'for Home'!

19th March
Reggie very bad. They have cut off his foot and most of his hand.
I feel he may yet pull through, for he has an intense desire to live
and that is more than half the battle.

20th March
Moses died this morning. He was shot in the head. They at first
thought he was doing well, then suddenly he went worse. Reggie
is doing better, but they cannot move him as yet.

There is trouble between the General and General Bowes[10]. The
latter is apparently weary, physically and mentally and, certainly,
has not proved himself to be very energetic. To make things worse,
he and H.are old and good friends. Not that H.would let anyone
stand in his way for sentiment's sake, and very rightly I suppose.

22nd March

It's my birthday and I received many pleasant letters and two huge cakes from Zoe and Nancy Lane. Went over to Armentières for tea, taking Nancy's cake with me. All well there. John Shea[11] motored me back to Bailleul in the evening and I went to see Reggie. He is again better and they think now that he will pull through. He is so maimed though, yet I feel he is the splendid sort of fellow who will bear it well and have a happy enough life[12].

23rd March

We are to take over the 27th Division line which embraces St Eloi. What joy!!

Apparently the 27th Division are in a hopeless state. I am sure it's all owing to that silly old man, Snow, and his Staff.

Spent the day at the 'Scherp' and then motored out to a cross-roads on the Dickebusch—Ypres road with the General and Colonel C. Evans[13]. We then walked up through a very smelly broken little place called Kruisstraathoek to Voormezeele. It was dark and one could see little, also damp, so our first impressions were not cheerful. Voormezeele is a much battered place about three-quarters of a mile from St Eloi.

We found General Charlie Fortescue and Colonel Thesiger in the Headquarters' cellar (a noisome abode) and very weary they all looked. They still have not brought in Kinkie's body, which apparently is very near the Mound and in too dangerous a place to make it possible to get near him — poor Dorothy[14]. However, now that we will be holding the place, I expect I shall be able to do something.

We are responsible for the line up to St Eloi, and the 85th Brigade move into this part of the line tomorrow. I forgot to say that we have the 85th Brigade in exchange for the 9th, as the 28th Division — like the 27th — seem unable to manage their business properly. We have found the 85th Brigade to be first-class in every way; General Chapman commands and Deveril is brigade major. I fancy this bit of line will need a tremendous lot of work to make it safe. The usual type of trenches are impossible owing to the wet, so it means long lines of continuous breastwork. The 27th Division, as can be seen on my former sketch of St Eloi, are contented to hold breastworks in the form of grouse butts with no connection and with rotten wire. No wonder the Germans got in. We don't move from Mont Noir till Snow clears out of Renninghelst.

The following memo from GOC[15] II Corps:

In carrying out the orders for extending our line northwards, it falls to the lot of the 3rd Division to hold St Eloi and the ground on either side of it. The enemy has been pushing forward at this point slowly but persistently, and the positions they have now reached are seriously menacing to our hold on Ypres. To prevent them making another foot of ground towards us, it is essential to push them back and to regain lost ground must be our immediate aim. For some weeks past, the enemy has kept the initiative. The 3rd Division must wrest it from him . . .

March 23rd 1915

28th March

We are still on our hill and in our château and still Snow sits in Renninghelst. The work has been set into with a will and, already, the place is different and more formidable. We have huge working parties down nightly and thousands of sandbags are filled and laid. The Germans are probably doing the same thing, for everything is fairly quiet and that, combined with a really good moon, makes the work a good deal easier.

The General and I went up to the Brasserie this afternoon. This is a big auberge used by the gunners as an observation post and an excellent one it makes; especially for the Mound and all the trenches as far as the Bois Carré. The Mound is an insignificant thing — about thirty feet high — and is nothing but a broken heap of earth. I could see no signs of sandbags or any work on top of it. St Eloi, what we could see of it, is in a bad way. The German trenches dominate ours in a most extraordinary way all down the line.

Everything is fairly quiet on this front, and now that the weather is so improved everyone is much more cheerful. I hear that some of Kitchener's Army is coming out very shortly. I suppose that will mean a general advance. Perhaps Cornwall and I will yet dine in London on May 27th! But I must say I doubt it. I remember three months ago we were quite confident of its possibility.

30th March

The General and I met General Chapman[16] just outside Dickebusch and walked up across the fields to Voormezeele. We had a look at the dug-outs along the stream, then set out to go up the communications trench to the Bois Confluent. It was bad going — the trench all too shallow. We were a long way from Mr German, but went along doubled-up. We were half-way when some

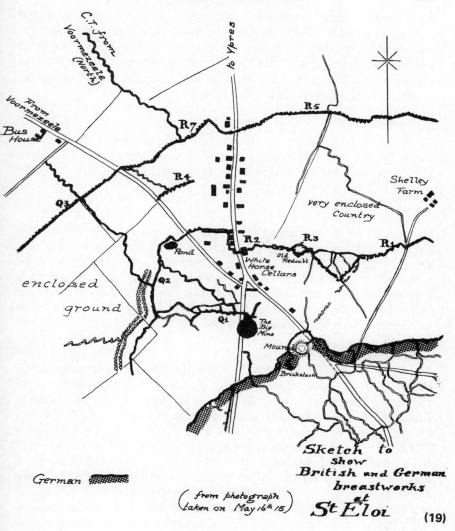

German ▬▬▬

(*from photograph*
taken on May 16ᵗʰ 15)

Sketch to
Show
British and German
breastworks
at
St Eloi

(19)

stray bullets came close. A halt was called and General C. said that it was dangerous to go any further. I am sure this was nonsense, but could not very well say so. So we returned, but I stayed behind a bit and got a fair look at the trenches between St Eloi and the wood. I then came back standing upright. There was no more a sniper at work than I thought.

4th April

Crichton has gone to do temporary brigade-major to the 8th Brigade, so I am doing his work and glad to have it to do. I wish I had it permanently. Hoskins[17] now commands the 8th Brigade, and Bowes has gone home!

7th April

We moved to Renninghelst today. It is not such a bad place. The General and I share a little house and are quite comfortable. We are split up in billets all over the village and it is really better than being all in one house. By day we are going up to some huts erected for us just behind Dickebusch. The St Eloi defences are really becoming formidable. I think that Mr German will have his work cut out to break through if he tries again.

12th April

I went up to Q1 last night with Wavell (the 9th Brigade have come back now). It was very interesting. We went up from Voormezeele to Bus House along the road. The most 'bullety' part of this bit is just as you come up the little rise from the stream towards the Bus House. From Bus House we cut across to Q3, which is more of a trench than a breastwork. In it were the Liverpool Scottish. I had been given to understand that Q3 and Q2 were joined by a communication trench. After much searching in the dark we found it. No wonder it took some looking for, as it was only about ten inches deep. Q2 is a fine breastwork with big parados, a very solid affair with firing steps in the parapet and dug-outs (or 'dig-outs', as the men call them) in the parados. We then went out through a hole in the parapet and walked up to Q1.

Walking up to Q1, one could see the black lump of the Mound looming up ahead, and when the flares went up one realised that it was safer to stand still. We arrived all right, and the trench was a duplicate of Q2 — very good.

We went along the trench to the mine-house[18] which is over the road, but one hardly realises, as the road has been cut through and the breastwork built over it. The mine-house is but a collection of bricks with some low walls. There were a few men in it, looking out for snipers on the Mound which is only fifty yards off. In the dark it shows up very clear against the sky and looks bigger than it really is. It consists of a mound of material for making bricks and is about twenty-five or thirty-five feet high. Behind it are two small stacks of bricks, into which the Germans have built a machine-gun. There was a sniper at work on top of the Mound, for I could see the flash of his rifle. The mine-shaft is in the house and is about fifteen feet deep; the gallery which is being carried towards the Mound is about twelve feet in now.

I went down and very dirty and hot I got, as one had to go down by a rope ladder which was no joke. I squatted in the gallery and talked for a few minutes to the miners who are specially enlisted fellows from some Durham coal-mine. A jolly looking lot they were, and working as happily as if they were in their native coal-mine instead of yards from the Germans!

The breastwork is being carried on slowly towards the other road, and I think this ought to be pushed forward quicker so as to join up with R3. The 5th Fusiliers[19] were holding the trench with Roddam in command. He is a good fellow. I made many enquiries about Kinkie's body, which I knew could not be many yards off. They said that there were still a lot of dead about, but that they were hard to get at. Roddam promised to try and locate Kinkie's body, and I said I would go up again if he thought he had done so.

13th April

This afternoon the General and I went for a long walk. The day was hot and before we had gone very far we were near melted, as one had to haul one's foot out of about a foot of mud. In the dug-outs behind the wood[20] we found some of the 4th South Lancs. Just as we got there the Germans started on these dug-outs with 'whizz-bangs' (this term now embraces all forms of fairly small high-velocity shrapnel shell), so we took shelter with some speed with one of their officers, who seemed to be on the most intimate terms with his servant who shared the dug-out. I, for some time, couldn't make out which one was the officer! The servant was doubtless worthy of this intimacy though, for he provided us with some excellent luke-warm cocoa; in our exhausted state, it was true nectar.

14th April

From R1, one gets an excellent view of the Mound sideways on.

The Brickstack shows up better too. There is another mine in White Horse Cellars. This goes towards the fork roads and is making very good progress. I arrived back very late and very tired, having been out all the previous night too. This evening I am going over to Armentières.

Editor's Note On 11th April, Billy Congreve had received word that his father was ill with bronchitis. An asthmatic all his life, his father was dogged with ill-health throughout the war. His health was further attacked in August 1916 when he was laid low with cholera. When commanding a corps in early 1917, he lost his left hand through enemy shrapnel.

15th April

Dads still bad and, as yet, not on the mend. He will have to go home for a rest and change when he is fit to move. I got back just in time for a 'scare', about 11 p.m.

The Germans blew up a big mine just in front of the mine-house in Q1. They followed this up with a very heavy shelling and rifle fire, but made no infantry attack. I think that this was probably due to the fact that our own guns opened fire so promptly on the enemy's breastworks that their infantry funked. Mercifully, the mine was not exactly under the house or the road, but as I have marked it on the sketch [page 118–*Ed*.]

The damage caused by the explosion was considerable. The shaky walls of the mine-house collapsed, burying several men and blocking up the mine-shaft. Also the barricade over the road fell down with a good deal of the left end of the breastwork. About twenty men were killed and injured in all. It might have been much worse. Several people showed great pluck in getting men out especially as the Germans threw bombs into the ruins and kept up a heavy fire. At first it was feared that all the miners must have been killed, but when light came in the morning a thin column — or rather wisp of smoke — was seen coming out from the blocked up shaft and this was pronounced to be cigarette smoke! So it was, and the miners, not the least upset by the affair, were fairly soon liberated.

The RE experts say that the charge to make so big a hole and explosion must have needed at least 500 lbs of high-explosive. Lucky for me that the Germans chose Wednesday night, and not Monday or Tuesday.

Saturday, April 17th
We received the following memo last night:

> To 3rd Division.
>
> The 5th Division is to carry out a small operation on Saturday evening at 7 p.m. Mines will be fired under an advanced hostile trench which will then be rushed by our infantry. The ground gained will be made good.
>
> II Corps. 8.10 p.m.
> 16/4/15

This is due to take place in a very short time now. It's quite time the old 5th Division had a bit of excitement.

Editor's Note Another artificial mound — this time the highest of three spoil heaps composed of earth excavated when a railway cutting was made during the construction of the Comines—Ypres railway. It was known as Hill 60 from the ring contour marking it on large scale maps. Mining began when the 28th Division held the line there. The 5th Division continued the galleries after relieving the 28th Division, which left its mining parties behind for that purpose. Because of the surrounding flat landscape, Hill 60 took on a huge military importance, as it was situated on the crest of the Ypres ridge with excellent all-round observation. Five galleries were run under the hill and packed with high-explosives — two with 2,000 lbs each, two with 2,700 lbs each and one with 500 lbs. Detonation would commence at 7.05 p.m. on 17th April. Something else caught Billy Congreve's attention that day, which in time would even dwarf the impending horrors of Hill 60:

*

We had an alarm a few days ago. About 7 p.m. the following message marked 'Secret' arrived, and we all prepared for a great attack. This is the report we received:

> A reliable agent of the French Army in Belgium reports that an attack on the Ypres salient has been arranged for the night of 15/16th. A prisoner of the 234th Regt 16th Corps, taken on 14th April near Langemarck, reports that an attack has been prepared for noon on the 15th. Reserves have been brought up and passages have been prepared across old existing trenches in the rear of the present German trenches to facilitate bringing forward artillery.

> The Germans intend making use of tubes with asphyxiating gas placed in batteries of twenty tubes for every 40 metres [along the front of XXVI Corps]. This prisoner had in his possession a small sack filled with a kind of gauze, which would be dipped in some solution to counteract the effects of the gas. The German morale is said to have much improved lately.
>
> It is possible that the attack may be postponed if the wind is not favourable, so as to blow the gases over our trenches.

Of course, as is always the case, it was a false alarm, and the night went very peacefully[21]. Anyhow, if the attack does come I fancy it's not likely to come on us here, and this gas business must be pretty good nonsense. I can't think they will be quite such devils as that.

18th April

The Hill 60 attack was quite a success. We exploded mines along the top of the hill and our infantry got up there without any losses[22]. They were heavily counter-attacked and at present it is a regular hornet's nest up there. The German heavy artillery are giving us an awful time up there. So far we have kept all the ground taken, but now suffering heavy losses ourselves.

Most of our trouble is caused by their bombers who work wonderfully well with the infantry. Our fellows are mostly untrained in bomb throwing, so it is rather an uneven contest — especially as we are issued with about six different patterns of grenades. If one man knows one sort, he probably doesn't know the others. It's months and months ago since the urgent need for a good hand-grenade was realised, and we haven't one yet!

I like the way the Corps referred to it as a 'small operation' — it's rather developing into a bigger one. Evidently the Germans set great store by the Hill. Our fellows now up there say the reason they do so is obvious, as one can see all the ground into Ypres and all the roads.

21st April

The 5th Division are having an awful time on Hill 60. The men who are lucky enough to come back say that it is the worst fighting in the war. I believe that, to date, we have lost about 60 officers and 1,700 other ranks in five days on a place about the size of the centre part in Trafalgar Square[23]. We are so hopelessly out-gunned at present, for what little artillery we have has all been taken away. Presumably to take part in the 'push that's coming' further south[24].

The Germans, not content with shelling Hill 60 out of existence, are now putting 16-inch crumps — super-super-crumps! — into Ypres [25]. Poor Ypres, it seems so long that I saw it in November, an almost unharmed and lovely place, and now it's burnt and broken and hopeless — and still they go on battering it to pieces. The last refugees and other civilians are leaving now in streams.

In the evening, Colonel Wilson-Sopwith[26] and I went up to Q1. It has been considerably altered by the explosion of the mine, but really I think on the whole stronger. The miners were hard at work and the 'foreman' persuaded me to go down again, which I did to please him. The rope ladder seemed more eel-like and muddy than ever. The gallery is now about seventeen feet out towards the Mound. They had some trouble at first in going on with the gallery, as the soil (which is blue marl) was much broken up by the mine. However, they have now passed this bad bit. I felt a bit anxious to get up to the top again, for I couldn't help thinking of what another mine might do. It would be so vile a death to be buried alive — not that this worries the miners! I doubt if ever they think of it.

I had a look for Kinkie's body, but was disappointed, as I only found that of a second-lieutenant of the Royal Irish who seemed in the dark to be about the right size. One can't get much nearer the Mound, for the flares are such an awful nuisance. When one comes down close by one and burns on the ground, one feels that one *must* be seen. Yet by lying flat and *perfectly* still, one never seems to be seen, even though it can't be much more than thirty yards from the Germans. However, the flares had the merit of showing one where one is, and what one is looking for.

Also got in a body of a man in the KOYLI. How he got there I cannot think, for his regiment has never as far as I know been there. It must have been very long ago. We buried them behind the trench. One gets very callous I find. It was a poor sort of funeral, no service, nothing; just an old greatcoat over the face and a few odd curses by some man at another's clumsiness. There is also the risk of a stray bullet, for naturally one wishes to bury the body as far back from the trench as possible, but one doesn't much like leaving the shelter of the parapet, so the graves are dug just about two yards behind the trench.

CHAPTER SEVEN

Gas and 'Second Ypres'

After a brief but glorious period of hot sunny days, the Belgian weather turned cooler from 19th April. If anything, the fall in temperature was noted with a shrug of the shoulders in the Allied camp. On the German side, however, interest in the weather was more profound, particularly on the subject of wind direction. For some time the enemy had eagerly awaited the right climatic conditions in which to launch a terrifyingly new weapon. And that weapon was contained in numerous iron cylinders, each 1.4 metres in length and stored in places of safety along the front line. On removing the cylinders' caps, poison gas would issue forth under pressure in voluminous clouds. When the moment came to do so, then the Second Battle of Ypres would commence.

As Captain Billy Congreve had chronicled, circumstantial evidence on the enemy's intentions was there for those in Allied high command to see. The French Tenth Army had even published a warning on the future employment of asphyxiating gas in its bulletin of 30th March. On 16th April, information also came from Belgian Army sources on the enemy having just manufactured in Ghent some 20,000 'mouth protectors' for use 'against the effects of asphyxiating gas'. Unknown to 5th Division, cylinders of gas had been buried for future use on Hill 60 — a fact that worried the Germans when they lost the hill. The report that Billy Congreve saw was of inestimable value. Unfortunately the French general who passed it to the British Second Army — General Putz — refused to believe it. He was not alone in his assertion when the threatened gas attack failed to materialise on the pre-announced day. It was on that note that 22nd April made its appearance with all its implications. Even so, little of consequence occurred until later in the day. Billy Congreve:

*

22nd April
A long dull day. Hill 60 is fairly quiet again now, but it is an awful

shambles up there. All these exploding mines and the terrible quantity of crumps have brought to light many things that were better buried, especially large quantities of very old Frenchman. These added to our own and German dead, make things very bad.

About 5 p.m. heavy shelling started up Bixchoote way. I suppose the French are up to some game[1]. At 7 p.m. I went again to Armentières and, on arriving back, I heard the bad news that the noise we heard at 5 p.m. was the forerunner of a very heavy attack by the Germans on the junction of the Canadian division and the French. We have little news of it as yet, except that the Germans used poison gases (as we were warned they were going to) and drove back our extreme left and the French right a longish way — exactly how far or what the situation is now none of us know as yet.

Ypres is being more heavily shelled than ever. Streams of belated inhabitants and, sadder still, French soldiers are coming back through here. Apparently the French troops there were Africans, as I have seen several of them coming back[2]. Queer-looking coves they are with their coal-black faces and baggy red trousers. I suppose this gas business is too much for them.

23rd April

A very cold, windy day and a lot of dust about. We met a lot of refugees coming from Ypres, a sad sight, old men pushing a few household treasures along in wheelbarrows, and husbands shifting wives in the same conveyances — all wearing their best clothes, poor people.

The Canadians, as far as I can make out, did not give way, but the French troops, consisting of Turcos and Zouaves, did. The Germans came streaming through the gap they left and nearly into Ypres. The Canadians fought like heroes; shoved all the men they could up on to their left flank and were eventually supported by the 85th Brigade[3], who prolonged the Canadian left. The French were driven out by the gas. The filthy brutes of Germans have a lot of this gas which they carry in tubes, and turn on when the wind is the right way for it. The effect on our fellows, as far as I can find out, is that they are unable to open their eyes, saliva comes from the mouth, and they are quite useless for at least an hour.

24th April

Everyone rather anxious, as the Germans keep on shoving hard.

The Canadians were attacked last night and, again, the Germans used gas. The Canadians stuck to their ground wonderfully well, though they are now being slowly forced back. The bombardment is quite continuous. They even put a few shells into Poperinghe this morning; goodness knows where from, as the nearest point of their front line to Poperinghe is seven miles.

25th April

It rained last night and the wind has died down as last. The news is better now, but everything is still in a pretty good mess-up. The French II Corps has now arrived on the scene, and are said to be one of their crack corps. I hope so. The French have really let us in badly this time. They were holding a long front most absurdly weakly and with no reserves at all. This seems so criminal, as on the night of the 15/16th we were warned to expect an attack by a deserter and a French spy. They even said, 'If the wind is not favourable, the attack may be postponed until it is so' — so I can see no excuse for the French GOC whose name is General Putz. He ought to be sent very hurriedly to Limoges![4]

26th April

Last night, Cory received news that his brother, Bob, was missing. He is in the 57th Highlanders (Canadian)[5]. This was about 8 p.m., so we found a car and, after dinner, set off together. He was naturally very much upset. We left the car outside Ypres, as the shelling was very heavy. Luckily it was a bright moon, so we could pick our way along fairly easily, which was lucky, since we had to cross all sorts and kinds of debris in the streets. Just as we got to the level-crossing at the north-west corner of the town, a big crump landed almighty close, throwing all sorts of stuff about us. Two dead horses were there, evidently just killed. Two shells a minute (and big 'uns) were coming on to this place. A dead civilian was there too, a grotesque-looking muddle at the side of the road with a huge bundle of his wordly goods wrapped in a sheet. He was the only civilian I saw in the town last night. a little past the dead horses was a dead soldier.

Everything was a horrid mess and the town was on fire in several places. It was a rummy scene: the big battered town, the very still moonlit night, the scrunch of broken brick and glass underfoot and no sign of life, except for the occasional motor ambulances rushing through. Then several times a minute, one would hear the coming wailing of some big shell getting closer

(*Left*) Cloth Hall under enemy shell-fire. Photographed by Billy Congreve from *Rue de Lille* on 16th June 1915. (*Top right*) Result of 17 inch German shell on Railway Square, Ypres, 18th June 1915. The GSO3 of 3rd Division, Major Sanders, standing in the shell hole. (*Bottom right*) A wash in a biscuit tin.

A badly creased photograph, but it shows a rare light-hearted moment when Billy Congreve's servant, Private Cameron, poses as a German soldier complete with Flammenwerfer.

and closer, then the crash as it hit some building and a roar as it burst.

We threaded our way between the Cathedral and the Halle. Here I noticed that the vile statue was still standing of the gentlemen in frock coat and baggy trousers — the only whole thing left in Ypres! We went into the square and then turned down to the left along the Bruges road, where we met a string of horse transport which was making a detour around the town. It was making an awful noise. I know no such intense noise as G.S. waggons on a *pavé* road! One can't help feeling that the Germans must hear it so clearly. Whether they did or not I don't know, but a crump and two shrapnel arrived simultaneously, making me jump. We turned right here towards St Jean. The road was packed — columns of waggons and infantry going both ways. Luckily the road was wide and the shelling less, although each corner or cross-roads had its quota of dead horses, showing the accurate registration of the German guns.

We were looking for the 15th Battalion and, by great good fortune, found them in St Jean, for nobody knew where anyone else was or indeed anything else. Half-way along to St Jean, I said to Colonel George, 'I suppose it is my imagination, but my eyes are smarting a good deal.' Of course I was thinking of the gas. He said nothing, but slightly further on he suddenly said, 'Well, there is no doubt about it now.'

Sure enough, we were well into a belt of it — this, mind you, was a good one and half miles from the front line. Tears ran down our cheeks and it was an abominably chokey chemical smell, rather like ether. It was not unpleasant, reminding me of oranges and lilac, but even so it was a 'wicked' scent.

With some trouble, we found the 15th Battalion in a field close by — 160 of them with one officer: the second-in-command — Maitland I think is his name — a fine fellow. They were all cheery enough, for they knew that they had done good work, as indeed they had.

This battalion was on the extreme left of our line next to the Turcos. They were extremely rude about the latter, who they said had run, making no attempt at a fight. The Canadians tried to stop 'em, but it was no good and, next morning (the 23rd), they found themselves almost surrounded, especially at that part of the line which had drawn back its left on St Julien. Cory's brother was here. From all accounts he made a gallant fight, for after the rest of the battalion had retired, he was heard to be going on fighting with his machine-gun and the remnants of his company. So that is all they knew about him, and he may be dead or wounded, and anyhow, a prisoner.

They said the gases are awful, and that many men were certainly killed by them, but they also said that they had killed a lot of Germans who came on in long extended lines and were very determined and brave.

Eventually Colonel G. and I came away, but we had many a scare on the way home. We cut across the Plaine d'Amour and never have I seen a place so ill-named! A misery it was, dead things, shell holes and broken trees. I was very tired and my eyes hurt. It is a new horror to this already horrible war, and there is something depressing in this gas. However, I dare say we shall get used to it.

Editor's Note The gas layer experienced by Congreve and Cory was part of the enemy's second gas offensive that began after midnight on 24th April. Having already made inroads in the French line, a German attack developed on Belgian positions to the north of Ypres in which a huge quantity of gas shells were fired. In danger of being enveloped, the Belgians managed to contain the attack and, with difficulty, linked up again with the French on their right. At 4 a.m., after a sixty-minute heavy bombardment, the Germans released cloud gas along a thousand yards of the Canadian front. Immediately in its path stood the 8th Battalion (Winnipeg Rifles) and the 15th Battalion (known also as the 48th Highlanders of Canada). The gas cloud, like a fifteen foot high fog bank, had not far to travel — between two hundred and three hundred yards to the 8th Battalion's trenches and, for the 15th Battalion, half that distance. As they tried to protect themselves with wetted handkerchiefs, towels, cotton bandoliers and such-like, the gas cloud engulfed them.

Men choked and collapsed, but others somehow scrambled to the parapets to ward off the infantry attack that closely followed the cloud. The enemy managed to penetrate only a small section of the line, but finally the effects of the gas and heavy casualties forced much of the battalion back to its second line — yet two platoons grimly held on. Among those bravely stubborn men in the two depleted platoons was Lieutenant-Colonel George Cory's brother. Taking into account the earlier gas attack, 15th Battalion's losses amounted to 17 officers and 674 other ranks in the period 22nd—24th April.

A trying time all round for the Allies, with weather observation taking on a new significance. Billy Congreve summed up both when continuing his entry of 27th April:

*

All counter-attacks up to date by us and the French have failed, chiefly owing to this gas. Oh, if only the wind would change and blow from the south.

5.30 p.m. Terrific shelling going on. Everyone agrees that it is the heaviest since Le Cateau back at the beginning of things. I wasn't there, but it is certainly worse than the last Ypres battle in November.

30th April
It is not easy to find out what the French are doing, but whatever it is, it is not very desperate in its energy and the line remains the same.

I see that all our papers at home treat this Ypres affair almost as if it were a victory for us, and talk about our 'vigorous offensive'. What offensive we have made has been badly handled and quite useless. As regards regaining the ground lost, we cannot do more until the French shove up on our left. Our papers are damnably incorrect, or else Sir J. French is lying.

1st May
Last night I took Sanders, the new GSO3, up to St Eloi (Crichton has gone as brigade-major to 83rd Brigade and was badly wounded a few days ago in St Jean). It was a lovely cool night after the very hot day, and we walked straight up to Q1. There was extraordinary little shooting from the Mound and neighbourhood, even though the moon was just coming up. Q1 is now a regular fort. The mine is going steadily forward; they now have seventy feet of heading down there — 35 feet towards the Mound and 30 feet along and under Q1 itself, so as to blow it up should the worst happen and the Germans get in. I could find no signs of Kinkie's body — it must be nearer the Mound. The ground is so hopelessly broken up that one can make little out in the way of distinguishing objects.

We walked on and they near caught us. Up went a flare just as we were half-way across the gap and it fell mighty close to us. I think we were spotted, for though we dropped and lay like stones they opened rapid fire. The bullets, however, all went over us.

In P1[6], we had a long talk with the HAC[7], who were happy enough. From there we cut up to the south corner of the Bois Confluent. It was very bright moonlight and the rifle shots at that place make a loud echo in the wood, so that the cracks of the German rifles sound almost as if they are fired into one's ears. Above all this noise out of the wood came the singing of a nightingale! It was really wonderful. The wood is shelled by the Germans every day, and is only 400 yards from their trenches. Bullets are constantly knocking up against the trees, and yet there was Mr Nightingale singing away to his lady-love as if there was nothing wrong with the world at all. I wonder, will he nest there and bring up his family? I hope so.

The General and I went into Bailleul this morning to enquire after young Lowther, who is badly shot in the head. Colonel Leek, who runs the No 2 Clearing Hospital, told me that several gas cases had died in the hospital, and that Dr Haldane the expert on gases had just come out from home and, after careful investigation, decided that the gas which the Germans use is chlorine and bromine mixed. We are all to have respirators, as the gas has the effect of an intense irritant. When it gets into the throat and lungs, it causes the membranes to give off a secretion which gets thicker and thicker, and gradually the patient dies of suffocation. Beastly.

2nd May
Last night they turned on gas and fired gas shells against our men on Hill 60 and, I fear, killed many with the gas. I saw some of the men in Bailleul this morning. They looked very bad indeed, so bad that the doctors are hardly able to save a single case. Oxygen is but little use, and they just get more and more acute and die. Some turn quite purple — horrid to see. It was fearful seeing the rows and rows of stretchers in the yard, all gasping and in misery.

Editor's Note The gas attack on Hill 60 on 1st May is of historic

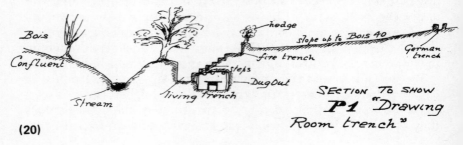

significance, because it was the first time that the enemy gained no advantage from the employment of gas. Holding the hill at the time was the 1/Dorsets with the 1/Devons and 1/Bedfords in support. The gas was released after an intense artillery bombardment from less than one hundred yards away. When the cloud reached the Dorsets' trenches, hostile rifle fire opened up whilst bombing parties attacked both flanks of the battalion. The gas came over so thickly and quickly that no one had time to protect himself from it, but a few of the Dorsets retaliated with rapid fire — giving enough respite for the support battalions to charge through the advancing gas cloud and rally to the Dorsets' defence. By gallantly sticking to their posts, officers and men of the Dorsets suffered dearly. Of the battalion on Hill 60, ninety men died from gas poisoning either in their trenches or before reaching a dressing station. Those who were brought to a dressing station, of whom 207 were gas victims, forty-six died almost immediately and twelve after long suffering[8]. More died at clearing hospitals, as seen by Billy Congreve at Bailleul.

3rd May
All is now more or less quiet up north, and tomorrow night or tonight the 27th Division and the 28th withdraw their lines towards Ypres, so as to cut off the nose of the salient. This will not bother us here. If they have to make another withdrawal though, we shall have to leave St Eloi and fall back on a line we are making which runs from P1, past the Bois Confluent, and down the line of the communications trench to Voormezeele. Then Voormezeele becomes a defence post. After going around it, the line turns right back to the Kruisstraathoek—Ypres road. It will make a funny sort of a salient of this piece of line, and I don't much like it.

4th May
Got all the things off Kinkie's body last night. He was simply riddled with bullets and, of course, very far gone. He must have walked into a machine-gun at least. I can't account for the number of holes any other way. The body was in the ruined houses opposite the mine-house and further forward than I had looked before; in fact, only about thirty yards from the German trench round the Mound. Even though they were hardly firing at all, I think it's too difficult to try and get the body back. I have sent

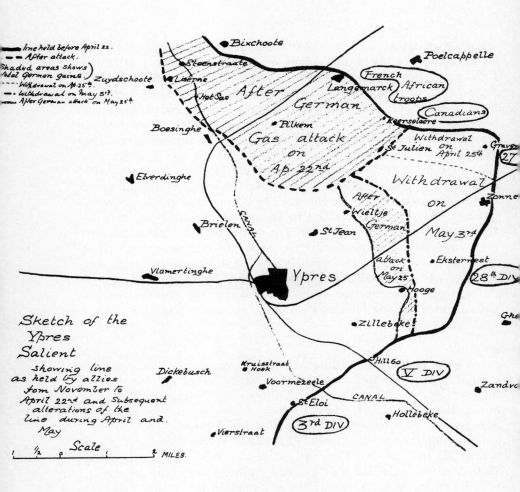

Sketch of the Ypres Salient

showing line as held by allies from November to April 22nd and subsequent alterations of the line during April and May

Scale

all he had on him, which wasn't much, to Dorothy. The glasses were too smashed and the torch too gruesome[9].

5th May
There is the sad news that, last night, our men were gassed off Hill 60 and that the Germans now hold it. It's anxious work this gas — they are devils to use it. Shall we be gassed tonight or not? The wind is just right for it.

Editor's Note The gas attack on Hill 60 took place at 8.45 a.m.,

5th May, after the defenders had spent a sleepless night in countering hostile fire from the German trenches, just one hundred yards away. As the fatigued defenders slept, except for the usual sentries, the Germans released gas at two points from the flank. Although a sentry gave the alarm, it was of little use, because the gas moved along and not over the battered trenches. There it hung in a thick cloud, completely overcoming anyone who stayed there. Counter-attacks followed with little success. Billy Congreve:

9th May

There has been no German attack on our part of the line, but all the 5th Division's attempts to get back on to Hill 60 failed, and the Germans have been shoving in the north of Hill 60. Our line was drawn back as arranged and now runs through Hooge and Frezenberg. Yesterday and the day before, strong German attacks with lots of artillery support came on against Frezenberg[10]. The Germans broke through and, yesterday evening, got into Velorenhoek and Wieltje, both of which they were turned out of last night with the bayonet. The 4th and 28th Divisions are those chiefly concerned. The 28th losses are, I am afraid, very heavy[11].

We have been ordered by the C-in-C to hold on here at all costs and can expect but little help from the outside, as the big push actually started this morning. At 5.40 a.m. the 8th Division were over the German first line trenches. The question is now whether we can hold the Germans up here with the troops we have, while the good work goes on down south. I think we can, even if it means bringing back the whole line on to the Ypres ramparts. Our arrangements for the 'Voormezeele Switch' are now completed.

They may find the southern offensive unpleasant, for it had been kept very secret. Yet I don't like another offensive at the same place. It means that you go to a locked door and give it a tremendous whack (Neuve Chapelle), but the door doesn't break down. So you go away and two months later come back with about the same strength in your fist, and give it another whack. Then you are surprised that the door barely shakes, because the man inside saw the danger of the first blow and has profited by the lesson, and has built it all up very strongly so as to be sure of no further accident. However, this view may be unduly pessimistic, and it is not shared by others.

Editor's Note This southern offensive was an Anglo-French affair
with the British objective being the capture of Aubers Ridge by
divisions of Haig's First Army. It was an unmitigated disaster from
the start, as Billy Congreve reluctantly predicted. The battle
started a day behind schedule with a forty-minute bombardment
that was largely ineffectual. The Germans were too well dug-in
and protected by expanses of barbed wire that was mostly uncut
by shrapnel. With a thinly-held firing line, they had in-depth
defences with murderous machine-gun nests and entrenched
infantrymen relatively unscathed by the bombardment. Again,
there was a shell shortage. The heroism displayed by British and
Indian infantrymen was not enough and, by the end of the day,
Haig had lost 458 officers and 11,161 men. On Billy Congreve's
front, however, the situation was quiet:

*

It is not pleasant to sit so close to everything. One longs to be up
and doing something. Hill 60 is, I hear, now not held by either side
— it's too impossible. The place is a pile of dead, probably some
5,000 on a hill which only resembles a heap of broken earth. The
actual length of the hill top is only about one hundred yards. It's
truly an awful place.

The show in the Dardanelles apparently goes on all right, but I
can't help feeling that it is a mistake. One can't run two wars at
once, especially when we are unprepared to run even one, and here
we are engaged in about six different campaigns. I think we ought
to turn all our attention on to one point first and finish it.

17th May
The poor 28th Division has been so smashed up that it had to be
taken out and replaced in the line by cavalry. Now the cavalry
have had an awful time too, all from the German heavy artillery
which concentrates its fire on this wretched salient from every sort
of direction. All the new line we took up in the salient is still
intact, but our casualties have been very heavy. I heard from
Roger Mostyn-Owen today that they amount to 41,000 since
April 22nd — this is just in the salient alone.

Down south things go ill. Dads[12] heard from Colonel Reggie
Stephens[13] today, and he says: 'The 2nd Battalion was the only
one which got into the enemy's trenches with very heavy losses.
We hung on there for twenty-four hours, no one being able to help

us, and were subjected the whole time to heavy shell-fire, rifle, machine-gun and bombing fire. In the end I withdrew, as our losses and the enemy's increasing numbers made it impossible to stay on. I could only collect 1 unwounded officer and 140 other ranks. 'Daddy' Sherston[14] and a whole heap of the boys are gone.'[15]

It's awful. Poor old Chaw[16], he was too gallant a fellow to get through this war alive. In October, near Meteren, he got a bullet through the chest which should have killed him, and now having just come back cured, he gets killed. The whole show was somehow badly messed up. If our lack of bombardment was due to shortage of ammunition, then those thousands of casualties in the 8th Division were absolutely murdered, for time after time has the lesson been learnt by us and sent back to St Omer[17] that unless you *absolutely* smash up the enemy's trenches, it is murder to send in infantry to attack. They all know this, yet once again were our men sent to a useless and certain failure.

Somebody must be responsible. Asquith in Parliament, a few days or weeks ago, got up and stated that 'no operations of the British Expeditionary Force had ever been hindered or stopped by lack of ammunition, nor would this happen in the future.' This is a lie. If he didn't know it to be so, he is just as much to blame — for it shows that he is being served by liars, and he is responsible. Murderers they are, and would to goodness they could be treated as such.[18]

Sir Horace S-D has gone home. In a letter he said that he felt himself obliged to resign his command, as the C-in-C refused to allow him free action which he considered under the circumstances to be an insult.

I knew that there had been trouble in this quarter for a long time. Sir Herbert Plumer takes over his command — Second Army. I fancy that the whole row is that Sir Horace strongly advocated giving away the whole Ypres salient, and wished to fall back on the line Bois Confluent—Voormezeele, the Ramparts and Canal — and very wisely too. This was not looked on with joy by GHQ and so the trouble began. I think anyone who knows the salient agrees with Sir H., but of course GHQ don't know it. Everyone is very sad here at his going, for he always did us jolly well.

Thursday, May 27th
The poor old salient has been further knocked in, both on the 4th and 27th Divisions' front. The Germans started using gas in

the night, then broke through us at Hooge and further north at Bellewaarde Farm. So far we have failed to get back the lost ground in spite of our counter-attacks. Owing to the exhaustion of the men, and as every inch of ground is to be fought, orders have come in that we are to go up and relieve the 28th Division. The 6th Division is also coming up from Armentières to take the place of the 27th Division. This is most thrilling. It will mean that the 5th, 3rd, 6th and 4th Divisions will be holding the salient, and I guess we shall make a job of it. Of course we shall still be in this shell trap and, day after day, be shelled silly. I hear that our casualties since the 22nd April have now risen to 70,000[19]. If Sir Horace had been allowed to have his way, we would have saved perhaps half of these casualties, if not more.

The 8th Brigade have already left here and have gone into the salient, taking over from some of the 28th Division. The General and I went up to see them before they went on Tuesday. We also went into Ypres, which is now a more or less complete ruin. Even the old gentleman outside the Cathedral in top hat and frock coat is down, and his head bust off. He is rather like Bismarck — I am glad he is done for.

The 14th Division (a Kitchener division) under General Vic Couper come in here and we, alas, go under the orders of the V Corps. A VI Corps has been formed and it's been given to General Keir, late GOC of the 6th Division. So I am hoping to hear at any moment that Dads has got the division[20].

Italy declared war some days ago[21]. Even if she doesn't do wonders, it shows she realises which way the fortunes of war must go in the end. I still have hopes of being home this year, though in the winter the 'Agent'[22] and I seriously planned to dine in state in London on May 27th, his birthday. It's curious when I think how seriously we thought it possible that the war should be over by now.

CHAPTER EIGHT

Again the Salient

With both sides exhausted, 'Second Ypres' officially closed on
25th May after a battered 4th Division withdrew to a new line. By
coincidence, orders had been issued to enemy front line troops the
previous evening to cease operations. The reduction in the bitter
struggle came just in time for the British Army, as there was
scarcely any artillery ammunition left. The latest withdrawal in
the salient had, however, stabilised the Allied line, and the area
held on 25th May was less than a third of what it had been on
22nd April. The position was so critical that if a couple of fresh
German divisions had made an appearance, 'Second Ypres' could
easily have become a German victory. Fortunately for the Allies,
such enemy reserves were in Russia.

On the day it ended, a coalition was formed in England with
Asquith still as Prime Minister. It was of minor importance to the
fatigued men in the Flanders trenches, but Major-General Haldane
derived some satisfaction, as there was no love lost between them,
from the news that his cousin, Lord Haldane, was no longer a
member of Government, having been sacrificed along with
Churchill in order for Asquith to form a coalition. However gleeful
of his cousin's departure from the mainstream of politics, Haldane
was more concerned with moving his division into the salient,
which was less than three miles away. Billy Congreve:

*

Monday, May 31st
We packed up at the huts last night and slept for the last time in
Westoutre. Today, we left at 8 a.m. and motored through to the
far side of Ypres. The road leading into the Grande Place is
unpleasant, as houses on both sides were on fire. We left Harrison[1]
amongst the ruins at the east end of the square and walked
through to the Sallyport, where we found General Kennedy
commanding the 7th Cavalry Brigade. We then went on over the
pontoon bridge and across to fields to the Ecole de Bienfaisance.
It's a huge place and in a much more battered condition than

when I was in it in the far off days of early November. It has
excellent cellars though, in which General Bulkeley-Johnson (2nd
Cavalry Brigade), General Hoskins (8th Brigade) and General
Ravenshaw (83rd Brigade) all have their headquarters. Just before
we reached the school, the Germans put two or three shrapnel
over us. We visited all three generals and had a long talk to all.

At present our divisional command consists of a cavalry division
(the 3rd under General Briggs) and the 83rd Brigade. In a few days
time we will get back the 8th Brigade from the 28th Division and
should be able to get things properly straightened out, for I've
never seen such a bad show. If the Germans come on again now, I
think things will go ill. At least it would be very difficult. I am
going out this afternoon to make a reconnaissance, hoping to be
able to find out more about our position — which is vague to say
the least.

The General and I did a bit of looting in the town this morning:
A beer mug and a looking-glass. I saw a lot of things that will be
useful for our mess, and which will only be destroyed if left. Our
new day HQ is quite nice, a big sunny farm, and the General and I
have a nice clean room. Really, we are better off than we were at
the huts.

On Saturday evening, I rode off to look for Ronnie[2] who is
now out here commanding the 8th Battalion[3], which is in the
14th Division. Eventually I found him in a farm between Neuve
Eglise and Bailleul. I much admired the general appearance of the
good Riflemen. They may be new, but they look splendid, and
have such a fine lot of officers. Archie Todd[4], second-in-command;
Joe Parker[5], adjutant, and plenty of other good fellows. Ron gave
me dinner and, afterwards, I walked up as far as Neuve Eglise with
the battalion, which was going up for its first taste of the trenches.
I felt quite an old soldier! I had a long ride back in the dark, but it
was well worth going, and it was grand to see Ronnie and Joe
again.

Later: Sanders and I went up and saw a good deal of the ground
this afternoon. We went out of the town through the Sallyport
and up to a little ridge marked 60 on the map. We did not stay
long there as we were too far back to see much, so went on to
Gordon Farm. There, we found a communications trench leading
up to the front line and running parallel to the Menin road. The
GHQ line runs through Gordon Farm and is in a very bad state. It
has apparently been used as a shelter for all sorts of odds and ends
of units.

We eventually made our way up to a ruined farm just short of the 8th Brigade trenches and, from here, had an excellent view of Hooge and Y Wood (so-called from its shape on the map, which I believe to be incorrect). We could also see Sanctuary and Zouave Woods. The Germans hold Y Wood, but have as yet little wire in front — whereas our line in front of Y Wood and all the way to Zouave Wood is very strongly wired. Of Hooge we could see but little. The bit of high ground between the east end of the village and the woods to the south is held by the Germans, and completely overlooks the valley which we had just walked up. It is one of the three places in this area where they have — as it were — got on to the lip of this saucer. The three places are Hill 60 to the south, this unnamed hill and Y Wood with Bellewaarde Farm behind it.

After, we moved up the slope to the south. On the way, we found one of our dead men and a whole heap of abandoned rifles and equipment. The whole of this area is in a most disgraceful condition, and reflects the worst possible credit on the 27th and 28th Divisions. Everywhere we went we found traces of bad discipline and worse. The 8th Brigade told us that on taking over from the 28th Division, many wounded men were found still lying out; no attempt having been made to collect them. In one ruined cottage alone, twenty men were found. All had been wounded and had been collected and placed there. Nineteen were dead from lack of attention, and the only living man — a CSM in the 60th — was nearly so. It's terrible and I can see no possible excuse. There are many more instances of bad Staff work, but this is perhaps the worst.

My tent at our new night HQ, is quite a palace, thanks to Cameron. Our mess room is small, but we could easily be worse off. The camp is in a field about a mile out of Poperinghe.

Tuesday, June 1st

Last night cavalry patrols went into the château at Hooge, and we are now holding it. Sopwith says that the whole place is too awful. He actually had to wear his respirator. There is an awful lot of work to be done up there. If only we could get out of this infernal mixture of units and get the line into the hands of our own brigades, we would soon have things straightened out. As it is, things are still at sixes and sevens. This V Corps, which we now belong to, is the very devil. I have never seen such bullying and incompetence.

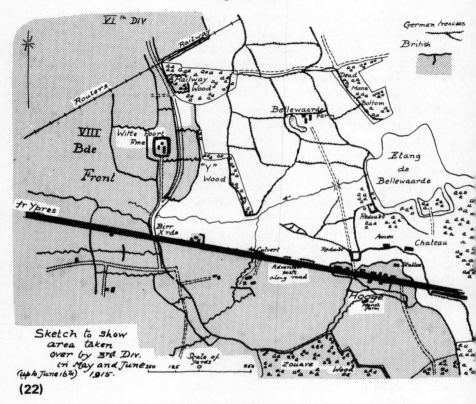

Sketch to show area taken over by 3rd Div. in May and June 1915. (up to June 16th)

(22)

The General and I went up to the École this morning and saw Generals Hoskins and B-J. The Germans were shelling St Jacques Church on our way back — wonderful shooting it was too. One hit the spire just as we were passing under it and properly made us jump. After a hurried lunch, the General and I went off to Ypres again. We took Cameron who we left [in Ypres] with Harrison to do some looting for the mess.

We left Ypres by the Lille gate and thence east along the railway past Tuilerie and along the high ground to the cottage which Sanders and I had found. We walked back straight across country to Gordon Farm. We should have gone up the communications trench, as no sooner were we well into the open, than they started to snipe us with whizz-bangs and bigger shrapnel. Luckily, they hadn't quite got the range, so we arrived at Baird's HQ all right and had a long talk with him[6]. Y Wood is the burning question of the hour. When we returned to the town, we found that Cameron and Harrison had the car looking like a Pickfords van.

2nd June

Went up to the École in the morning and everything seemed all right, except for a little more German shelling than usual. Since then, the shelling has got worse and worse and, I fear, they have had a desperate time in Hooge. The cavalry are still there, poor fellows.

Later: Most of the shelling was on Hooge and Zouave Wood. The Gordons on the south of the Menin road were also heavily shelled. The cavalry losses in Hooge are, I believe, heavy, and also most of the trenches and works are destroyed. Having shelled our fellows several times, the Germans got into the château and have occupied it — also the partly finished redoubt we were busy on.

3rd June

No more shelling now. The casualties in the cavalry and in 8th Brigade totalled about 300 — a pretty big bill against Mr German. He, of course, did it all without any losses. Arrangements are now being made to retake the château and unfinished redoubt tonight, but it is hopeless to try and work any scheme as long as we are mixed up with the cavalry.

Later: The Lincolns were sent up to help the cavalry, but the attempt failed although we did get the stables. None of us knew that the Germans had occupied the stables and, personally, I don't think they had. I knew there would be a mess-up of things up there, for everyone was knocked silly by yesterday's shelling. Nobody knew where anyone else was or much about anything. Now we are going to be content for the present to do without the château and works. The 7th Brigade will have to get a deal of work done to make good the rest of the village. I feel very sorry for the cavalry. It's not their job — their units are much too small in comparison with the size of their staffs. Altogether, it is a shame to use them in this sort of place.

4th June

The V Corps Staff has been an awful worry ever since we came up here. The poor General is near driven mad. General A.[7] is, I think, a bully and not a brilliant soldier. General J.[8], his Chief Staff Officer, is already very cordially disliked — it's an unfortunate combination.

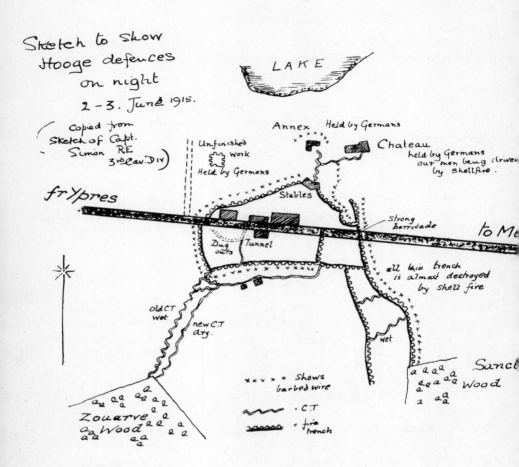

Sketch to show
Hooge defences
on night
2 - 3. June 1915.

copied from
Sketch of Capt.
Simon RE
3rd Cav. Div)

LAKE

Annex   Held by Germans

Chateau
held by Germans
our men being driven
by shellfire.

Unfinished
Work
Held by Germans

fr Ypres

Stables

Strong
Barricade

to Me

Dug
outs   Tunnel

all this trench
is almost destroyed
by shell fire

old CT
Wet

new C.T
dry.

Wet

Sanct
Wood

x x x x x Shows
barbed wire

· C.T

= fire
trench

Zouarve
Wood

5th June

The cavalry went off this morning and we now have the 8th, 7th
and 9th in line. I believe the 9th Brigade is to come out soon again
to be fattened up for some battle. It's dreadfully hot now and the
flies are becoming an awful nuisance — almost as bad as the
V Corps. We go back to the Camp tonight, as peace now reigns
again.

8th June

The General and I have been up to Hooge. We went up via
Sanctuary and Zouave Woods, where we found Blake in a dug-out
(he now commands the Wilts[9]). Everything was fairly peaceful —
they still shell Zouave Wood, but not Sanctuary. Blake took us up
to the 'village', then to the stables. It was hard to make anything

Desolation at Hooge in August 1915. Billy Congreve's photograph shows a small part of the crater with dug-outs.

Captain The Hon. William Fraser of the 1/Gordon Highlanders. Western Front – Winter of 1915.

out, as the General was in such a hurry, and the place is such a maze of works and debris that one needs a day up there to realise where one is and what is best to be done. Suddenly, down came the rain. The heat had been awful and now we were soaked through. The trenches were a few inches deep in mud and water almost at once.

We went to the Island Posts and tunnel after going to the stables. The tunnel and the dug-outs there are of French make and very good indeed. Even the bad shelling of 2nd June had done them no damage. The main dug-out was made with a roof of steel beams bent semi-circular, so that it looked just as if one was inside an over-turned boat.

We were both exhausted when we reached the car in Ypres, and I could have embraced the worthy Harrison who had looted a bottle of red wine and a glass. I felt better after it and, being an old vintage, it made the General quite garrulous and amusing. He almost waved his hand to the men who saluted him. I pulled down the blinds!

9th June
We have been ordered to do an attack on Bellewaarde Farm. The date of the attack is the 14th. It's now the 9th and, of course, it is the most desperate business to get everything ready in four days. It is almost ludicrous and would be, if it wasn't so desperate; all the orders and reconnaissances to be done and a thousand other things.

The 9th Brigade have now been out for nearly a week, so will have had some small chance of training themselves, but the 7th Brigade, which is to co-operate, is still in and will only come out on the night of the 12th or 13th. They will have no rest, no chance to organise all the little details that are so essential. The artillery too are going to have a very hard task. The ammunition supply is very limited, and any programme we are likely to put forward will be probably jumped on as being impossible with the ammunition available. Altogether, it is no pleasing job. The General has already made up his mind, I think to fail. I think there need be no failure, but it is not a bit satisfactory.

The front of the attack will be roughly from the Roulers Railway to the Menin road. It means taking the 'E' end of Railway Wood—Y Wood, and then forcing a way up to Bellewaarde Farm and Lake. Once here, the line has to be established. It is no small task and the general situation of the ground, and the enemy's

guns, makes it still harder. All ought to go all right, but that will
be on the merits of the 9th Brigade and not on those people who
have ordered the attack. The excuse is that it is to be done on this
date, so as to take attention from a large French offensive down
south — which is always futile.

11th June
We may now, I hear, get a day or possibly two days extra. The
General and Colonel Evans[10] are almost balmy. As well as the
many natural worrying details, there is always the horrid
atmosphere of the V Corps. General A. comes every day and sits
talking for ages, and generally finishes by saying how easy the
whole thing is — and being generally somewhat displeasing. It
doesn't trouble me, but it is a bore having the Staff bothered.
Luckily Heywood and Sandy don't care a damn, but Evans is
taking life very seriously at the moment.

I went into Ypres this afternoon to look around the ramparts,
as we are to have our advanced HQ somewhere there. I think we
shall all be able to fit into the casements, for General Ballard[11]
will have to be further forward. I saw Sopwith who is busy digging
assembly trenches for the 7th and 9th Brigade. We had a pioneer
battalion of the 14th Division (K's Army) up to help dig. They
were a little shelled and only about a quarter of them turned up
for work. This is a beastly place to bring them to learn what war is
like. It's enough to demoralise a brick wall, let alone eight-month
old soldiers.

We are staying at the farm[12] tonight and move up to the
ramparts on Tuesday evening; the attack being now timed to take
place early on Wednesday morning, the 16th.

Saturday, June 12th
The arranging is now nearly over and the Corps are not worrying
us quite so much for the moment. The General presented some
medal ribbons to the 9th Brigade this morning. I always hate
inspecting troops who are just going into a very gory battle. These
next few days are going to be hard for everyone, but I much envy
those who have the fighting to do.

15th June
The old Germans were evidently expecting the attack to take
place this morning. Last night they shelled all the roads and tracks
by which we might bring up troops. Of course nobody was there,

except for some working parties who were coming up to finish off the assembly trenches. The pioneer battalion of the 14th Division were out on this job and did not like it one bit. In fact, many of them ran away, which bears out what I have already said — that it is no good shoving untried troops into unpleasing situations. The assembly trenches were finished off by our own people, but only just in time. What a scramble the whole thing has been.

17th June
We have not had a glorious victory, but it has been by no means a failure. Here is a timetable of more or less what happened:

2 a.m.	7th and 9th Brigades reached their assembly trenches.
3.20 a.m.	Artillery bombardment commenced — fire very effective.
4.15 a.m.	Artillery lengthened to 2nd line German trenches — infantry at once assaulted front line.

The first line German trenches were captured without much resistance. There were many dead and wounded Germans in the trenches. The unwounded were completely demoralised by our shell fire and were 'hands up' in almost every case — others were shot. The Wilts worked up the long trench towards Hooge, taking sixty prisoners and one machine-gun — this was all bombing work.

The pace of the infantry advance was beyond all expectations. For this reason, they reached the second and even third line German trenches before our artillery could lift their fire. The Royal Fusiliers[13] were within thirty yards of the lake, but then had to retire, partly owing to our own artillery fire and partly owing to the German trenches not been sufficiently bombarded there, and were capable of resistance.

5 a.m.	The Royal Scots[14] and Liverpool Scottish seized the trench south-west of Bellewaarde Farm. The Royal Scots Fusiliers[15] reached the trench east of Bellewaarde Farm (this appears doubtful).

At this moment, it seemed as if the attack had been completely successful.

5.20 a.m.	Enemy heavily shelling all ground our troops had

advanced over. This prevented supports moving up, and greatly disorganised the units who had moved up to Y and Railway Woods in support.

The Wilts who had forced their way a long distance up the Hooge trench were now running out of bombs, and being slowly forced back by German bombers.

7.40 a.m.	Weak counter-attack by Germans against Bellewaarde Farm easily repulsed.
9.20 a.m.	German infantry massed in Dead Man's Bottom and then counter-attacked. Our guns got well into them and the attack was repulsed.

The German shelling was now very intense, and men began to fall back on Y Wood. This left us in possession of the 1st line German trenches. Major Crossfield with a few men (4th South Lancs) held on to the trenches around Bellewaarde Farm until 3 p.m.

The casualties were now considerable, and the units much disorganised by the heavy shelling and heavy losses in officers.

9.15 a.m.	Orders issued to General Douglas Smith[16] to send General Ballard up to reorganise units in Y Wood.
9.30 a.m.	The 42nd Brigade of 14th Division were ordered by V Corps to move up to Y Wood from Ypres.
10 a.m.	Units of the 7th Brigade failed to re-occupy the ground previously gained, owing chiefly to very intense and accurate hostile shelling, which wiped out the attack.
12 noon	Orders to GOC 9th Brigade to organise a new attack and to (if necessary) use the 42nd Brigade (then on its way up).
3.30 p.m.	GOC 9th Brigade ordered two battalions of 7th Brigade, supported by two battalions of 42nd Brigade, to start attack; objective being the edge of the lake and Bellewaarde Farm. The attack was preceded by a twenty-minute bombardment.

The two battalions of the 42nd Brigade were heavily shelled on their way up and arrived too late to be of any use. The attack by the two battalions of the 7th Brigade failed. No sooner had they left Y Wood, than they were swept away by shell and rifle fire.

All the officers were almost instantly killed or wounded. The 149th Brigade, holding Hooge, had orders to co-operate by seizing the redoubts. The Border Regiment's CO, seeing the initial failure of the 7th Brigade, did not deliver his assault.

6 p.m.	Orders were received from the Corps to consolidate all positions gained. The 8th Brigade ordered to take over the new line as soon as it was dark.
7–8 p.m.	Very heavy hostile shelling.

Casualties were worse at this moment than at any other period of the day. After dark, the 8th Brigade took over the new line, the 7th, 9th and 42nd Brigades being withdrawn to billets. There were no serious counter-attacks and all ground won was made good during the night. The result was that an important part of the Bellewaarde position was left in our hands. Casualties were: officers, 25 killed, 109 wounded and 9 missing; other ranks, 341 killed, 1,907 wounded and 1,169 missing. Total 3,560.

The German losses must have been considerable, but not so heavy as ours; it is impossible to form any accurate estimate. We took about 200 prisoners and some hundreds of dead were buried. It is probable that many more were killed by our men who reached the German second and third lines; also by our artillery, especially in Dead Man's Bottom.[17]

Causes that led to the attack not being completely successful: the great difficulty of absolute co-operation between infantry and artillery; inadequate supply of hand-grenades and that several different types were issued – we have said ages ago that we wanted one sort and one sort only and that's the 'Mills Grenade'; disorganisation of units in support, caused by the enemy's shell fire; troops engaged were not long enough out of the trenches to reach the necessary state of efficiency; the whole of the arranging from start to finish was hurried, owing to a French attack down south – one cannot quite see the reason for only giving us a week, the French knew for months that they were going to attack on a certain date.

We were heavily shelled in the ramparts, but none landed on top of our house. Several pitched into the moat, throwing water over the tops of the trees on the ramparts. It was extraordinary to see a heavy shower of rain coming out of a clear blue sky! Old Allenby, when he saw it, said he thought that, 'The last shell must have broken a cloud.'!

18th June

All yesterday the Germans went on shelling Y and Railway Woods, causing a good many casualties in the 8th Brigade — rather hard on them, after thirty days in the trenches, to have to go back again in *such* trenches too, and *such* sights.

19th June

Around the line with the General. Interesting, but horrible — as is always the case after a big or fairly big fight. We left the École about 2 p.m. and went along the railway till we came to the Gordon Farm communication trench, then to just south of Birr

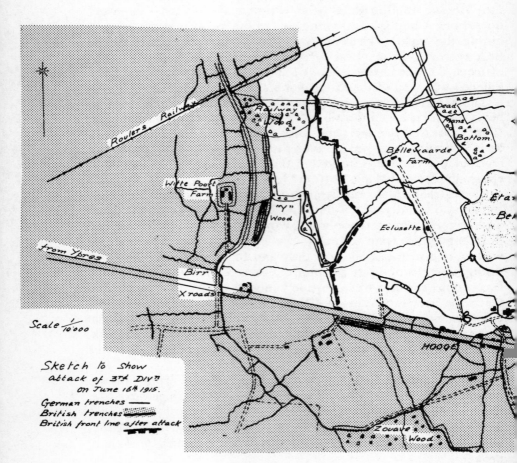

Sketch to show
attack of 3RD DIVn
on June 16th 1915.
German trenches ——
British trenches
British front line after attack

(2

crossroads and up the trench towards Witt Poort Farm. It was here that the first unpleasant signs met one — a man's foot sitting all by itself made the General jump a bit. It did look rather sad. It was about here that the Germans put most of their heavy crumps, and the place was badly chewed up. From just south of the farm, we cut across to Y Wood through the assembly trenches. Half-way there we found Baird, who is commanding the Gordons. He was very jumpy and looked ill, and sitting amongst a whole lot of beastliness which nobody seemed to much worry about. We left him, as he was past reasonable conversation.

Y Wood was in a bad state. Our bombardment must have been beastly. The big 9.2-inch and 6-inch shells had knocked all the trees endways and most of the trenches, but a good deal of these were still undamaged and were very good — deep and narrow with formidable machine-gun emplacements and very strong dug-outs. Signs of their barbed wire were few. There was a certain amount about and that was much torn up. The lyddite fumes had coloured everything bright yellow. I noticed a lot of the prisoners brought into the ramparts were bright yellow too. I think that our big howitzer shells must be as unpleasing as theirs.

There were a good many dead Germans lying about, but three or four times as many of ours; that I suppose must always be the case in an attack[18]. There was every sort of thing lying about, both ours and theirs.

We went down to the south end of Y Wood and out along the old German communication trench towards Bellewaarde Farm, which was now converted into an excellent fire trench. It was a good sight to be able to look *down* into the German trench that runs up towards Hooge. The first time, I think, during the war that I had looked down on a German trench, for always are they looking down on to us. Not only did we look down into the particular trench, but we also absolutely had it in enfilade. The Wilts[19] bombed it up just half-way before they were out-bombed.

We went on round till we arrived due west of the farm and, there, a sap ran way out to the east, at the end of which we were building a fire trench. I went down it to see how they were progressing and looked over the parapet to see where the German trenches were. I thought I saw something half-way between the lines, and there was some poor fellow lying wounded. He kept on waving his hand. It was awful. I longed to go out and get him in, but of course couldn't with the General there. The men, though, promised to go and fetch him in as soon as it was dark, and that was all we could do. He must have been fifty yards from where we were. I shouted to him to tell him that we knew he was there. Perhaps he heard. He must have been lying out there for three nights.

Eventually we worked our way to Railway Wood. Here the mess was very bad. Also the Germans were very close, only about fifteen yards. A burial party of some sixty men arrived and got to work, so I hope that when the 14th Division takes over, things won't be quite so bad, for it's a shame to put new troops into so bad a place as that. Everything was quiet while we were up there, hardly any snipers at work in the German lines and no shelling. There is no doubt about the value of the ground gained. Looking back towards Ypres from the trench between Railway and Y Woods, one can see every bit of ground. How it is we ever moved about by daylight beats me. I suppose Mr German has too wholesome a respect for our snipers.

All the men were in very good spirits. Everyone of them was sporting something German, either a helmet or cap or rifle or bayonet. I wonder if any of them will ever get home.

The Wilts go up to take over Hooge tonight. Blake now commands the Wilts and does it well. I expect they will put Hooge to rights fairly soon.

20th June
Last night they shelled Railway Wood and Cambridge Road with gas shells. This shelling went on while the 42nd Brigade was relieving the 8th Brigade. All went off all right, however, but the 42nd Brigade — as do all new units — brought up *many* too many men, in spite of our telling them not to do so. It is such foolishness to crowd men into a vile place like that where they can be so heavily shelled.

The General and I go up to Hooge this afternoon. Nothing much doing in other parts of the world, though I think that there may be a great event before long — the departure of the General and me to London for a few days leave! He needs it and I think I want it, except that Pam is still laid up.

21st June
We had a good look round Hooge yesterday, but it was an awful day to do it on, very hot and 'muggy'. By the time we reached Blake's HQ in Zouave Wood we were nearly dead. However, we had a nice look at the German redoubt from Island Posts, or rather

the hedge in front of the redoubt. I could see no wire in it. There is a plan afoot for this redoubt to be taken. Personally, I believe the way to do it is to rush it during the daytime when everyone is more or less asleep — it's only about twenty yards. If there is no wire, the machine-guns would never have time to get going and we would be in. I cannot see why one shouldn't do this. I should like to have a go myself with two platoons of good riflemen. I told the General so!

Later: It has been decided that the Wilts are to have a go at the redoubt tomorrow night, about dark. There is to be a half-hour bombardment first, also a simultaneous attack by the 14th Division on a small German work just outside Railway Wood. To my mind the half-hour bombardment by a few guns is just like giving a fellow notice that you are going to kick him — but it's a Corps plan. Though why the General doesn't definitely say what he intends to do, and not to be bullied into doing something he doesn't like, beats me.

22nd June
The attack failed absolutely.

23rd June
Apparently the shelling was not effective enough. The Wilts came under heavy fire as soon as they showed themselves. The Boche was all warned and ready, so naturally it failed. I am fed up with this sort of half-hearted show. It's not fair on anyone, and must make the Germans laugh. The 14th Divison 'attack' also failed. The Germans shelled the École hard this morning, as a sort of retaliation, I suppose.

Editor's Note Captain Congreve left for England early on 25th June. He stayed at Edward Hudson's London home at Queen Anne's Gate where his girl-friend, Pamela Maude, joined him, much to his pleasant surprise as she was still recuperating from a serious operation. He returned to the front on 1st July:

The General and I came back together, a good journey. We arrived into camp about 4 p.m., having left London at 8.30 a.m. I came over on the boat with Lutyens[20] and also saw Henry Yarde-Buller, now a brigadier-general. He is chief liaison officer between Joffre and the War Office, and has nothing to do with our GHQ. From all that I heard at home, there is a good deal of friction between GHQ and the War Office — talk of Sir John's lack of 'greatness', also much gossip as to his various sins, which may be true or not, but are anyhow poor hearing. I don't think that anyone out here *does* regard him as a great man, or indeed anything approaching it, but he is, I suppose, as good a figurehead as anyone else.

4th July

It's been very hot today, a real summer's day, so thinking that the Boches would perhaps be bathing, we turned shrapnel on to all the known (from aeroplane) bathing places — rather a dirty trick, perhaps! The results, I think, must have been satisfactory, because the German guns retaliated by knocking a fresh set of holes in the unfortunate École.

7th July

Went up to Zouave Wood today. We cut across from the Tuilerie towards Maple Copse instead of sticking to the Zillebeke communication trench. The result was that we were very properly whizz-banged. It was just as we were going through a chicory field. The first burst some way ahead, perhaps one hundred yards, and we did not think much of it and went on. The next was closer, but to the right front. The General was in front of me and I saw the flash of something bright come through the tops of the chicory flowers. The next thing was a dull whack, and the General fell backwards with an awful grunt and lay gasping and groaning. It gave me a bad fright, for I didn't know what quite had happened, though as soon as I had time to realise what the flash meant I knew he couldn't be really much hurt. It was the fuse of the shell and it had taken him right in the middle of his tummy!

I rubbed his tummy for him and he soon grew coherent in speech. I then hurriedly searched for and found the fuse (which burnt my fingers), and then got him a few yards forward into a ditch behind a good thick hedge. Just as well we moved, as the next two burst exactly where he had fallen and would have made us look very silly had we been there. They went on for about twenty minutes, so we sat in our ditch feeling fairly secure. We finally made it to the wood and back again with no further misfortunes, though it came on to rain and we were drenched.

9th July

Last night a deserter came in and gave himself up to the men in C1. He was an Alsatian and said that the Alsatians were so badly bullied by their officers that, were it not for fear of being shot by us, they would all desert. He hadn't much useful information to give; they very seldom have, or else won't give it. This cove was only too willing to talk, but knew nothing. I often wonder if our men when taken prisoner talk freely and give away information. I expect they are very surly, and they again will know nothing worth giving away, for they hardly know their officers' names!

14th July

They[21] are having good fun up in Hooge now with a .450 Express rifle. We use it to smash up the German loophole plates and it has splendid results. The bullets are steel-nosed and generally one shot is enough to smash the plate or knock it down. I only wish we had a few more of them.

The 9th Brigade go off tonight and come under orders of the 5th Division. The forming of the Third Army is meaning the withdrawal of several Regular divisions from here. In fact all corps in future are to be Regular/Territorial/New Army divisions, so the 5th and 4th Divisions leave this part of the world, and the 9th Brigade goes down to take over some of the 5th Division line. Colonel Sanders is off to do GSO2 to the Third Army. I hear that there is a chance of my having to go to the Second Army as GSO3, and that doesn't suit me at all. I'd be sitting in an office day and night and never see anything more exciting than an aeroplane going over.

17th July

All is well — I am GSO3 here. Poor Sandy is much disturbed at having to go to an Army Staff; it will be fearfully dull.

The 18-pounders had a naval engagement today. The infantry at Hooge spotted a barge being used by the Germans on Bellewaarde Lake, so we turned plenty of shrapnel on to them and the barge was run ashore — a wreck we hope. I expect that they used it to bring up rations etc.

18th July

We are to loose off the mine tomorrow night. It ought to be a real good explosion, as we are putting into it 3,000 lbs of ammonal, over 1½ tons! The mine-shaft is in Bull Farm, and we hope the gallery end to be exactly underneath the redoubt. The idea is that when the mine goes off, the Middlesex are to seize the crater and the trench in front of Island Posts and make them good. If we do this, it ought to improve our position in Hooge enormously.

Editor's Note Mining was carried out in difficult circumstances by Major S.H. Cowan's 175th Tunnelling Company, Royal Engineers. Working in water six inches deep and constantly contending with sub-soil problems, Cowan's men had managed to drive a gallery 190 feet in length to a position that was calculated to be beneath the strongly fortified enemy redoubt. A chamber was excavated just above the water level in which was laid a charge of 3,500 lbs of ammonal. It was later discovered that the enemy had also commenced mining operations, but had ceased the work on account of the water.

19th July
A quiet morning. All the preparations are complete for the mine affair — it is to be touched off at 7 p.m.

Later: The mine went off most successfully and the Middlesex took the crater without much trouble, also the piece of trench in front of Island Posts. The Middlesex worked down the trench to about Point 'X' shown on my second sketch, but were unable to stay there as they ran out of bombs. It was a real bombing battle. The crater is huge, and the explosion greater than we thought possible; so great that several of the storming party were burned by falling debris, in spite of the fact that they were all withdrawn south of the main road.

It is very late now (about 1 a.m.) and about twenty prisoners have been sent back, miserable fellows of the 126th Regiment (Würtembergers). They were all much shaken, and small wonder. Their accounts of the show were naturally useless. The only fellow who seemed to have his wits about him was a NCO, an artillery man, who had been in the trench opposite Island Posts with his officer, who was up observing. He was surly, so also was useless. I did not keep them long, but passed them on to Corps after a brief examination. I have a good fellow of the HAC who can speak German well. His name is Herbertson.

The Corps are kicking up no end of a fuss on the number of bombs used. It's so silly — as though we threw bombs by way of amusement. As it was, they gave us too few and now are creating trouble when we ask for more.

Editor's Note The Germans were completely caught off balance by the explosion, and two companies of the 4/Middlesex promptly occupied the resultant crater. Bombing parties drove the enemy back for about three hundred yards before they ran out of hand-grenades. The rapid advance of the bombing parties also deprived them of much needed artillery support to counter the ever-increasing enemy resistance. Consequently, they were forced to give up much of their territorial gains.

20th July
All seems all right up at Hooge. The Germans turned on a heavy artillery fire after the attack. We had a good many casualties, but all is otherwise well and we have all we wanted to get. Busy collecting maps etc for the 14th Division who are to relieve us in Hooge. It seems a foolishness to shove them into such a hot corner when they already have a bad place in Y Wood and Railway Wood, but apparently we have to go down to St Eloi again.

21st July
When I went to the ramparts in Ypres yesterday, I found that General Hoskins and everyone else were up at Zouave Wood, so I set off to find them. I went to the Middlesex HQ at the 'tail' of Zouave Wood and discovered Fraser and Macready. Burn, Heywood and General H. were on their way back. Fraser was just going up to Hooge, so I went with him to see what there was to see before returning to the ramparts.

There was a certain amount of shelling going on, but mostly down towards Birr crossroads and nothing worth speaking of in Hooge. Fraser had to go down to the wood again to see about bombs. I said that I would go on and look at the crater, and then come back and join him. I went down to Island Posts and, just as I arrived, the 6-inch German shell began to arrive a good deal close, and a whizz-bang knocked bricks and dust all around me. I went up the new trench into the old German trench, which one entered by crawling through a hole in the hedge. The trench was a fine strong one — deep and splendid dug-outs down about six feet with at least that amount of earth and timber on top. The best of these had been cleaned out and were already occupied by our men. Several of them though were still occupied by dead Germans. One had an officer in it, dead. The Middlesex must have thrown a bomb into his happy home just to keep him quiet, to judge by his unpleasing appearance. There was a lot of German equipment about, and a German machine-gun already turned round and dug in so as to deal with its late owners.

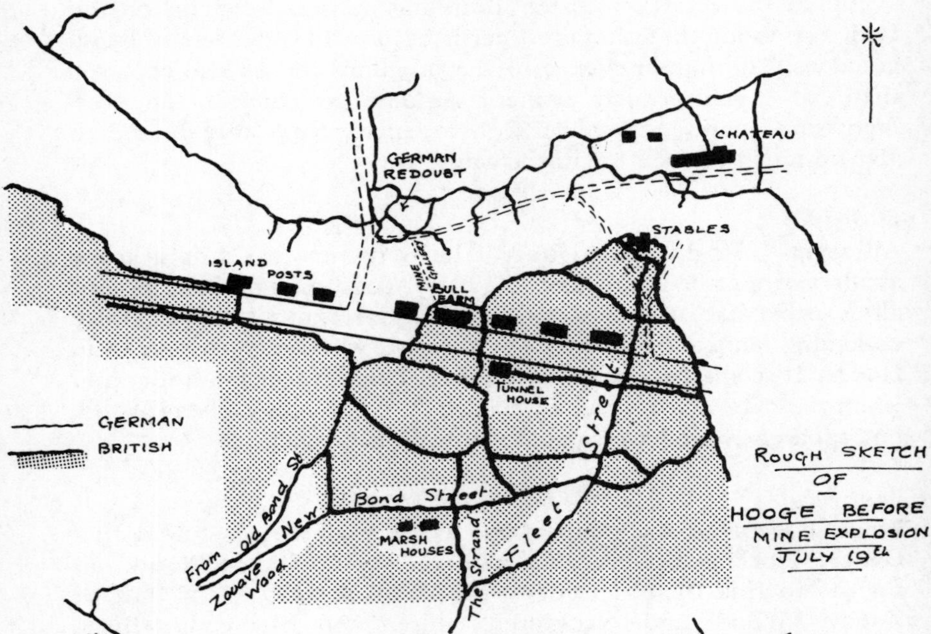

GERMAN REDOUBT

CHATEAU

STABLES

ISLAND POSTS

BULL FARM

MINE GALLERY

TUNNEL HOUSE

The Strand

Fleet Street

GERMAN
BRITISH

From Old Bond St.

New Bond Street

Zouave Wood

MARSH HOUSES

ROUGH SKETCH
OF
HOOGE BEFORE
MINE EXPLOSION
JULY 19th

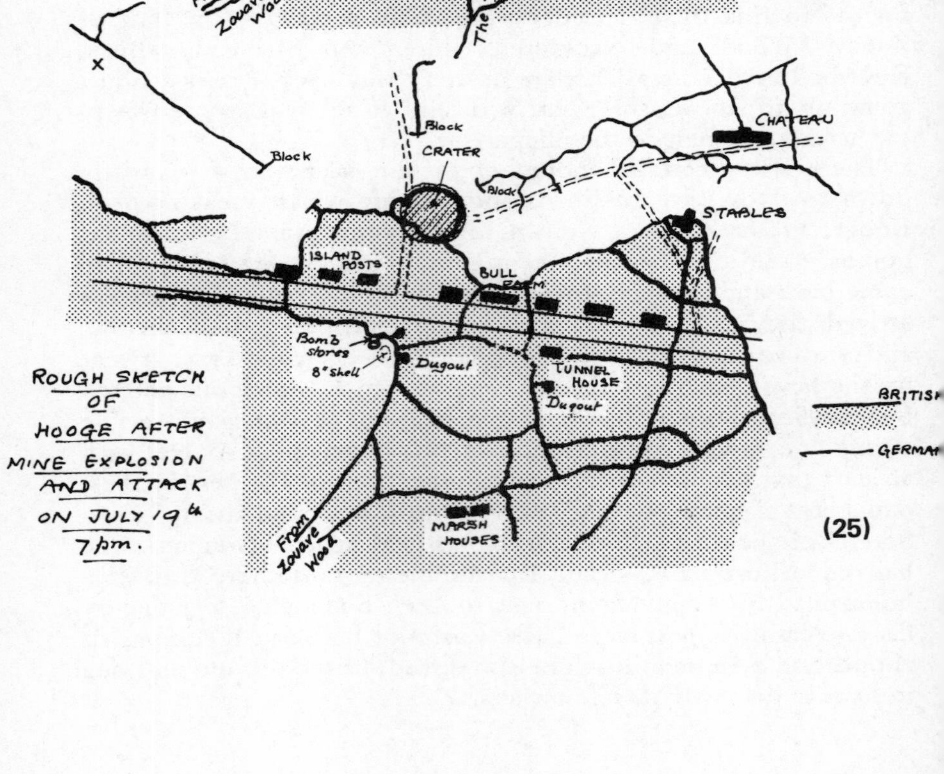

X

Block

Block

CRATER

Block

CHATEAU

STABLES

ISLAND POSTS

BULL FARM

Bomb stores

8″ shell

Dugout

TUNNEL HOUSE

Dugout

BRITISH

GERMAN

ROUGH SKETCH
OF
HOOGE AFTER
MINE EXPLOSION
AND ATTACK
ON JULY 19th
7 pm.

From Zouave Wood

MARSH HOUSES

(25)

At the end of the trench nearest to the crater, I had a most wonderful view of Bellewaarde Farm and Y Wood. No wonder the Germans wanted the place — it's a strong little position. To get into the crater from here was not easy, as no trench had been completed into it. However, by keeping low, one could get in at the back. It was a sight I shall never forget. The hole was huge, at least forty yards in diameter and thirty feet deep, but these figures give no idea of what the place looked like. The earth had been thrown up into a high 'lip' all round. On the north and east side of this lip, our men had made a good sandbag parapet and parados. They sat on the great lumps of earth inside the hole, smoking and laughing, while others kept a look-out over the parapet and finishing off the two machine-gun emplacements.

At the bottom of the crater was one dead German and a few empty tins of beef and jam. Outside the crater I had seen a few more German dead, all a good deal crumpled up, so I expect that most of them had been blown to bits and the remainder buried. From each side of the crater, one obtains a good view of the lake and the château. In fact, it's a most commanding point and our being there must irritate the Boche.

I met a subaltern of the Rifle Brigade (8th Battalion) looking around. We were talking when suddenly a very fat crump landed south of the road. There was a moment's pause, then I thought the end of the world had come, and then I thought the Germans were making a great bomb attack! Something caught me a whack on the back and I looked up to see the sky full of sorts of things. It was the bomb store — *the* bomb store — which had blown up, and bombs kept on exploding. When the 'bombing' started, everyone had rushed to their posts with shouts of ' 'Ere they come!' and we all laughed when it was realised there was no attack.

I went off via Bull Farm to see what had happened. The shelling was now becoming considerable, whizz-bangs in plenty and the 6-inch and 8-inch crumps, all south of the road and where I had to go! I had covered some distance when I met an agitated cove who said, 'For God's sake, come along.' I asked him who he was and why he was so worried. He was the adjutant of the Worcesters, and he told me that all his HQ was blown up and the men buried or killed.

Sure enough the big crump had done 'some damage'. Most of the men (there must have been a dozen there) had vanished. The first one I met was in two halves and blocking up the trench. It was a wicked sight. I then found a poor fellow buried up to the neck and crying most miserably — said he couldn't breathe. I found a shovel and got going on him. The adjutant was quite useless, half balmy. There were two other fellows buried up to the thighs, both unhurt. One of them, by leaning forward, was able to help me dig. I fairly dug and kept on trying to cheer up the poor little man, who was in pain. I soon realised that it's very difficult to dig out a man, for one fears to stick the shovel into him, also one is working in a cramped space. Noble help now arrived in the form of a gunner signaller or rather a telephonist, a good fellow, and he soon found himself a shovel.

Just as we had the man half undug, and he was beginning to stop crying, when another 8-inch landed almost twenty yards off. There had been plenty of all sorts about, but not so close as this. The gunner and myself were knocked violently on top of the buried cove and something hit me a dreadful crack on the head. So I lay still, thinking, and heard the gunner say something about, 'The poor bloke getting knocked out too,' which effectively cured me and we went on digging. It seemed to take a very long time, but at last he was out and, after a bit, was able to hobble away. We then freed the other two, who also departed, leaving the gunner and I alone in our glory, for I had long since been extremely rude to the adjutant, who had gone off.

The damage was bad. One bomb store was completely destroyed and the other filled up with earth and men. Luckily the telephone dug-out could still be cleared. It was really an advanced battalion HQ, so we did this and by great fortune found a wire which led to the Gordons' HQ. I talked to Fraser and told him I would stay up till things quieted down. It must have been about 5.30 p.m. or later. The shelling was getting worse, so I set about trying to find out what would happen if the Boche attacked. I found that there were no men south of the road at all, and Dinwiddie, who commanded the company of the Gordons in the crater, said he had too few men. I went back to my Headquarters (!) and had a look eastwards. In the tunnel I found about thirty Gordons and two stout NCO's who I took off with me to keep as a bodyguard.

It was beginning to get dark and, to add to our joys, the Germans started with the big *Minenwerfer*[22] . This is a *beast* — about 12 inches in diameter and 2 foot 6 inches long, range about 700 yards. The first thing I knew about him was when I heard him coming. I looked up and saw him. He looked quite innocent.

'Wuff, wuff, wuff,' he said. Then he suddenly steadied himself and came straight down.

A moment's pause, then the most almighty big bang. Unlike a crump, there were no bits flying about — just a crash, a cloud of black smoke and then the sky blackened with lots of things. The first seemed to drop about Bull Farm and then they continued coming about one every five minutes. It was the nastiest thing to see and I could not help wondering when or where the next was coming. I would sooner live with crumps than spend a few minutes with these aerial torpedoes. I went to the telephone and tried to get our guns on where I thought our friend to be — somewhere up the Menin road.

I was told that all the Middlesex were to be relieved during the night by the 1st Gordons. These reliefs soon started and the night became a nightmare after dark. We only had the one trench, already virtually wiped out and nowhere giving more cover than up to one's shoulders. I had a very good sergeant in the Gordons who was a great help. One burst of 'woolly bear' did a lot of damage to us. The trench in a moment was blocked by dead and wounded, and it was extremely difficult to clear. One poor fellow had had his arm blown off, and he was so hard to pick up in the narrow trench. At last we got things cleared again, but not before my sergeant friend had been hit. All night long we kept passing men along, the double traffic being the very devil and the wounded worse.

I went to see Dinwiddie several times. He was running out of bombs. I managed to get some more up to him, also some Very lights, and so it went on till 1 a.m. when the shelling mercifully seemed to die down. One had almost ceased bothering very much about it till it stopped, and then it really was lovely. Everybody became sort of hilarious. The rest of the night I was getting wounded sent down and the worst part of the blown-in trenches dug out again. Dinwiddie in the crater was fine, but the platoon holding the trench around Bull Farm had almost been destroyed by the big torpedoes. I went round at first light and it was a horrid sight.

Who should turn up after but Cameron! A grin on his face and, better still, the elements of breakfast. We had a good breakfast. I was very hungry.

Daylight did not improve the look of things a bit. Before I left I set parties on covering things up and digging out the buried bombs, many of which had not gone off.

22nd July

That infernal *Minenwerfer* is still busy up at Hooge, doing a lot of damage and shooting at the crater. It is a very wet evening and the 8th Brigade are being relieved by the 14th Division. I can't help feeling anxious at their being put into such a vile place as Hooge, especially in its present state. We have asked if we may stay on a week to put things right, but it has not been allowed.

Editor's Note The 14th Division's 41st Brigade took over 8th Brigade's positions, with the 7/Rifle Brigade relieving the 1/Gordon Highlanders in the front line at Hooge on 22nd July. Thanks to their technical ability to listen in to British telephone conversations, the Germans knew that they now faced relatively inexperienced troops — unlike the recently departed Gordon Highlanders. The 3rd Division, meanwhile, marched a few miles south to the St Eloi area:

23rd July

At twelve noon the whole line from the Vierstraat road to 134B (about half-way from the canal to Hill 60) came under our command. It really is maddening the way we are sent first to one place and then to another. One never has a chance to get settled down.

26th July

The General and I went up to the 8th Brigade line north of the canal today. Our trenches are everywhere on a level with the Germans and, at the Bluff (which is really part of the canal bank), one looks right down into the German trenches in a most satisfactory way. The Boche is busy mining at St Eloi. He blew up one tonight, but did no harm as it was short. It is difficult to see exactly what his game is. I personally think that he is very scared of being blown up himself, and this mine of his was a defensive one to destroy our shafts and galleries, but failed to do so.

29th July

Early this morning the Germans attacked the 14th Division in Hooge, and have apparently captured the whole place. It's too sickening. I hear the 8th RB are the people who lost it. I am dreadfully sorry for poor Ronnie. We have no news at present of what actually happened, but there is a rumour that the Germans used *Flammenwerfer* — liquid fire.

Editor's Note They had, just after the 8/Rifle Brigade had relieved the 7th. Again the Germans knew that they faced unseasoned men who were strangers to Hooge, and so they quietly allowed the relief to take place during the night of 28th/29th July and bided their time. Then they pushed unobtrusive pipes through their parapet and launched horrifying streams of liquid fire towards the British line that was just a few yards away. At the same time an intense three minute bombardment took place on the 8/Rifle Brigade's positions. The result was catastrophic and not one 8th Battalion man in the firing trench lived to tell the tale. By 5.30 a.m., even the 8th Battalion men in the support trenches had been driven back to the edge of Zouave Wood. The 7th Battalion returned and with the 9/King's Royal Rifle Corps, together with remnants of the 8th Battalion, tried to counter-attack during the day against a storm of enemy machine-gun and rifle fire — and against the advice of the brigade commander on the spot, whose objection to the counter-attack had been over-ruled at divisional level. At the end of the day's fighting, casualties in 8/Rifle Brigade had risen to 19 officers and 469 men and, in 7/Rifle Brigade, 16 officers and 300 men. All to no avail, because the enemy still held Hooge and the crater. In company with his divisional colleagues, Billy Congreve's fears were fully realised.

30th July
Everything is in a fair old muddle at Hooge. The fools have been doing those useless counter-attacks and have not only done no good at all, but their losses have apparently been very heavy. We are right back along the edge of Zouave Wood. It is devilish, really it is, all our work and trouble wasted. The whole division is very cross.

This afternoon I went around some of the 7th Brigade line, and an old man in the Irish Rifles asked me what all the noise had been about, so I told him, and he said: 'It's a sure thing that we shall be sent back there to clear up the mess, don't you think so, sir?' I am pretty sure he is right! I saw Dads tonight. He thinks he will have to go to Hooge. I bet *one* of us does, and hope it's him!

1st August
The 7th and 9th Brigades are being relieved by two brigades of the 17th Division, and go up to the 6th Division line to relieve two of their brigades who are to be used to retake Hooge. So Dads has a jolly little job on his hands. If anyone in the world can do it, I

know it is he and the 6th Division.

4th August
Heard this morning that poor Joe Parker was killed in Zouave
Wood (he was doing adjutant to Ronnie); also Gilbert Talbot[23]
who is a friend of Pam's. The 8th Battalion have had very heavy
losses. It is a bad job.

6th August
I took Simson (who is attached here) around the St Eloi-Canal
trenches, very wet and muddy. Some of the communication
trenches were deep in water and mud. Their snipers are fairly
good. One made me jump considerably — bursting a sandbag by
my head.

Went over to see Dads this evening. Great preparations are going
on for the retaking of Hooge. I am sure they will get in all right;
the question is how they are going to stand the subsequent
shelling? Our artillery are giving the Boche something to think
about up there. His artillery are giving Zouave Wood a bad time
too, but we have now very few men in it. The Boche has the whole
of Hooge, his front line running through Island Posts to Marsh
Houses. Dads says Geoff[24] is likely to turn up very shortly, which
will be a great event.

8th August
The 6th Division attack went in at 3.15 a.m. As far as we can hear,
it has been a great success.

Editor's Note The 6th Division regained all the ground lost by the
14th Division. The attack began with a bombardment of enemy
positions from 2.45 a.m. to 3.15 a.m. Under cover of the
bombardment, infantrymen left their trenches and crept as close
as they could to the German line. As the bombardment stopped,
they assaulted the enemy positions and made good the line. It was
then that the enemy heavily shelled the newly-won positions,
causing most of the losses amongst the 6th Division troops. In all,
the division suffered approximately 1,100 casualties, but certainly
inflicted huge losses on the enemy. Major-General Congreve visited
the crater on 10th August with his GSO1, Lieutenant-Colonel
Boyd. He estimated that there were nearly two hundred dead
Germans in the crater, excluding the enemy dead in the battered
trenches at Hooge. 'It is a bad place altogether,' Congreve wrote,

'Everywhere dead men, some days old and some blown to bits. You step over them in the trenches and see them wherever you look out of the trenches.' On his return from Hooge, he was visited by his son:

10th August
Went in early to the ramparts and saw Dads who told me all the news. They hold a line (I think) from the crater to somewhere near Bull Farm and then down to the Marsh Houses, then back to Zouave Wood. This is a strong line which denies Hooge to the Boche, but I think that they will have to shove forward a bit when things get quieter. At present we do not hold the stables.

They killed a lot of Boches during the attack. The Durhams were especially fierce owing to Hartlepool (the Zepp was it, or the cruiser shelling?)[25]. About fifty Boche were found hiding in the crater and they were all dealt with most unmercifully. Dads told me a nice (?) story. He was going round seeing some of the DLI — one old man he asked, 'How are you now?' 'I be all right, thank'ee, sir. Slept foine last night, better than I did night before.' 'Why, how was that?' 'Well, you see, I come up to a trench and in I tumbles, roight on top o' two other blokes. One on 'em was dead, t'other aloive. The aloive one 'ad a great long whoite beard as long as my granfeyther's!' 'Well, what did you do then?' 'Do!' (unutterable scorn), 'Whoi *do*; put 'un on the point, o' course.' Poor old white-bearded Boche!

It is a hot muggy day. Geoff should arrive tomorrow night.

11th August
Geoff turned up early this morning — about one in the morning, couldn't find me (I was sleeping in the office), so went to bed in the Belgian interpreter's tent! As I was sitting in the office after breakfast, he turned up, much grown. It is great having him there. We went up the Scherpenberg this morning and had a good look round. After lunch we went up to see General Hoskins, who is taking him around the 8th Brigade trenches tomorrow. After we had been there some time, we walked back through Ypres, which is always an impressive sight, and finally fetched up at Vlamertinghe where we found Dads. I left Geoff there.

12th August
Called for Geoff about twelve. He had properly changed his appearance: Dads' breeches and puttees, which fitted very well, a

private soldier's jacket, which he filled only moderately, and a trench cap (with a General's badge), belonging also to Dads. We set off and went to the Lille Gate — they were putting a few crumps thereabouts. Geoff's first baptism! We had lunch with General Hoskins and then Geoff and he went off together. I had to return to the office. He eventually arrived back at Reninghelst, having had great adventures, at 11 p.m. He had a shot with a rifle, very nearly met a *Minenwerfer*, saw some shelling and, in fact, had a great day of it.

13th August
Colonel Brown (1st Gordons) and I went all round the Bluff trenches. The Bluff is a very pretty place to snipe from. One Boche kept on showing his head; it was a long shot, but we scared him properly. Another Boche was walking along the trench, showing his cap on the end of a stick. We could see the stick, being on higher ground, so he did not draw our fire. The Gordons should get a good bag up there.

15th August
Dined with Dads tonight. Geoff has spent the day up in Hooge! He went up with 'Uncle' Harper[26] and saw all the gruesome sights there were to be seen. He came back with various Boche loot and intends taking the articles back to his battleship. I wish he hadn't to go back, for he is excellent company. He is off tomorrow, going down, I think, with General Nicholson[27].

Editor's Note On 17th August, his father visited Hooge with Major-General Haldane in preparation for 3rd Division to relieve 6th Division — not a welcoming prospect for Haldane's men:

21st August
Here we are, holding Hooge again. We hoped against hope that we were on the Canal line for the winter, and worked hard at getting everything put to rights. Now all our work goes into others' hands and we come to this beastly place, where everything has to be done over again.

Hooge is in a poor way. Its condition after the 6th Division attack was too awful and, ever since then, the 17th Brigade have been working hard to get it straight, but it's a hard job. The dead bodies, old and new, made everything so fearfully slow, for one cannot dig a yard without coming on some grim relic which has either to be reburied or dug round. 'Uncle' Harper tells me that they have buried over 1,000 bodies. I went up there yesterday and found the 3rd Battalion in Sanctuary Wood. I met Prideaux-Brune[28] commanding a company; also saw Kewley[29] who is now adjutant, and Bob Pigot[30] commanding. I found all my old friends in the signallers and it was good seeing them again. They all seemed very cheerful.

The situation at Hooge still appears a bit vague. The 17th Brigade say that they hold the stables. I am pretty sure that they don't.

Editor's Note The following day, 22nd August, having recently said farewell to his younger son, Geoffrey, Billy Congreve's father was surprised to be visited by his youngest son, Christopher John, then aged twelve and dressed in his Boy Scout's uniform. Christopher was spending his school summer holidays in France, helping his mother who was nursing at the Anglo-American Hospital at Ris-Orangis just south of Paris. According to Christopher Congreve, who in later life also joined the Rifle Brigade (retiring in 1946 with the rank of major), his greatest adventure on that holiday was visiting the front line and walking along it with his father, coming in for the odd crump and burst of small-arms fire: 'This must have intrigued the soldiery for, coming round a traverse, and finding two of them, one was heard to exclaim: "Blimey, Bill — 'ere's a bleedin' Boy Scaht!" ' Christopher Congreve's visit was to last until 11th September. It is possible that he was the youngest British person to visit any Great War front.

23rd August
The South Lancs have done first-rate work up in Hooge and we have now reached the stables, but cannot dig a trench round the Boche side of it — as the latter has brought *his* trench up very close there. A good deal of bombing there last night with no definite results. We shall have to content ourselves with digging a trench on our side of the stables, and holding bombing posts on either side of it.

The Wilts found a 14th Division machine-gun in the stables, which proves that the 17th Brigade could not have been there. The Worcesters[31] also found a *Flammenwerfer* just south of the main road. It was in a sort of a cupboard, let into the side of the trench and was in perfect condition and complete. It is full of the most filthy stinking sort of tar stuff. The day the 6th Division attacked, they also found one. The crater is being made into a happy home! The 6th Division started good dug-outs and we are making more. The bottom of the crater contains now at least 250 dead Boches and a good many of our own fellows. I heard today that we are likely to have to do a further attack on this front. Of all places to choose on the British front, I suppose this is the worst. I only hope the General puts his heels in and refuses point-blank to do any such mad thing. Both Guffin[32] and I agree that it's a hopeless job.

24th August

There is no doubt that we are to do this attack. General Allenby was here again today, and I suppose has bullied the General into the job. We are to attack from the B4 Salient to Bellewaarde Lake. It is a mighty tough proposition and, if we do take the beastly place, I know that we shall get shelled out of it again. I believe that our show is merely to co-operate with something big down south, which will mean the old game of not getting enough gun ammunition. Apparently modern tactics call for these feint attacks, though I can't see that they do any good.

We are to start bombarding the Boche trenches almost at once — daily bombardments. There is a doubt as to whether we are to have any 9.2-inch ammunition. If we do not have this, it's a poor show.

25th August

The Boches shelled Hooge today in retaliation, but not very seriously. We are all very hard at work now preparing things. I spend my time at air photos, drawing maps, collecting information from brigades and am also up at Hooge most days. It is very difficult to tell exactly the state of the Boche defences, for the whole of the ground is so desperately broken up. There is no doubt that their wire is formidable in many places, and this we must destroy by our bombardments. We are shoving forward some mines from B4, so that part should not present many difficulties — that is to say if the mines are done in time, but we cannot get any definite news as to the date, which is troublesome.

Editor's Note The 3rd Division's subsidiary battle hinged on the date set for the proposed main Allied offensive, but that date had already been postponed from the first week in August to the end of the month and, as yet unknown to 3rd Division, would again be postponed until 8th September, then finally to 25th September.

What was this much vaunted southern offensive that caused so much concern in 3rd Division? For the answer, it is necessary to look to Joffre's strategy rather than to the British Commander-in-Chief's. Joffre's belief was that a successful break-through in Champagne and in Artois, followed by a general offensive of all the French and British armies on the Western Front would 'compel the Germans to retreat beyond the Meuse and possibly end the war'.

Brave words and spoken by a man who sincerely thought that he had learned a valuable lesson in May and June when, on the plains of Artois, a French offensive had bled into the ground after a 3,000 yard penetration of the German lines. Haig's First Army was detailed to be the British trump card for this latest offensive. His troops would advance eastwards, but on surveying the ground that his troops would have to attack over, he formed the opinion that a rapid advance was an impossibility. Haig made his views known to Sir John French. He too was worried, but Joffre dismissed their pessimism. Joffre was of the opinion that the area where the British were to attack, between Loos and La Bassée, was particularly favourable. In reality, it was quite the opposite; a fact that could well have been a contributory element that impelled Haig, a year later, to tell Billy Congreve's father that Joffre was not very good at reading a map[33]. Be that as it may, the British attack would be made across that terrain once a date was fixed. In 3rd Division's headquarters, meanwhile, the last days of August were spent in frantic activity:

2nd September
A very busy few days these have been and, this evening, there was a very serious bombardment of Hooge — an obvious set piece in retaliation for our daily 'hate'. The shelling went on for about two hours and was very intense for most of the time. The poor old Wilts had heavy losses, and I hear that the state of the defences is hopeless — smashed to bits everywhere. The crater came in for an especially heavy dose and proved a death trap. All the newly built dug-outs were destroyed and many of the Wilts with them.

4th September
It rained all last night. This stopped all work. Unless we get fine weather now we shall not have everything ready for this attack.

There is a fearful lot to be done. All the old trenches have to be opened up again to act as assembly trenches for the attack. The Strand and Fleet Street have also to be opened up and communication trenches cut forward. The work on the old front trenches is terribly hampered by the dead bodies. These are very numerous and all are in an awful condition. To add to this, Hooge itself has to be put straight again, so we at the moment do not look like getting things through by the 8th, which we hear may be the day.

This rain has flooded most of the communication trenches, and it is hard work in getting up to Hooge now by day. I have started a system that may help to keep the communication trenches in order; each trench having trench wardens — about ten men and an NCO who live in the trench and are responsible for keeping everything in order. At present, of course, many of the trenches are too hopeless to be dealt with by ten men and need more like one thousand.

8th September
The attack has been put off, date still vague. I was up at Hooge all last night and arrived back about seven this morning. Took Cameron with me and, as soon as it began to get dark, I went up to the Appendix and warned the HAC, who were there, that I would be coming down the old F1 in half-an-hour's time. It was as well to do this, for when one is about after dark outside one's own trenches, men are apt to shoot first and ask who you are afterwards.

Cameron and I got into Sanctuary Wood all right (without even being challenged) and then went up to the Worcester's HQ who gave me dinner in their dug-out. Hankey, who commands them, is a good fellow. They knew little about Hooge. I generally find that the people holding the trenches have this failing. After dinner I slept in Colonel Hankey's dug-out till about 2 a.m., when the moon came up and made things fairly visible.

Evans arrived from Brigade HQ and he, Colonel Hankey and I set off to Hooge to go round the old C3, C2 and C1[34]. We were likely to meet a Boche patrol, so went pretty slowly. I knew the ground best and went first. We found the trenches in an awful state, all blown to bits and a great many dead in the ruins of them. These poor fellows were in a bad way and the rats made me feel horrid, like wanting to be sick. However, they reduce the bodies to skeletons fairly quickly — such rats they are, big as rabbits, and so bloated that they hardly take the trouble to run — beasts. It was rather jumpy work. We stalked a tree stump for several minutes at one time, I with a somewhat wobbling revolver trained in the direction of its tummy! Then we ran into one of our own patrols who were coming from the south — they ran away!

We returned to the Worcesters HQ about 6.15 a.m., and I woke up Mr Cameron and returned home. Went over to see John[35] at Vlamertinghe. He is having a great time and already knows as much about everything as most officers do out here.

9th September

I went up to Hooge again last night and again took Cameron. Hooge is still in a pretty bad way, and I don't know how the 2nd South Lancs are ever going to assemble behind the stables. I found some fine cellars in the one but last ruin of the north line of houses. One has to drop in through a hole, but once inside it is fine: two rooms, tables, chairs and a full-length looking-glass, a truly astonishing thing to find in Hooge. There was a *Daily Mirror* of May 30th which had not been read, so the cellar was, I think, last used by the cavalry before we relieved them. These cellars must be very nearly crump-proof, for there is about ten feet of brick and timber and debris on top. Cameron saw a black cat (I saw it too), and he said that we were going to have bad luck. I thought that they were lucky! It's a wonder how that cat has stayed in Hooge. It must live in some hole in the ruins and I suppose gets plenty of victuals by eating rats. The wonder is that the bombardments have not killed it. It must have more than its proper complement of lives, I think. Cameron had brought some food and cold tea, which gave us dinner and which we shared on the edge of the Menin road.

It was very quiet up there; the Boche was working hard at repairing and strengthening his works and our people were not doing nearly enough to hinder him. I got them going with rifle grenades and catapults, but unless one *forces* them to do things they are quite content to sit down and do nothing. They are like children, the modern officer and NCO. One has to start them on a game and then they love it and go on playing it till they get bored, when one has to invent something else to amuse them!

10th September

Tonight, Dads and John called for me here and we went to the 'Fancies' in Poperinghe. It was a very good show. One man sang awful well — in the Queen's Westminsters he was. After it was over I had to say goodbye to John, for he returns to Paris via Boulogne tomorrow. The poor man is a bit sad and it was horrid having to say goodbye to him.

11th September

A lovely fine day. I went up to the 7th Brigade about 7 p.m., and Evans and I spent the evening in Hooge. I got home about midnight. It was very quiet up there. We cannot stop the Boche working at present, as we have so much work to do ourselves in exposed places. An Irish regiment last night was working on the old C1, C2 and C3 line and, after working a short time, the whole 400 bolted! The whole affair, I think, started due to the Irishman's fear of ghosts. The line, as I have said, is very full of dead in all sorts of conditions. That and the rats were too much for their nerves. Whatever it was, they came back and had to be driven out again by their enraged officers. Of course it's very bad, but almost laughable. Evans and I met two tonight who were on patrol and they were shivering with fright. They nearly shot us, and then could give no coherent account of what they were doing. We were very angry, yet I could not help laughing when we eventually put them back where they should have been. The work up there is going ahead now with the fine weather, and I think that everything will be ready in time.

27th November

Today the 'G' office was completely destroyed by fire. I had just gone out of it, when the silly ass of an orderly tried to light the fire with a tin of petrol. I heard the explosion and in a moment the whole place was in flames, for it was only made of wood and canvas. The man was badly burnt and it was lucky nobody else was. Everything we had was burnt; all the papers, typewriter, maps — in fact, all that was left was a bundle of unimportant papers that happened to be in the mess hut.

My diary was burnt, and a good many other papers and books of mine. The only good thing was that it was a freezing day, and I got proper warm trying to put the fire out. Also wet, as one man threw most of a bucket of dirty water over me in his excitement. Poor Glassfurd's[36] dismay when he returned was ludicrous, for all his precious 'grenade file' was gone. I don't feel much inclined now to go on with a diary. So much that was interesting was burnt, all the September 25th fighting up at Hooge, and I can't be bothered to write it all out again.

CHAPTER NINE

Brigade-Major

Undeniably, Billy Congreve's diary entry for 25th September would have cast further light on 3rd Division's subsidiary attack at at Hooge, an attack that coincided with a huge French offensive in the Champagne and a combined Anglo-French offensive in the ancient province of Artois. The Hooge operation was just one of many side-shows up and down the Allied line on 25th September, and included an attack by 3rd Division's neighbour, 14th Division, on the Bellewaarde Farm position.

It was all part of Joffre's grand scheme and backed by Lord Kitchener, Great Britain's Secretary of State for War, to make September the pivotal month towards victory and the ending of trench warfare in favour of the Allies. 'Artois had taught me,' wrote Joffre, referring to the bitter French campaign in May and June when 400,000 French troops became casualties of war, 'that simultaneous operations by several armies would prevent the enemy from making full use of his reserves and force him to accept battle with limited means.' His reasoning was based on the fact that the Germans were still outnumbered along the Western Front through Eastern Front commitments. Joffre was also heartened by the growth of the BEF which would exceed a million men by September 1915. On the reverse side of the coin, German High Command had calculated months before that it was a mathematical impossibility for the Allies to punch a large hole through their front, as there was no flank to turn and their defences lay in depth.

Of the two planned main thrusts, it was the Champagne one that Joffre favoured, with its force of nearly half a million French troops under Pétain's command. The Anglo-French Artois operation, involving Haig's First Army and d'Urbal's Tenth Army under General Foch's co-ordination, meant an eastward thrust to Tournai, Valenciennes and Le Quesnoy. If successful, then cavalry would continue over the Belgian frontier towards Mons. Enemy-held Vimy Ridge lay across a stretch of d'Urbal's path, whilst Haig would have to contend with the mining village of Loos. If all augured well, both armies would converge on Pétain's force advancing in a northerly direction.

Unfortunately for the Allies, very little went right. Haig's First Army employed gas for the first time ever in British military history, but what wind there was proved fickle. In the end it inconvenienced the British spearhead battalions more than the Germans. Certainly, Loos was taken and, for the second time in the war, a small penetration was made through the enemy lines. To Haig's frustration, many of the badly needed reserves were held too far in the rear to exploit such a situation. As Sir John French had more than a casual hand in the placement of the reserves, it would prove to be the end of his career. To be fair to Sir John, because of limited forces and inadequate artillery resources, he did not want any British infantry involvement when Joffre first mooted his grand scheme. On observing the ground which his First Army would have to move over, Haig also voiced his opposition. Both men, however, were over-ruled by Kitchener in order to 'do our utmost to help France in their offensive, even though by so doing we may suffer very heavy losses.'

And so it was. Exclusive of the subsidiary attacks, British casualties from 25th September to 16th October were 2,013 officers and 48,367 other ranks. The German losses from 21st September to 10th October (casualty returns being made on a ten day rota) were around 20,000 officers and men of whom fewer than 5,000 were killed.

The French Tenth Army attack came to little consequence, and so did Foch's offensive in the Champagne. Their casualties were vastly heavier than the British. As for 3rd Division's attack at Hooge, some minor gains were made and, as for its neighbour, 14th Division whose front extended from Railway Wood to the Menin road and whose attack was confined to 42nd Brigade, the result was a costly fiasco. Indeed, reporting on the action the 42nd Brigade commander wrote of the 'great difficulty in getting reliable information as to what actually happened owing to the fact that only one officer in the whole of the assaulting columns returned unscathed.'

All told, British subsidiary attacks chalked up a total of 453 officers and 10,880 other ranks in casualties.

Fighting at Hooge continued, with the enemy particularly active in shelling 3rd Division's lines. On 9th October, 3rd Division lost its trusty 7th Brigade to 25th Division in exchange for 76th Brigade, the latter being an amalgamation of two Regular battalions (2/Suffolks and 1/Gordon Highlanders, both from 8th Brigade), one Territorial battalion (4/Gordon Highlanders, also from 8th Brigade) and two New Army battalions from the 25th Division (8/King's Own Royal Lancs and 10/Royal Welch Fusiliers). The change stemmed from a policy that was introduced after the Battle of Loos, whereby new divisions — such as 25th Division — were to be stiffened with some brigades and battalions from old divisions. The 76th Brigade moved into billets at Poperinghe as 17th Division relieved 3rd Division at Hooge during the last week of October. Although still GSO3 of 3rd Division, the advent of 76th Brigade would shortly mean a new position for Captain Congreve.

In the immediate future, however, and with his involvement in the Hooge attack already recognised with a mention in despatches on 15th October, Billy Congreve was informed that France had awarded him with the *Croix de Chevalier, Légion d'Honneur*. He received the accolade from General de Boiselle, commander of XXX Corps, who pinned the decoration to his chest in front of a parade of French and British troops. Among the onlookers was his father who, six days later on 12th November, heard officially that he was to take command of XIII Corps in General Allenby's Third Army.

Having passed over the command of 6th Division to Major-General Ross the day before, his father (promoted to temporary lieutenant-general[1]) bade a sad farewell to his staff on Sunday, 14th November. He left with his son at 3 p.m. by car for St Omer before travelling on to Doullens. It had been a dreadful day of partings, then when Lieutenant-General Congreve thought all was done, he and Billy found that the road ahead was lined with soldiers of 6th Division. The resulting scene motivated Billy Congreve to write in a letter:

I was filled with pride and then almost reduced to tears when hundreds and hundreds of men rushed out all along the road and cheered him — *real* cheering. It made me quite miserable and I think he nearly wept — lieutenant-generals can weep!

Known affectionately to the rankers as 'Old Concrete', Lieutenant-General Congreve was also moved to put his thoughts to paper, concluding with: 'Dear, dirty fellows, how I do hate leaving them in all the discomforts and dangers of those parts. If only I could have brought them with me.' As a commander who believed in sharing danger and hardship with his men, he sincerely meant what he had written, having recently escaped death himself from hostile shelling, only to receive a bullet through his tunic that left behind no fewer than nine holes in various garments.

At the time of Congreve's departure from 6th Division, all three brigades of 3rd Division were resting at Steenvoorde. Their respite from front line activities finished on 22nd November when they relieved 24th Division at St Eloi the next day. Just over a week later, Billy Congreve recommenced his diary:

*

1st December

I hear that there is a good chance of my going to the 76th Brigade as brigade-major, which is good news. It's all quiet nowadays up in the trenches[2], especially in the right sector where most of our trenches have most terribly fallen into decay. I suppose we have the combined efforts of the 17th and 24th Divisions to thank for it.

8th December

Have today been appointed brigade-major to the 76th Brigade. General Pratt (late of the DLI) commands and is, I believe, a very pleasant old gentleman. I shall, I think, move up with Cameron to Woodcote House[3] tomorrow. Cameron does not appreciate the prospect of the change, and thinks it would be better if I went to a corps staff! He says we would do well to keep away from the trenches.

9th December

Today the Navy arrived to be shown trench life. A petty officer, four seamen and a marine turned up, and were hearty looking fellows. Admiral Jellicoe had sent a message saying that he was anxious that the men should see as much of trench life as possible, as he had pointed out to them that 'although their life afloat is monotonous, they live in much greater comfort than their brothers ashore'. This meant that we had to arrange sundry strafes for their benefit. As luck would have it, their arrival in the trenches was greeted by the Boche trench mortars. This got our mortars and artillery strafing, so that they had a lively time and, I must say, appeared to thoroughly enjoy it!

The old Boche went clean balmy last night and shelled the main road outside here till *we* near went balmy from not being able to

A W. Heath Robinson cartoon captioned 'Christmas Eve with the 3rd Division 1915'.
Never before published, the cartoon was a Christmas gift to Billy Congreve from W. H.
Robinson himself 'with his best wishes'.

Wedding day: 1st June 1916. When this photograph was taken, Billy Congreve had seven weeks to live.

sleep. Maddening it was. About 4.30 a.m., I got up and turned on
our guns to give them a doing. After that, they dried up — but we
had a poor night.

15th December

Heard from the division that we were likely to have a Boche gas
attack during the next few days. Terrible excitement! I must start
trying now to like wearing my [gas] helmet. I don't somehow
think that they will attack here. It is all very quiet at present,
except for our own grenadier work and our brave Belgians who
shoot like heroes.

Editor's Note His reference to 'grenadier work' related to the
firing of rifle grenades — a vast improvement on the impoverished
and patented catapults employed in earlier trench fighting. Stokes
mortars had made an appearance in the front line during the latter
half of 1915, and most welcomed by the British troops.

19th December

We have had a horrible day. At 5.30 a.m., I was happily asleep
when the deuce of a bombardment started. It was hard to say
where the shooting was most intense, though at first I thought it
was mostly well to our north. I rang up the Welch who said that
they were being shelled, but that there was no sign of a gas attack.
A few minutes after this, we smelt the gas strongly ourselves; from
then till about 8 a.m., we had a miserable time of it. It only
affected the eyes, but that was bad enough and we sat about
weeping copiously.

The Boche only shelled on our front. We heard later that the
real attack had been on the 6th Division up Wieltje way. The
helmets are so hot to wear that it was pleasanter to weep. So we
wept and swore. About 3 p.m., the old Boche joined in our
strafing (for we had our guns going early) and gave the 1/Gordons
a bad doing for an hour.

(11 p.m.). We are sending some of the 4/Gordons[4] to help clear
up the mess in the 1/Gordons' trenches. I am afraid that we have
had about twenty casualties. Wright (Capt) was killed in his dug-
out — had his head taken off.

23rd December

We had a Zepp over last night, at least everyone says there was
one. I doubt it myself. I am making out a gorgeous Boche strafe

for Xmas Day — just to show him how much we really can 'hate'.

24th December

Awful rot; a wire came in from the division this morning, saying: 'No action is to be taken by us on Xmas Day which is likely to provoke retaliation on the part of the Germans.' Was *ever* such an order given before? I expect the corps commander is leaving off trousers and putting on skirts. I am especially annoyed, as I had taken some trouble in organising our 'hate'. However it will do for New Year's Day!

Cameron is making everything lovely for tomorrow. He has looted a fearsome sort of wreath of paper roses from Ypres, which is festooned on the ceiling of the dining-room, and he has got holly and mistletoe from somewhere, which is splendid. My bed has a large piece of the latter above it and a beautiful *Wishing you a Happy Christmas* in my best drawing inks (I think); at least, I know no other source of such various colours. Some parcels have come for me, but these also has he taken from me! Even Pam's letter, marked 'for Xmas Day', has been stolen from my table.[5]

Editor's Note As well as noting that Billy Congreve's Christmas Day (artillery) programme was cancelled, the 76th Brigade's war diary for 24th December also quoted V Corps' (Lieutenant-General H.D. Fanshawe) order. The officer responsible for writing up the war diary for that date, stonily remarked: 'No reason given for this.'

Xmas Day

This morning when I awoke I saw hanging above me a large sack. For some time I was too sleepy to realise that it was, but eventually remembered. It was my Xmas stocking. Almost all its contents were from Pam — parcels of sweets and books, and a silver banknote holder. I had a happy time. Cigarettes there were too.

It has been a windy wet day and I have been very lazy. Some day! And tonight we had a great banquet: a goose and fiery plum pudding. The Boche has been quiet, his only 'offensive action' being that he started singing some rotten German stuff which the King's Own wanted to get our guns going in reply, but I had to say that we had been ordered to be peaceful, though I think Boche hymns do almost call for artillery retaliation.

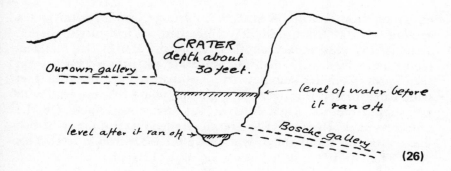

CRATER
depth about
30 feet.

Our own gallery

level of water before
it ran off

level after it ran off →

Bosche gallery

(26)

30th December

Some excitement today. About 7 a.m. this morning, all the water in the big Bluff crater suddenly disappeared with a rush and left exposed in the south-west corner of it the entrance to a Boche gallery. Brisco[6] at once went up and started off down the gallery by himself, leaving a man armed with a rifle at the entrance.

After going about sixty feet, he heard somebody coming towards him, so he slowly retired. When he had got close back to the entrance again he waited and, as soon as the Boche shoved his head round the corner, fired with his revolver. He missed. The man who was with him, in his excitement, let off his rifle. It flew up and hit Brisco a whack on the nose that nearly knocked him out, so the Boches got away.

I went up in the afternoon to see how things were and found the crater almost dry. Many tons of water must have run off down the Boche gallery. Brisco had blocked up the entrance to the gallery with sandbags and was awaiting developments. I also found three grenadiers of the RWF sitting on top of the block! These I hurriedly withdrew to a safe distance. About half an hour later the Boche blew up his gallery from the inside without doing us any damage, so now all is quiet again. It has shown us, however, that he is still working in the neighbourhood and we shall have to be on the look-out.

It must have been the gradually increasing weight of water in the crater which eventually broke down the block that the Boche had built in the gallery. Our only hope is that some Boches were drowned! As his gallery undoubtedly runs straight down to the Canal, he probably has other workings branching off this one.

Editor's Note Holding a sector of V Corps operational area, which extended from south of St Eloi to Hooge, 3rd Division had a section of the front line that embraced an irregularly shaped artificial hill (yes, indeed another one in the almost flat Flanders landscape) which was called 'The Bluff'. It was situated yards from the Ypres–Comines canal where, in that sector, the 120 feet wide canal passed through a long cutting which was terraced with the spoil from the canal when it was first constructed. On the northern bank, the top of the terrace ended just inside the British line and stood about thirty feet above the local ground level. This was 'The Bluff' and, whoever held it, had one of the best observation posts for miles around. The Germans had twice exploded mines near it during 1915 and, although the craters made by them destroyed a section of the British firing line, the British troops occupied the nearest lips of both craters. In so doing, denied the enemy complete occupation. It was the larger crater of the two which drained its pool of water.

2nd January 1916

We are gradually getting the wire thickened up along our front, especially opposite the Bluff. It is very slow work and, most nights, I go up to egg it on. The Boche snipes a good deal which makes the work harder, but there are surprisingly few casualties.

10th January

For some reason or other we are on a very strict ammunition allowance again; a sad affair, as it means we cannot go on with our organised strafing. Up till now, we have had two or three good bombardments a week on to the Boche trenches with the result that he has become quite tame. I cannot believe that we are really short of ammunition and expect it is that we are saving up for some 'great offensive'.

The work at the Bluff is now really going ahead and I am getting very proud of it. It is by no means finished yet, but as compared with what it used to be, it is now beautiful.

The new tunnel ought to be through in a few days. The loop still needs a lot of work done to it, and Angle Trench is still bad. Both these will, I think, be through in a few days. We are also making a new trench off 29R, and will be a big improvement on the North Canal Trench which is in a fearsome state. We are going to call this new trench Xmas Trench, because it was about Xmas Day that we decided to make it.

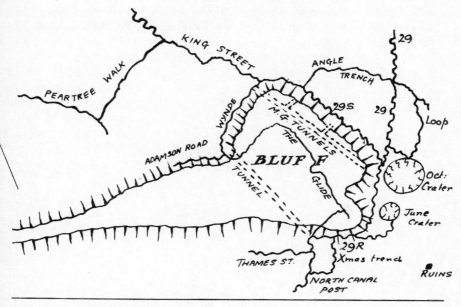

CANAL

(27)

We are having real fine weather just now, and that makes all our work and life generally much easier.

Editor's Note His duties as a conscientious brigade-major were long and strenuous. If time had been available, he would doubtless have commented on Sir John French's historic departure in December and of Sir Douglas Haig assuming the mantle of Commander-in-Chief. On a personal note, he omitted any reference on New Year's Day when he was mentioned in despatches for the third time (the second time being on 15th October 1915), nor to his award of the Military Cross for gallantry at Hooge which was gazetted on 15th January. Two days later and no doubt due to pressures of brigade work, Billy Congreve penned his last entry:

17th January
Some of the Belgian batteries are now being withdrawn. This is very sad, for we all love them. They are such sportsmen and shoot

like blazes whenever one wants them to. Our grenadiers gave the Boche 150 rifle grenades, and the Belgians let go their salvoes in fine style.

CHAPTER TEN

Journey's End

As the year of 1916 dawned on a war-torn Europe, preparations were already underway for a co-ordinated offensive that would be launched simultaneously by France, Great Britain, Russia and Italy. Joffre had calculated that Russia would not be in a position to do anything before June, so June became the target date for the offensive. The logical place to launch the offensive on the Western Front was at the point where both French and British Armies met, namely the Somme. Firstly though, Joffre wanted to extract the French Tenth Army from between the British First and Second Armies at Arras. He also wanted the British to wear down the enemy through a series of preliminary attacks before the main thrust. Haig, now Commander-in-Chief of the BEF, agreed in principle to both requests. He sent Rawlinson, who was about to take command of the new Fourth Army, to make a feasibility study of the Flanders area with an eye to mounting an attack there two weeks before the main one.

So a date had been set for the offensive as well as the place and, hopefully, the proposed blow would obliterate the enemy's defences, paralyse his mobility and destroy his morale. It would be achieved by creating a gigantic gap in his lines for the cavalry to exploit in order to roll up his flanks.

There was just one snag — the enemy struck first. The blow fell at Verdun on 21st February. Bearing the code name *Gericht,* translated as the 'place of execution', the German offensive was staged on a very narrow front and limited to no more than seven miles wide. Verdun was French Army territory and General von Falkenhayn had launched the offensive with attrition in mind. His primary objective was to break the back of the French military resolve. In the event, he nearly succeeded. Before the attack on Verdun was initiated, it had been decided by the enemy to conduct a series of operations against specific sectors along the Allied front. The Germans, having exploded a mine in front of the Bluff on 22nd January, shelled half a mile of front line trenches, including the Bluff itself, on the afternoon of 14th February. The defenders were battalions of 17th Division's 51st Brigade which had relieved 76th Brigade seven days previously.

A single platoon of the 10/Lancashire Fusiliers held the Bluff when the Germans mounted their assault. With their positions blasted by artillery, survivors of the platoon sought refuge in the Bluff's tunnel.

It proved to be a death-trap for all but three men, because the enemy exploded a small mine beneath it and buried the occupants. The Germans occupied the Bluff in time to annihilate another platoon which had come up to replace the victims of the mine explosion. The captured trenches were consolidated by nightfall and repeated counter-attacks failed.

On studying the reports emanating from 17th Division, it became clear to the V Corps commander that the lost ground could not be regained except after deliberate preparations and bombardment. He also judged that the attack should be conducted with troops who knew the ground intimately. For that reason, Brigadier-General Pratt's 76th Brigade was recalled from reserve and, on the night of 16th/17th February, placed at the disposal of 17th Division for the proposed attack. A field artillery brigade and a 3rd Division RE field company came into 17th Division's operational area to join 76th Brigade.

As brigade-major, Billy Congreve was actively involved in the planning and preparations of the assault. With the help of aerial photographs, an exact representation of the German position was accomplished to practise the forthcoming attack. No date could be finalised on account of the weather. After much discussion, it was settled that the assault would begin on the morning following the first fine day that would allow for artillery registration. Brigadier-General H.C.C. Uniacke, GOC Royal Artillery, V Corps, was brought in to arrange artillery co-operation.

All four of 76th Brigade's battalions were to take part, together with the 7/Lincolns and 10/Sherwood Foresters from 51st Brigade. The plan called for the 2/Suffolks, supported by the 10/Royal Welch Fusiliers to storm that part of the line where the Bluff was situated, as well as the canal bank where the enemy mine workings were suspected. Companies of the 1/Gordon Highlanders were detailed to attack on the left flank, leaving the 8/King's Own to take care of the centre. Each assaulting battalion would have its own tunnelling party and RE section. The 7/Lincolns would be in broad support behind them with the 10/Sherwood Foresters in brigade reserve.

At a conference attended by the Second Army commander, General Herbert Plumer, it was ultimately decided to bombard the enemy's positions from 5 p.m. on 1st March. The duration would be forty-five minutes and laid down in such a way as to convey the belief that an infantry attack was imminent, but in the end had failed to materialise. The enemy, hopefully, would be caught off-guard when the real moment came. To prevent the Germans making good their battered defences in the meantime, their lines would be subjected to a 'casual' but accurate fire that would not unduly raise their suspicions. If all went well, a surprise attack by the infantry was scheduled for the next day at 4.30 in the morning. A daring scheme, and one in which Billy Congreve had played a decisive role in its formulation.

The Bluff, because of its height advantage for surveillance, presented a special problem. It was considered impossible for the 2/Suffolks to cross No Man's Land without fire cover — and fire cover could easily expose the whole scheme. Two minutes was the time estimated for the 2/Suffolks to advance over the open ground and, somehow, a way had to be found to keep the defenders' heads down during that very brief but critical period.

It was Brigadier-General Uniacke who hit upon the solution. He would arrange for a battery to fire a salvo at the Bluff, followed by another salvo two minutes later. The same pattern to continue at irregular intervals day and night until zero hour. Then — and only then — one salvo would be fired. While the Bluff defenders stayed under cover for the anticipated second salvo, one company of the 2/Suffolks would cross over and storm the position before the defenders were aware of the ploy.

On the night of 1st March, infantrymen filed quietly into their allotted assembly trenches to await zero hour. With the Germans still unsuspecting, Brigadier-General Pratt reported that the infantry would go in without a preliminary bombardment as planned. The enemy was completely taken by surprise and, except for the tragic loss of one of the tunnelling parties and half a company of Gordons mown down by machine-gun fire, all objectives were achieved with little resistance.

The Bluff operation went like clockwork in spite of its sensitivity. Duped by Uniacke's artillery tactics, sentries were startled to find the 2/Suffolks on top of them. Many of the Bluff's garrison were discovered sheltering in the crater caused by the mine explosion of 22nd January. It was a bitter-sweet moment for the Suffolks, because the 76th Brigade was holding the Bluff when the mine was blown which inflicted some seventy casualties in the unfortunate company occupying that section of the hill. In a letter to his father at the time, Billy Congreve described the effects of the mine explosion:

> The mine destroyed the pride of my heart: the Bluff defences which we had just completed. It's the hugest thing in the mine line I have ever seen — about four Hooge's rolled into one. It blew up 3,500 tons of earth. The crater is 60 feet deep (from the top of the Bluff) and 50 yards by 40 yards across. The actual depth from ground level is about 30 feet, and it blew off the end of the Bluff. The Boche made no attack and did very little shelling. I cannot describe it all, but no volcano or earthquake will have fears for me in the future. We have now remade the whole place and, I think, it is stronger even than before.

After all the difficult and dangerous work in making good the Bluff's defences, it rankled with the men of 76th Brigade when the position was lost to the enemy on 14th February. Selected to recapture it, they had not only regained that stretch of line, but had even improved the position by capturing more ground. It was, as the *Official History* states, an excellent example of a 'set piece', well carried out. Brigadier-General Pratt's brigade-major, 'whom the officers engaged unanimously regard as the leading spirit in the attack, was Captain W. La T. Congreve'.

The battalions which had taken part in the action were relieved during the night of 3rd/4th March, midst a chilling snowstorm that reached blizzard proportions. Rest for the 76th Brigade's troops was short-lived, because 3rd Division took over that part of the line from 17th Division at the beginning of the second week in March. By 11th March, it was 76th Brigade's turn to relieve another brigade in 3rd Division and subsequently found itself occupying the Bluff again. It was there on 20th March that a young lieutenant, by the name of John Glubb, went up to the Bluff trenches with his CO. The purpose of their mission was to acquaint themselves with the area, as their division was about to relieve 3rd Division. Still in the line were troops of 76th Brigade.

> We went round the trenches with young Congreve, who was the brigade-major. He was famous as a brave man. When we were walking with him in the line, between the Bluff and the canal, he suddenly spotted a broken machine-gun lying in the open on top of the Bluff spoil bank itself. He calmly climbed out of the trench and walked up the slope of the Bluff in

the open to look at it. He must have been in full view of the Boche line for miles. Presumably none of the enemy was looking, as nobody would have ever dreamt that anyone would walk there in daylight.

Congreve had a great effect on the morale of his brigade. When they were relieved by the 3rd Division, the 17th Division were very much shaken, and were crawling about on all fours, for fear of snipers. The 1st Gordons of the 3rd Division came in full of beans to relieve them, and all stood on the firestep at once, à la Congreve, to look over the top and see where Jerry was. *

The last week of March saw 3rd Division moved to another hotspot, one which its experienced soldiers knew a year before. It was the St Eloi sector, and units of the division were re-arranged for an assault south-east of the village. The 1/Northumberland Fusiliers (the 'Fighting Fifth') and 4/Royal Fusiliers of 9th Brigade were detailed for the attack, scheduled for the early morning on 27th March. The night of 26th/27th March was exceedingly cold, and both battalions waited in chronic muddy conditions for the signal to go over the top.

It came at 4.15 a.m. with the tremendous eruption of six carefully laid mines, totalling 73,000 lbs of explosive, along 600 yards of the enemy-held front. Both battalions immediately advanced across No Man's Land. The craters literally transformed the landscape, but soldiers of the 1/Northumberland Fusiliers managed to secure their objectives with the loss of one man. Their comrades in the 4/Royal Fusiliers were less fortunate. Held up by barbed wire and with hostile machine-gun fire wreaking havoc in their ranks, they tried desperately to gain entry into the German trenches. Some of them finally made it and hung on grimly, but many of the battalion's objectives stayed in enemy hands.

Total casualties from the action amounted to 40 officers and 809 other ranks. On 3rd April, it fell to the lot of 76th Brigade to improve the situation.

A daunting task, but the brigade commander knew it required doing despite the awful weather conditions. After half an hour's bombardment and with the 8/King's Own chosen for the job, the order was given to advance. It was two o'clock in the morning and, as well as the darkness, the troops had to contend with a thick mist. Trying to stare through it, they groped their way towards the

*Lt-General Sir John Glubb: *Into Battle*.

unseen enemy. Fortunately the mist hampered the enemy's observation too. On bombing and shooting their way across the German firing line, however, hostile shots were heard from their rear. The momentum faltered as troops peered around in an attempt to visually isolate the pocket of resistance. After some delay, it was discovered that the firing came from an unknown number of Germans occupying a mine crater behind the newly-won positions. The crater (later designated as No 5 Crater) had been missed in the fog and, being on high ground, its occupants were able to shoot down on positions around it. Their firing had subsequently stopped movement in the vicinity, thereby jeopardising captured trenchwork from being put into a state of defence. Billy Congreve arrived on the scene as a very misty dawn was breaking. With the responsibility of the attack's outcome resting on his shoulders in his capacity as brigade-major, and extremely fatigued from his night-long exertions, he found the situation chaotic.

On being briefed about the problem, Congreve hurried to a trench that was some fifty yards from the crater. No one knew how many Germans were defending the crater, but he realised that they had to be neutralised quickly before the situation deteriorated any further. Just as he wondered how it could be achieved, he saw a sandbag being hoisted up on the end of a stick and then waved from side to side. The shooting, however, continued. Assuming that some of the Germans wanted to surrender and others not, he determined on a piece of audacious bluff. Instructing a nearby officer and four men to go with him, he pulled out his revolver and made a bee-line for the crater.

He freely admitted in a letter home that the first moments were anxious ones, expecting to be shot at any second. Half-way up the crater's side, he was fired on without result. He kept going, hoping that their tiny presence would dupe the enemy into thinking that the attack was already a success. He then reached the rim of the crater and looked into it.

> Imagine my surprise and horror when I saw a whole crowd of armed Boches! I stood there for a moment feeling a bit sort of shy, and then I levelled my revolver at the nearest Boche and shouted, 'Hands up, all the lot of you!' A few went up at once, then a few more and then the lot; and I felt the proudest fellow in the world as I cursed them.

After collecting the officers' revolvers, Congreve made them march in front of him with the other prisoners coming along in the rear. They were taken to the support trenches where he left them with his fellow officer and the four men, so that he could return to the front. After a swift head count, he was later informed that he had brought in 4 officers and 68 men. The *Official History,* for the record, quotes a higher figure: 5 officers and 77 men captured.

His father knew very little of his son's achievements at the Bluff and at St Eloi, he being busy himself with the change in plans that was brought about by the sudden German assault at Verdun. It was no longer a question of launching a Somme offensive, entailing thirty-nine French and twenty-five British divisions as conceived by Joffre and Haig. With a heavy French commitment at Verdun, plans were being drawn up for an offensive on the Somme to take the heat off Verdun, with the BEF making the largest contribution. For Joffre, it could not be soon enough. As well as Rawlinson's preliminary attack in the Flanders area which was scheduled two weeks before the Somme offensive, Haig had also discussed with Allenby the possibility of a preliminary attack in the Somme area by Allenby's Third Army. Both schemes were shelved in the embryo stage in favour of one big push at the Somme. Part of the new strategy called for Lieutenant-General Congreve and his XIII Corps to be transferred from Allenby's Third Army to Rawlinson's Fourth. The transfer was officially carried out on 1st March.

For Lieutenant-General Congreve, it was but one of a series of unexpected events that would personally confront him in the coming weeks. The next event was a pleasant one. It came in a note from his son, Billy, who informed him that he proposed to marry soon. Then, while at Fourth Army headquarters on 30th March, he met Lord Kitchener who told him that the war would certainly last over Christmas 1916, but the supply of men would not. Kitchener's solution was to put into the front line more of those employed behind, whom he could replace with unfit soldiers.

The morning of 5th April began surprisingly cheerful. In his mail was a letter from a colleague who had written to say that his son was the best young officer he had ever met. The compliment was followed by a verbal one from Brigadier-General Uniacke who not only echoed the same sentiments, but said that his son ran the Bluff and St Eloi attacks, and that he considered him fit to command a division. Uniacke added that he would be proud to serve under him in it. Hearing such heartening news about his son, whose twenty-fifth birthday was a fortnight before, pleased him immensely. It helped to ease the hurt when, at a corps commanders meeting later that day, Rawlinson told him that his XIII Corps plans for the Somme offensive were not dashing enough.

More letters in praise of his son arrived the next day, one of which was from General Plumer who concluded his letter by saying, 'He is really first rate.' There was also a letter from the Fourth Army commander, informing Congreve that he would be in XIII Corps area the next day. His meeting with Rawlinson on 7th April was humiliating. In his diary that night, he wrote:

> Sent for to see Army Commander who told me that as he did not consider me fit to take command of five divisions in coming operations. He had been to C-in-C who is sending Horne to take over two of mine: 7th and 21st and the left attack.[1] I to keep 18th and 30th, and do the right attack. I had expected something of the sort from the combination of Rawly and Haig, both of whom consider nothing and no one of use unless from First Army. A severe slap in the face all the same . . .

Rawlinson's decision was to have an ironic twist to it on the first day of the Somme infantry assault. But the offensive lay in the future and Congreve's immediate concern was the re-housing of his headquarters, as his present HQ was accommodated in the area which Horne would command. With difficulty, he found a place in the small town of Corbie. Meanwhile, he had heard that his son's action in the St Eloi battle had been recognised. Recommended for the Victoria Cross, Billy Congreve was awarded the Distinguished Service Order for conspicuous gallantry. His citation in the *London Gazette* read: 'Congreve William La Touche Capt, Rifle Brigade. For conspicuous gallantry. He consolidated a newly-won position under very difficult conditions at a critical moment, and by personal courage brought about the surrender of a considerable body of enemy officers and men.'

On 1st June, Billy Congreve married Pamela Maude in London. The wedding ceremony took place at St Martin-in-the-Fields with the Rev. Sheppard and the bishop of London officiating. It was a happy but moving occasion for the bishop. He knew the Maude family well and they had shared his grief when his youngest son, Lieutenant Gilbert Talbot, was killed at Hooge on 30th July 1915. The best man at the wedding was a 1/Gordon Highlander officer, Captain Hon. William Fraser, who in later years was to become a brigadier-general and an intimate member of both the Maude and Congreve families.

The newly married couple departed after the wedding breakfast for Beaulieu where they spent an idyllic though brief honeymoon. Within a matter of days, Billy Congreve was on his way to the front again to rejoin his brigade at Meteren.

Behind the Anglo-French front in the Somme area, preparations were well underway for the approaching offensive. The British contribution would be mainly a New Army affair with only a sprinkling of Territorial and Regular divisions taking part. Haldane's 3rd Division was not one of them, at least not for the opening phase, and 76th Brigade was detailed for reserve. By 12th June, the brigade had been marched and railed to a Second Army training area, followed by 3rd Division's 8th and 9th Brigades a few days later.

The assault date, having fluctuated during June from the original date of 1st July, was advanced to 30th June and then to 25th June. It returned to 30th June, but was postponed for twenty-four hours at virtually the last moment. The reason was due to bad weather, and so Saturday, 1st July, became the fateful date that would forever sear the pages of British military history.

A misty dawn gave the promise that Saturday would be warm and sunny. For a week, artillery had pounded the enemy along the British eighteen mile front. There was an hour's bombardment on that morning, which ceased just two minutes after the last detonation of a series of mines that had been laid beneath specific points of the German firing line. The first wave of infantrymen went in at 7.30 a.m., comforted by the many promises that the enemy could not live through such a devastating barrage. Advancing on the extreme British right were battalions of 18th and 30th Divisions belonging to Lieutenant-General Congreve's XIII Corps, with 9th Division held in reserve. Squeezed between XIII Corps and the north bank of the River Somme were French troops of General Balfourier's XX Corps. A corps of Fayolle's Sixth Army, Balfourier's infantry had also advanced in line with the British. Two more corps of Fayolle's Sixth Army on the south side of the river were due to attack at 9.30 a.m., which meant that the weary Germans facing them had another two hours of merciless bombardment.

Five corps of Rawlinson's Fourth Army and one corps of Allenby's Third Army were actively engaged on 1st July. Due to the lack of heavy artillery on the part of the British, which meant stretches of uncut wire and the failure to destroy numerous German deep dug-outs, British casualties that day rose to nearly

60,000 by nightfall. An alarming figure and nowhere justified by the small amount of enemy territory taken. Indeed, only one British corps had been successful in fully achieving its initial objectives that day, and that corps was Lieutenant-General Congreve's. His 30th Division, commanded by his brother-in-law, Major-General John Shea, was remarkably successful in that it captured the vital village of Montauban by 10.30 a.m.

Ahead of 30th Division's victorious troops lay a valley full of Germans retreating to their shaky second line of defence. Astride the horizon was the sloping Bazentin ridge with High Wood dominating it. Less than two miles to the right of it was the untouched village of Longueval nestling up to Delville Wood. Shea's men could also see the tranquil woods of Mametz to their left, Bernafay and Trônes to their right.

They wanted to go on. Congreve wanted them to go on. He even telephoned Rawlinson for permission to do so, but permission was refused.[2] Balfourier's infantrymen on Congreve's right had been equally successful. They also eagerly awaited the opportunity to press home their advantage, but they needed XIII Corps to advance again in order to cover their left flank. Congreve, a stickler for obeying orders, regretted that he was unable to comply. Rawlinson's orders were clear — capture and consolidate the definite objectives allotted to each corps.[3] For the XIII Corps commander who had two divisions taken from him, because he was 'not dashing enough', it was the supreme irony. By the early hours of the next morning, the gap created by XIII Corps had healed.

Congreve was visited on Sunday by General Sir William Robertson (CIGS) to congratulate him. Seeing that XIII Corps had been so successful, Congreve proposed that it would be better to utilise the success by an advance northwards rather than eastwards as originally planned. Robertson agreed and, shortly afterwards, Congreve's proposal was adopted for further Fourth Army operations. The change immediately brought into focus the hope of a break-through between Contalmaison and Longueval. On Tuesday, 3rd Division joined XIII Corps. Haldane, his three brigade commanders and Billy Congreve (now a brevet-major), arrived at Congreve's HQ for a conference.

Held in reserve, Haldane's 3rd Division was called forward to relieve Maxse's 18th Division on 6th July. It was none too soon, as 18th Division had suffered over 3,400 casualties since the start of the offensive. The bloody struggle for the various woods was in

(*) The ruined village of
~~~~~val, September 1916.
(*) Memorial tablet
~~~~~ed by Lutyens in Cor-
~~~~~rch.

A LA MÉMOIRE GLORIEUSE
DU COMMANDANT
WILLIAM LA TOUCHE CONGREVE
DU RIFLE BRIGADE, DE L'ARMÉE BRITANNIQUE.
CHEVALIER DE LA LÉGION D'HONNEUR,
DÉCORÉ DE LA VICTORIA CROSS DU
DISTINGUISHED SERVICE ORDER ET
DE LA MILITARY CROSS.

HOMME SANS PEUR, SOLDAT VAILLANT,
IL TOMBA AU CHAMP D'HONNEUR LE 20
JUILLET 1916 À LONGUEVALLE, SOMME
A L'ÂGE DE 25 ANS À L'AURORE D'UNE
BRILLANTE CARRIÈRE, AIMÉ DE TOUS.

Il repose à Corbie

MAJOR
W. LA TOUCHE CONGREVE
V.C., D.S.O., M.C.
RIFLE BRIGADE
20TH JULY 1916

FOR VALOUR

LEGION D'HONNEUR
IN REMEMBRANCE OF
MY BELOVED HUSBAND
AND IN GLORIOUS EXPECTATION

Billy Congreve's headstone in Corbie Communal Cemetery.

full swing by the time 3rd Division had completed the relief operation on the night of 8th/9th July. Horne's XV Corps on Congreve's left was also battling to take Mametz Wood.

A critical time and Major Billy Congreve was active wherever his presence was required and, on some occasions, where he need not have been. 'Very wrong of him to be out on such work,' wrote his father in his diary, but adding, 'bless him.' His seemingly unflagging energy aided the combined XV Corps and XIII Corps surprise dawn attack on 14th July, an attack that won valuable ground 1,400 yards in depth and brought about the capture of 6,000 yards of the German second position. By noon, British infantrymen were thrusting at the Bazentin ridge and, in consort with the South African Brigade of 9th Division, were locked in combat for supremacy of Longueval and Delville Wood. By dusk, the northern half of the village was still in enemy possession. The South Africans, however, had gained a foothold in Delville Wood and were to immortalise it with their blood. Battalions of 76th Brigade were also engaged in trying to drive the enemy from Longueval and, over the next four days, fighting continued at Longueval and in Delville Wood at a desperate level.

A further effort was made in the early morning of 20th July, employing for the purpose the 2/Suffolks and 10/Royal Welch Fusiliers of 76th Brigade. The Suffolks advanced from the west at the scheduled time of 3.35 a.m. The Royal Welch Fusiliers, due to a guide leading the battalion astray, failed to make an appearance at the allotted time. With their right flank exposed, the two leading companies of the Suffolks continued their advance and were decimated. The 10/Royal Welch Fusiliers duly arrived ten minutes late. Tragically, because of the time lapse, the battalion came under 'friendly' machine-gun fire and lost nearly all its officers.

Because of these circumstances, Billy Congreve took himself on another mission to the Longueval front. With him went Private Edward Roberts of the 10/Royal Welch Fusiliers as orderly. Congreve's features were drawn from lack of sleep and the physical exertions of the past days. The parlous situation arising from the early morning's failed attack added to his personal discomfort. He knew what was required of him as brigade-major, and it called for his individual appraisal so that the situation could be corrected. It was on that note that he and Roberts hurried as best they could over the pulverised ground to Longueval.

They first stopped at the 2/Suffolks' headquarters where they were joined by the battalion commander, Major Stubbs. He accompanied them to the battalion's front line sector where they entered a freshly-dug trench. The trench snaked along the side of a road, code-named Duke Street, on the western perimeter of the village. It was there that Billy Congreve saw a company of the 2/Suffolks busily engaged in lengthening the trench and generally consolidating the position. Stubbs left him for a few minutes as Congreve sought a vantage point from which he could observe enemy activity. On his return, Stubbs saw him in a disused German gun-pit and using his field-glasses to seek out the enemy's positions and strength. Every now and then, he would lower his field-glasses to scribble notes.

Suddenly, Stubbs felt anxious for him. He told him to be careful and to keep under cover for fear of snipers in the vicinity. Congreve acknowledged with a quiet laugh and continued observing the enemy's positions. All the same, it appeared to the battalion commander that he seemed depressed and yet gave the impression that he intended to right the situation as soon as possible. After speaking to him, Stubbs returned to his headquarters.

With four of his men, Sergeant Sheen was busily preparing a sap when, from the corner of his eye, he saw Billy Congreve climb down from the top of the disused gun-pit and into the main trench. He walked down the trench and spoke to Sheen, complimenting him on the sap.

> Just as he said the word 'work', he was hit. He stood for half a second and then collapsed. He never moved or spoke, and he was dead in a few seconds.

The fatal shot came from the direction of some standing corn. The bullet took him low in the throat and made its exit from the back of his neck. Sheen put the time of death at 10.55 a.m.

News of the tragedy reached XIII Corps headquarters by telephone. It fell to the lot of Brigadier-General W.H. Greenly, the senior staff officer, to impart the sad tidings:

> It was at a very important and critical moment, when the Corps were on the point of carrying out a very important and very daring operation, and where the direction of the corps commander was of the greatest importance. When I told him what had happened he was absolutely calm to all outward appearance and, after a few seconds of silence, said quite calmly, 'He was a good soldier.' That is all that he allowed to appear, and

he continued dealing with everything as it came along in the same imperturbable and quietly decisive way as usual.

I shall never forget the incident or lose the admiration I felt for the marvellous self-suppression of the 'man' in the capacity of the commander.

It had been Major-General Haldane who had telephoned XIII Corps headquarters. His feelings on the death of Billy Congreve were amply portrayed in a letter he wrote the next day to Pamela Congreve, who had only recently discovered that she was expecting her late husband's child.

. . . . . I am so upset by what has happened that writing is difficult. Still I must write and say how infinitely sorry I am for you and how deeply sad I feel. I confess that I have dreaded that he would not live till I could get him a brigade, where for the normal commander the risks would have been less, for his splendid standard of duty and great disregard of self made him think nothing too little to be done so long as anything remained to be done. He never spared himself and, that I trusted him as I have rarely trusted anyone in my life, was because I knew that no officer or man in the division and, indeed, few in the whole Army, had so high a sense of duty . . . .

On the 18th, when things were not going too well, and I had been obliged to use the 76th Brigade — which I was preserving for another operation — I went through the ruined village of Montauban into the valley south of Longueval, where the headquarters of the brigade were in a quarry. The enemy were very active, shelling heavily, and Billy had just returned from a dangerous visit to Longueval and gave me a lucid and manly account of what was going on there, I mean reassuring under the circumstances. He looked tired, but I knew that if I said he was overworking he would scorn the idea. That was the last time I saw him alive. Cameron, his faithful servant, who is heartbroken, and whom I saw yesterday, tells me that he was anxious and remonstrated with him for working at such high pressure and going so much to the front line where, of course, his example was priceless . . . . I took one look at the dear fellow. He looked beautiful in his last sleep, so handsome and noble, and not a trace of pain on his face. He was then half-way to Carnoy and, on my way back there, I met men of my regiment (Gordon Highlanders) carrying wild poppies and cornflowers to lay upon him, for his love for his brigade was amply returned by all ranks.

On the morning of 21st July, in accordance with Lieutenant-General Congreve's wishes, Haldane's two ADC's escorted Major

Congreve's body to Corbie. After attending a conference at Fourth Army headquarters, Lieutenant-General Congreve travelled to Corbie for the funeral. But first he went to see his dead son for a private and very personal farewell:

> I saw him in the mortuary, and was struck by his beauty and strength of face . . . . I felt inspired by his look and know that he is 'helping' me, as he used to say, and that he always will do so. I never felt so proud of him as I did when I said goodbye to him.
>
> A lot of flowers were sent by kind people, amongst them wild mallows from the fighting line by some of the men. These, I had put into the grave; and a huge wreath tied with the tricolour ribband from General Balfourier. I myself put in his hand a posy of poppies, cornflowers and daisies . . . . and with a kiss I left him.

With his coffin mounted on a RHA gun, closely followed by Lieutenant-General Congreve and Private Cameron as the chief mourners, the sombre cortege slowly moved towards the Corbie cemetery. There, in the south-west corner and overlooking the valley of the Somme, Billy Congreve was gently laid to rest.

The 76th Brigade commander, Brigadier-General Kentish, recommended Billy Congreve for the Victoria Cross — Kentish's officers, NCO's and men having unanimously and spontaneously requested that his name should be submitted for the highest military honour. Kentish, however, intended doing it before he received the wishes of his brigade. His recommendation was accepted. In the *London Gazette* of the 26th October 1916, the following citation appeared:

> William La Touche Congreve, Brevet-Major, DSO, MC, Rifle Brigade. Date of Acts of Bravery: 6-20 July 1916. For most conspicuous bravery during a period of fourteen days preceding his death in action. This officer constantly performed acts of gallantry and showed the greatest devotion to duty, and by his personal example inspired all those around him with confidence at critical periods of the operations. During preliminary preparations for the attack he carried out personal reconnaissances of the enemy lines, taking out parties of officers and non-commissioned officers for over 1,000 yards in front of our line, in order to acquaint them with the ground. All these preparations were made under fire.
>
> Later, by night, Major Congreve conducted a battalion to its position of employment, afterwards returning to it to ascertain the situation after assault. He established himself in an exposed forward position from whence

he successfully observed the enemy, and gave orders necessary to drive them from their position. Two days later, when Brigade Headquarters were heavily shelled and many casualties resulted, he went out and assisted the medical officer to remove the wounded to places of safety, although he himself was suffering severely from gas and other shell effects. He again on a subsequent occasion showed supreme courage in tending wounded under heavy shell fire.

He finally returned to the front line to ascertain the situation after an unsuccessful attack, and whilst in the act of writing his report was shot and killed instantly.

At Buckingham Palace on 1st November and on behalf of her late husband, Mrs William La Touche Congreve received the Victoria Cross, the Distinguished Service Order and the Military Cross from the sympathetic hands of King George V. The ceremony was unique, because no other officer had previously attained this triple honour. For his young and expectant widow, it was a proud yet poignant moment.

For Billy Congreve himself, whose sole guide had been one of duty, and whose mortal remains lay with other cut flowers of his generation, it was a triumph over death.

Notes

CHAPTER **O**NE: *Tipperary — A Long Way to Go*

(1)   Captain C.H. Meysey-Thompson, 3/Rifle Brigade's adjutant.

(2)   German troops moved into Luxembourg on the night of 1st/2nd August and Belgium on 3rd August 1914.

(3)   Great Britain actually declared war on Germany at 11 p.m., 4th August. Germany, on the other hand, did not *officially* recognise Great Britain's declaration of war until 23rd November 1914. Billy Congreve's friend, Tom, was Lieutenant Hon T.B.G. Morgan-Grenville.

(4)   Midshipman Geoffrey Congreve, his younger brother.

(5)   Captain N.J.B. Leslie of 3/Rifle Brigade. A first cousin to Winston Churchill, Captain Leslie was obviously privy to inside information, as Kitchener was appointed Secretary of State for War on 6th August. In 1910 Captain Leslie took part in the last duel fought by a Regular serving officer. His rapier is on display in the Royal Green Jackets' Museum, Winchester.

(6)   Billy Congreve's father, who was then Brigadier-General Walter Norris Congreve, VC, CB, MVO. Since he invariably signed his letters with his initials only, he was widely known as W.N.C. Another of his nicknames was 'Squibs' or 'Squibby', inherited from an illustrious ancestor who patented the Congreve Rocket which was used in the Napoleonic wars.

(7)   Celia, his mother.

(8)   Arthur Christopher John Congreve, his youngest brother.

(9)   Billy Congreve's aunt, Mrs Laurence Buxton.

(10)   Thanks to their heavy siege artillery, the Germans reduced the gallantly defended Liège forts to ruins over 14th—16th August. Built to withstand 210-mm artillery fire, the forts crumbled under the enemy's immense 420-mm guns.

(11)   1/Rifle Brigade. Billy Congreve was in 3/Rifle Brigade (6th Division).

(12)   The 1/Rifle Brigade sustained 374 casualties which included 345 other

ranks missing, many of whom were known to have been wounded when last seen. Major S.H. Rickman was second-in-command. Captain J.T. Coryton and Captain R.P.A. de Moleyns avoided capture, although both were wounded. Captain G.E.W. Lane was wounded and captured. It was Captain Lane who commanded the guard of honour at Harwich for the departing German Ambassador, Prince Lichnowsky.

(13) 'Wumps' was his eleven-year-old brother's white rat.

(14) Lieutenant Maurice Godolphin Osborne, a great friend of Billy Congreve's.

(15) His father was also embarking with the 6th Division, as commander of the 18th (Infantry) Brigade.

(16) When in field service marching order, an infantryman's equipment weighed 61 lbs. An officer's equipment weighed slightly less, not having the weight of a Short Lee Enfield rifle, a bayonet and the regulation issue of .303 rounds to carry. He would, of course, be armed with a service revolver.

(17) Sir John French's headquarters was at Fère-en-Tardenois, about half-way between Coulommiers and the River Aisne.

(18) Lieutenant-Colonel the Hon G.H. Morris.

CHAPTER TWO: *On Divisional Staff*

(1) His servant.

(2) Lieutenant-General Sir Archibald Murray: Chief of the General Staff. Murray's feelings on the French military top brass were reciprocated. They had a very low opinion of him as, indeed, they had of Field-Marshal French himself. It could be justifiably said that Murray was a prime example of an officer promoted above his capability level. His conduct during the retreat from Mons left much to be desired. Murray was replaced by Sir William Robertson in January 1915.

(3) Major-General W.P. Pulteney who took command of III Corps on its formation in France on 31st August 1914.

(4) When Brigadier-General Congreve's brigade rejoined 6th Division on 2nd October, he wrote; 'Our time with 1st Division cost me 51 officers and 1,000 men.'

(5) A French frontier fortress on the River Sambre, Maubeuge was to have been the jumping-off point for the BEF in the war. The German advance, and their victory in the Battle of the Frontiers, put paid to the prospect. Because of their astonishing advance, the Germans could have by-passed Maubeuge and have invested it at their leisure. As it was, laying siege tied up precious

manpower as well as badly needed pieces of heavy artillery.

(6)   His uncle, who was then Captain F.L. Congreve. He eventually rose to the rank of lieutenant-colonel and was awarded the DSO and MC.

(7)   It was on 27th September that Churchill also visited Sir John French at Fère-en-Tardenois, where they discussed together the 'advisability of joint action by the Army and Navy'. (French: *1914*). Churchill was First Lord of the Admiralty, an office which he held from 1911 to 1915.

(8)   Count Wedel Jarlsberg, Norwegian Ambassador from 1906 to 1930. He obviously favoured the Allied side, even allowing Allied personnel to visit him at his home in Paris. He was, in fact, one of the few diplomats to remain in Paris at that time.

(9)   'Crumps': a nickname for 5.9" HE shelling. The word was partly derived from the name of Krupp and partly from the noise that the exploding shell made. A 'crumpet' was a smaller shell exploding.

(10)   In her Red Cross capacity as nurse/driver, Celia Congreve left the doomed city in one of the last bus-loads of wounded men. It was an 'Old Bill' London omnibus that, by coincidence, displayed a large advertisement of actor/writer Cyril Maude's play. His daughter, Pamela, was Billy Congreve's girlfriend. For her services in Antwerp, Celia Congreve was awarded the Queen Elizabeth Medal by King Albert of Belgium.

(11)   René Duval, a Frenchman with the 3rd Division Staff who acted as interpreter.

(12)   Lieutenant-Colonel C.S. Wilson, commanding the division's Royal Engineers (56th and 57th Field Companies, also the 3rd Signal Company — signals being the responsibility of the Royal Engineers at that time).

(13)   The other infantry division in II Corps.

(14)   *Official History*, Vol. 1.

(15)   The three infantry brigades in the 3rd Division were: 7th (3/Worcesters, 2/South Lancs, 1/Wilts, 2/Royal Irish Rifles); 8th (2/Royal Scots, 2/Royal Irish Regt, 4/Middlesex, 1/Gordon Highlanders); 9th (1/Northumberland Fusiliers, 4/Royal Fusiliers, 1/Lincs, 1/Royal Scots Fusiliers). Order of Battle as at 13th October 1914. The 2/Royal Irish Regt, for example, was replaced in 8th Brigade by the 2/Suffolks on 25th October.

CHAPTER THREE: *The Crunch at Neuve Chapelle*

(1)   The 8th Division — the last British Army Regular division — was not to arrive in France until 6th November.

(2)   The fighting on 14th and 15th October cost II Corps 967 officers and men. Due to the nature of the terrain, which meant fighting in small detachments, losses among officers numbered 90 since 12th October.

(3)   2/Royal Scots in 8th Brigade.

(4)   III Corps infantry divisions, advancing on 3rd Division's left.

(5)   Major-General C.J. Mackenzie.

(6)   Major-General Hamilton's body was subsequently removed and reburied in England at Cheriton (St Martin) Churchyard, Folkestone, Kent.

(7)   4/Middlesex of 8th Brigade.

(8)   A wood just south-east of Neuve Chapelle: see Lieutenant Congreve's map on page 52.

(9)   To plug gaps, battalions were transferred from one brigade to another. The '5th Fusiliers' were the (1st) Northumberland Fusiliers, formerly the 5th Regt of Foot. Between 13th and 29th October, this battalion lost 13 officers and 351 other ranks. The 1/Royal West Kents lost 12 officers and an estimated 450 other ranks in operations at Neuve Chapelle.

(10)   Indian troops of the Lahore Division.

(11)   9th Bhopal Infantry.

(12)   Two companies of the 3rd Bombay Sappers and Miners.

(13)   The 47th Sikhs.

(14)   1/Lincolns.

(15)   1/Bedfords.

(16)   1/Cheshires.

(17)   Lieutenant-Colonel Forsyth.

(18)   Brigadier-General F.S. Maude succeeded Brigadier-General P.R. Holt when the latter was invalided home on 29th October.

(19)   GSO1: 3rd Division.

CHAPTER FOUR: *Ypres Salient*

(1)   Captain Norman Leslie of 3/Rifle Brigade was killed in action near

Armentières on 19th October at the age of twenty-eight. He was the son of
Sir John and Lady Leslie of Glaslough, County Monaghan; also a first cousin
of Winston Churchill as previously stated. Just before he was killed, Captain
Leslie had written: 'Remember we are writing a new page of history. Future
generations cannot be allowed to read the decline of the British Empire and
attribute it to us ... Some will live and many will die, but count the loss
nought. It is better far to go out with honour than survive with shame.' For a
man who had lived life to the full, it was a fitting epitaph.

(2)   Contrary to popular belief, the effects of being close to a bursting shell
were recognised at this time. Indeed, during August-December of 1914, there
were 1,906 hospital admissions for this type of casualty, and made up 2.55%
of the total admissions for wounds and sickness. Not until towards the end of
1915, however, was it recognised that *general* war strain could produce
neurasthenia, and this was also popularly called 'shell shock'.

(3)   Alan Paley was promoted to brigade-major on 1st November, eventually
being awarded the DSO (1915) and the CMG (1918). The day before he was
made up to brigade-major, his brother (Major George Paley) was killed at
Château Hooge when serving as GSO 2 with 1st Division. 'Charlie' was Billy
Congreve's cousin: Lieutenant C.R. Congreve. After the incident, he discovered
four bullet holes in his uniform.

(4)   Captain C.M. Meysey-Thompson, battalion adjutant, was killed in
action near Ypres on 17th June 1915. 'Snipe' was Major Lord Henniker's
nickname and 'Jellunda' was Lieutenant-Colonel R. Alexander's nickname —
the latter was on leave recuperating from a wound.

(5)   Lieutenant Charles Swan. He was made captain on 15th November.

(6)   Lieutenant Martin Alexander, promoted to captain on 15th November.

(7)   Rifleman Harris, Billy Congreve's servant when he was with the
battalion, was probably killed on 18th October. The 3/Rifle Brigade assisted
in the attack on the Prémesques-Perenchies ridge on the day. The attack
failed, costing the battalion 3 officers and 66 men in casualties. The ridge
stayed in German hands until October 1918.

(8)   Although the second to last Regular division to come into the line, the
7th Division under the command of Major-General T. Capper had suffered
heavily. The division was relieved on 5th November, having lost in eighteen
days 364 officers and 9,000 men.

(9)   The 3rd Division was now in I Corps, under Haig's command, and the
division was placed practically in the centre of the British line. The division's
part of the line ran from Shrewsbury Forest to Herenthage Wood and up to
the Menin road. Its line was approximately 2,500 yards in length and was
held by about 4,500 troops, including the company of Zouaves on its left.

(10)   Major-General J.A.L. Haldane was previously GOC of 10th Infantry
Brigade.

(11) The famous Cloth Hall of Ypres. Both St. Martin's Cathedral and the Cloth Hall, as Billy Congreve predicted, were reduced to ruins in the fighting. Both are beautifully restored today.

(12) Edward Hudson, founder and editor of *Country Life*.

(13) Brigadier-General F.C. Shaw, GOC of 9th Infantry Brigade.

(14) A German long range gun that fired a 280 lb shell.

(15) Commanding A Squadron, 15th Hussars.

(16) 9th Brigade HQ.

(17) Attack on 7th Brigade was repulsed. The 1/Northumberland Fusiliers repeatedly attacked by enemy.

(18) Brigade-major of 9th Brigade.

(19) See Billy Congreve's 'Sketch to Show 9th Bde Area' on page 78.

(20) All mention of 5th Fusiliers refer to 1/Northumberland Fusiliers.

(21) In his entry for 15th November, Billy Congreve makes reference to a very brave fusilier by the name of CSM Gilmour. Research has found that 'CSM Gilmour' was, in fact, CQMS Leonard Gillborn. This error has been corrected in the text as shown.

(22) Herenthage Château.

(23) The KOYLI with the Royal West Kents arrived on 13th November. The former placed in divisional reserve, while the latter took over line next to the KOSB's.

(24) Here, we glimpse the career in the making of a distinguished soldier, none other than Field-Marshal Earl Wavell, who also became viceroy of India during the difficult years (1943-47) which preceded the transfer of power. He was brigade-major from 16th November 1914 to 28th June 1915. He was wounded in 1916 when he lost the sight of one eye.

(25) 3rd Cavalry Brigade's 4/Hussars were shelled out of the stable on 20th November.

(26) Between 12th October and 22nd November, British and Indian casualties alone totalled 58,155. German casualties for the same period are stated as 134,315. Add French and Belgian losses for the same period — and the grand total rises to around quarter of a million. A few British Yeomanry and Territorial units had come into the line by 22nd November. Their casualties are also reflected in the figure of 58,155.

CHAPTER FIVE: *Entrenchment of Trench Warfare*

(1)   Point 76 was a small hill on the German side and was called Spanbroek Molen from the ruined mill on its peak.

(2)   King George V arrived in France on 1st December for a seven day visit. Among those to greet him when he landed was the Prince of Wales, who had been appointed ADC to Sir John French.

(3)   With all his adult family away at the war, Billy Congreve spent his leave at Edward Hudson's London home at 15 Queen Anne's Gate. Brown was Edward Hudson's butler.

(4)   2/Royal Scots and the 1/Gordon Highlanders of 8th Brigade which had rejoined 3rd Division on 27th November.

(5)   Captain Hon F.R.D. Prittie.

(6)   Captain Hon R.G.G. Morgan-Grenville (Master of Kinloss).

(7)   Major Alan Paley.

(8)   Major-General H.F.M. Wilson.

(9)   Chief of Staff of III Corps which 4th Division came under.

(10)   His friend and editor of *Country Life*, Edward Hudson, published a long letter of Billy Congreve's in the form of an article about trench life. Entitled 'From a Subaltern', it ran '. . . . . every beer barrel for miles round has been bought up and they are sawn in half and a little seat nailed across the top. In these the men stand or sit, and the water can do its worst, for nothing is so waterproof as a good barrel.'

(11)   1/Lincolnshire Regiment.

(12)   The KRRC

(13)   Brigadier-General Hon Charles Grenville Fortescue. He, in fact, became GOC of 80th Brigade.

(14)   A deep thinker as well as an astute observer in his capacity as 3rd Division's intelligence officer, Captain J.H.M. Cornwall occasionally put his private thoughts down in verse.

(15)   His uncle, Major Arthur King of the 4/Rifle Brigade which had embarked from Southampton on 20th December. Major King's nickname was actually 'Kingki', although his nephew spelt it 'Kinkie'. Major King was also one of the top eight Army marksmen before the Great War.

(16)   Lieutenant R.C. Hargreaves, 4/Rifle Brigade.

(17) Lieutenant Hon T.B.G. Morgan-Grenville, 3/Rifle Brigade. He was awarded the MC(1916), DSO(1918) and the OBE in 1945.

(18) Rt Rev Neville Talbot, chaplain to 3/Rifle Brigade and then chaplain to XIV Corps (1916-18). He was one of the originators of Toc H.

(19) In seniority alone, Billy Congreve's father should have been promoted months ago. The main reason why he was overlooked was due to 6th Division being retained in England in the early weeks of the war. By 30th December 1914, ten brigadier-generals had been promoted over him.

(20) When 3rd Division staff moved into their new headquarters on 21st November, a bed was discovered that was decorated with white ribbons in 'La Chambre de Madeleine'.

(21) Rev Gillingham, attached to divisional staff.

(22) Princess Patricia's Canadian Light Infantry, affiliated with the Rifle Brigade. Major Herbert Buller was ADC to the Duke of Connaught when Governor-General of Canada in 1911. Previously Buller had been adjutant to 3/Rifle Brigade, 1907-08. The Duke of Connaught was the Rifle Brigade's Colonel-in-Chief. The PPCLI were part of the 1st Canadian Division which arrived in February.

(23) Captain Sir Walter Pitt-Taylor, GSO3, III Corps; Brevet-Major Hon Maurice Wingfield.

(24) Major-General Wing was subsequently killed at Loos in September 1915, when commanding 12th Division.

(25) Brigade-Major H.V. Scott — died on active service on 1st September 1915.

(26) Later Field-Marshal Sir Henry Wilson. An ardent Francophile, Wilson on his own admission thought that he was more responsible for England joining the war than any other man. (Major-General Sir C.E. Caldwell: *Field-Marshal Sir Henry Wilson Bart., GCB, DSO, His Life & Diaries.* Vol 1, p 189).

(27) The party included representatives from *The Times, Reuters, Evening Standard, Daily Telegraph,* also an American journalist named Delmer. Ellis Ashmead-Bartlett of the *Daily Telegraph* was the most experienced war correspondent among them. Later in the year he went to Gallipoli where, in partnership with an Australian war correspondent called Keith Murdoch (father of the media tycoon, Rupert Murdoch), he managed to publicise the reality of the situation in the face of heavy censorship, thereby assisting in the downfall of General Sir Ian Hamilton and the termination of the Gallipoli campaign.

(28) Portugal, Great Britain's oldest ally, proclaimed her sympathy with the Allied cause on 7th August 1914. This link was strengthened when a German raid was made on the Portuguese post of Maziwa on the northern

frontier of Mozambique on 24th August. Several weeks later, Portugal provided 24,000 rifles to the British troops in the Cape, followed by fourteen batteries of 75's to the Belgians fighting on the Yser. The Germans, fighting in their African colonies, invaded Portuguese Angola on 24th December without any preliminary declaration of war. On 23rd February 1916, Portugal seized German ships which had taken refuge at the mouth of the Tagus. Germany retaliated by officially declaring war on Portugal on 9th March 1916. Austria followed suit within days.

(29) Wilson appears to have omitted the seven cavalry divisions.

(30) Captain M.M. Crichton, Royal Scots Fusiliers and GSO3 to 3rd Division.

(31) Following a beautiful summer, the winter of 1914-15 proved to be one of the wettest on record in northern France and Belgium.

CHAPTER SIX: *Spring Offensive and St Eloi*

(1)   Fortunately for the enemy, there were only thirty-odd shells available for the 15-inch howitzer, and some of those were faulty. The howitzer fired 12 rounds on 10th March, two of them at Aubers church which was thought to harbour enemy observers.

(2)   After a thirty-five minute bombardment, the first wave of First Army infantrymen moved in and captured Neuve Chapelle from a surprised enemy. They had created a gap 1,600 yards wide in the centre of a 3,500 yard frontal assault, which left the Germans still in possession of both flanks. For the first time in the war, however, a clean break-through had been made. Then everything went wrong, mainly due to the very narrow frontage and the cautious behaviour of some senior officers, all compounded by the withering enemy machine-gun fire from the flanks that was backed by counter artillery fire. The advance had ceased by nightfall, with infantrymen digging themselves in along the perimeter which they had reached during the day. The battle ended on 13th March with British losses at 583 officers and 12,309 other ranks. German casualties were estimated at about 12,000 which included the capture of 30 officers and 1,657 other ranks. Taking into account a territorial gain of a smashed-up village and a few square yards of churned-up mud, Haig's effort could be classed as a blood-soaked draw.

(3)   1/Wiltshires.

(4)   3/Worcesters.

(5)   Captain H.B.M. Pryce (Moses) commanded 'D' Company with Lieutenant Reginald Hargreaves as his second-in-command. Captain Pryce subsequently died from his wounds.

(6)   Son of a former CO of the 4/Rifle Brigade, Lieutenant (later Major) Stopford-Sackville was awarded the DSO for his bravery in the battle. He

was invalided in December 1919, and died in 1920 at the tender age of twenty-six.

(7)   Lieutenant-Colonel G. Cory, DSO — GSO2 of 3rd Division.

(8)   His servant.

(9)   Brigadier-General C.R. Ballard, who took over command of 7th Brigade after the First Battle of Ypres.

(10)   Brigadier-General Bowes took over command of 8th Brigade when Brigadier-General Doran was invalided on 23rd October 1914.

(11)   Lieutenant-Colonel John Shea, his uncle by marriage. Shea eventually rose to the rank of lieutenant-general and was knighted.

(12)   Lieutenant Hargreaves was awarded the MC and survived. He was promoted to captain in October 1915, and became King's Messenger in 1916 and later adjutant to 11/Royal Tank Corps in France in 1917-18. He retired (invalided) in 1922, but served as a wing commander in the RAF VR from 1939 to 1945.

(13)   GSO1: 3rd Division.

(14)   Major King's wife.

(15)   Lieutenant-General Sir C. Fergusson, Bt., CB, DSO, MVO.

(16)   Brigadier-General A.J. Chapman: GOC 85th Brigade, 28th Division.

(17)   Brigadier-General A.R. Hoskins.

(18)   Having already rejected a report of mining activity, 3rd Division's predecessor (27th Division) had just begun to counter-mine when further evidence could not be ignored. The decision to counter-mine came too late, as the Germans exploded their mine first. The Germans, however, had started to mine again — unknown by 3rd Division.

(19)   1/Northumberland Fusiliers of 9th Brigade.

(20)   Bois Confluent.

(21)   Not quite a false alarm, simply that the wind was unfavourable.

(22)   There were seven casualties — thanks to the massive mine explosions which completely surprised the enemy.

(23)   The struggle for possession of Hill 60 finally cost 5th Division 100 officers and 3,000 men.

(24)   Battle of Aubers Ridge which took place on 9th May.

(25) Among the heavy artillery used by the enemy on Ypres, was a 17-inch howitzer firing shells with delay-action fuses.

(26) The GSO1.

CHAPTER SEVEN: *Gas and 'Second Ypres'*

(1)   The 45th (Algerian) Division had just come into line along a five mile front between the Poelcappelle road and the canal at Steenstraat, NNE of Ypres. It was generally thought that the divisional artillery was registering guns on the enemy line. In reality the Germans, who had bombarded Ypres in the morning of the 22nd, re-commenced with a heavier bombardment on Ypres and the villages in front of the city at 5 p.m. The French 75-mm field-guns immediately retaliated, although the German field-guns kept silent from 5 p.m. to 5.10 p.m. so as not to disturb the gas clouds.

(2)   There were many Africans in the 45th (Algerian) Division.

(3)   The brigade came under 28th Division which was commanded by Major-General E.S. Bulfin.

(4)   Whereas 'failed' British generals were, more often than not, euphemistically 'invalided home', their French opposites were relegated *(limogés)*. As there is a town in France called Limoges, it was not long before the British sense of dry humour translated it as 'sent to Limoges'.

(5)   In all probability, he meant the 48th Highlanders of Canada.

(6)   A certain well-made trench, known also as the 'Drawing Room Trench' — see Billy Congreve's sketch which shows its cross-section.

(7)   Honourable Artillery Company.

(8)   *Official History:* Vol 3.

(9)   Killed on 15th March, his body found by his nephew on 4th May, Major King has no known grave today. His name, however, is commemorated on the Ypres (Menin Gate) Memorial.

(10) The beginning of the Battle of Frezenberg Ridge which lasted until 13th May.

(11) 28th Division's casualties during the period 8th-13th May were 163 officers and 3,726 other ranks.

(12) Major-General W.N. Congreve returned from England on 6th May.

(13) The 2/Rifle Brigade CO.

(14)   Captain S.A. Sherston.

(15)   Some time afterwards, a letter was found on a Roman Catholic's priest's body who had served in the ranks of the German Army. In it, he had mentioned the enormous resistance of the riflemen who had managed to fight their way into the German trenches: 'The hundred fellows who were in our trenches had brought with them an enormous quantity of ammunition, a machine-gun and one they had captured from us . . . . Almost every single man of them had to be put out of action with hand grenades. They were heroes all, brave and true to the end, until death . . . . men of the "active English Rifles Brigade". . . .' Casualties of the 2/Rifle Brigade in the Battle of Aubers Ridge were 21 officers and 629 other ranks.

(16)   Captain J.E.V. Isaac, DSO.

(17)   St Omer had been the GHQ until 27th April, when Sir John French and his staff moved to Hazebrouck from 28th April to 28th May 1915.

(18)   In the 21st May edition of the *Daily Mail*, just four days after Billy Congreve's personal criticism on the ammunition shortage, Lord Northcliffe made a swingeing attack on the Secretary of State for War on the same subject. Before the month was out, a Ministry of Munitions had been created under Lloyd George.

(19)   It would appear that this figure included the Aubers Ridge casualties, if we are to believe the official figure for Hill 60 and Ypres Salient from 22nd April—31st May, being a total of 59,275 casualties. Enemy losses in front of Ypres were 34,933 for the period 21st April—30th May.

(20)   His father took over command of 6th Division that day.

(21)   Having signed a treaty with the Allies on 26th April 1915, whereby she would share in the Allies' future acquisition of selected enemy territory, Italy denounced the Triple Alliance on 4th May before declaring war against Austria on 23rd May.

(22)   Captain J.H.M. Cornwall, MC.

CHAPTER EIGHT: *Again the Salient*

(1)   Major-General Haldane's chauffeur.

(2)   Lieutenant-Colonel R.C. Maclachlan. He was wounded in December 1915, awarded the DSO in 1916 and killed in action on 11th August 1917.

(3)   8/Rifle Brigade was one of Kitchener's New Army battalions.

(4)   A/Major A.A. Todd.

(5)   Captain W.M. Parker: killed in action at Hooge, 30th July 1915.

(6)   CO: 1/Gordon Highlanders.

(7)   Sir Edmund Allenby, CB. He took over command of V Corps when Plumer went to command the Second Army.

(8)   Brigadier-General H.S. Jeudwine.

(9)   1/Wiltshires of 7th Brigade.

(10) GSO 1.

(11) Brigadier-General C.R. Ballard, GOC 7th Brigade.

(12) The 3rd Division's day headquarters.

(13) 4/Royal Fusiliers.

(14) 2/Royal Scots.

(15) 1/Royal Scots Fusiliers.

(16) GOC 9th Brigade.

(17) According to German sources, it was estimated that the Germans lost 457 men in the battle, of whom 157 became prisoners.

(18) His observation certainly lends credence to the German estimated casualty figure of 300, excluding the 157 prisoners.

(19) 1/Wiltshires.

(20) Probably Sir Edwin Lutyens, RA, who was a close friend of the Congreve family. It was Lutyens, of course, who designed the Cenotaph in Whitehall.

(21) Battalions of 8th Brigade — the 7th and 9th Brigades being rested.

(22) The *Minenwerfer* was an ideal weapon for trench warfare. Capable of firing 20 rounds per hour, it took a high-explosive shell 207.2 lbs in weight with a calibre of 9.84 inches.

(23) The famous Talbot House in Poperinghe was named in Lieutenant Gilbert Talbot's memory. He lies buried in Sanctuary Wood Cemetery. Abbreviated to Toc H, Talbot House was the springboard for the Rev 'Tubby' Clayton's post-war Christian movement.

(24) His younger brother who was serving as a midshipman in the Royal Navy.

(25) Enemy ships raided three coastal towns — Hartlepool, Scarborough and Whitby — on 16th December 1914. Hartlepool (and West Hartlepool) suffered industrial and civilian damage from three German cruisers. Shelling lasted for nearly an hour from 8 a.m. The ships retired in a northerly direction afterwards, laying mines in their wake. The mines subsequently sank three British ships that night. Two days later Hartlepool received a warning to look out for a hostile airship, but no German airship appeared.

(26) Brigadier-General G.M. Harper, GOC 17th Brigade, 6th Division.

(27) Brigadier-General C.L. Nicholson, GOC 16th Brigade, 6th Division.

(28) Captain D.E. Prideaux-Brune. He eventually rose to the rank of lieutenant-colonel and was awarded the DSO and Bar in 1917.

(29) Captain E.R. Kewley. He became adjutant when Captain Meysey-Thompson was killed on 17th June 1915.

(30) Major Sir Robert Pigot, Bart.

(31) 3/Worcesters.

(32) Probably the GSO 2 of 3rd Division.

(33) Billy Congreve's father's diary entry for 4th July 1916.

(34) Trench identity codings.

(35) Christopher John, his youngest brother.

(36) Glassfurd, an Indian Army officer, replaced Guffin who was posted to GHQ in early September.

CHAPTER NINE: *Brigade-Major*

(1) Confirmed in January 1916.

(2) There had been very little action due to inclement weather.

(3) 76th Brigade's headquarters.

(4) 4/Gordons were attached to 76th Brigade from 19th October 1915, to 4th February 1916, and then transferred to 51st (Highland) Division.

(5) His engagement to Pamela Maude was announced in *The Times* on 23rd December.

(6)   Second-Lieutenant R.B. Brisco, RE.

CHAPTER TEN: *Journey's End*

(1)   Lieutenant-General H.S. Horne's corps (XV Corps) would compose of 7th, 17th and 21st Divisions for the opening of the Somme offensive.

(2)   Martin Middlebrook: *The First Day on the Somme*, page 213.

(3)   Fourth Army Operation Order of 14th June 1916.

Index

should be A.K. Hargreaves